# Ambassador from the Prairie
## *or Allison Wonderland*

# JOHN M. ALLISON

# Ambassador from the Prairie

## or *Allison Wonderland*

HOUGHTON MIFFLIN COMPANY BOSTON

1973

FIRST PRINTING   W

Printed in the United States of America

Library of Congress Cataloging in Publication Data
Allison, John M.
     Ambassador from the prairie.
     1. Allison, John M.   2. United States — Foreign Relations
— 1933–1945.   3. United States — Foreign relations — 1945–
I. Title.   II. Title: Allison Wonderland.
E748.A197A32      327'.2'0924[B]      73–13823
ISBN 0–395–17205–5

*For Toots*

# Acknowledgments

No book of this sort could have been written entirely from memory. Although I never kept a diary, I did keep a vast file of clippings from contemporary newspapers and magazines, copies of public speeches, and a few letters and memoranda regarding what seemed important matters. However, much of the detail concerning my career from the time I became Assistant Secretary of State for Far Eastern Affairs, in the last year of the Truman Administration, until I retired seven years later, is due to the courtesy of the Department of State in making available to me its records covering my activities during this period. Dr. William Franklin, Director of the Historical Office of the State Department and his associate, Dr. Arthur Kogan, could not have been more helpful. In the detailed searching of the files, Wilmer P. Sparrow, head of the Reference Section, and Miss Jessie Williams of his staff were of the greatest assistance. Dr. Peter A. Poole, of Howard University, a former Foreign Service Officer and a specialist in Southeast Asian Affairs, took over the reading of the files when I had to return to Honolulu, and his summaries and comments were of great value. Under Secretary U. Alexis Johnson and members of his staff broke precedent and forwarded copies of certain documents to the Office of the Political Adviser to the Commander-in-Chief, Pacific, in Honolulu.

There, through the courtesy of Admiral John S. McCain, Jr., and the assistance of Oscar Armstrong, the Political Adviser, and his staff, I was provided with an office and materials to study and make notes from the documents.

My former colleague in the Foreign Service and associate at the University of Hawaii, W. G. (Greg) Hackler, read most of the manuscript and gave me valuable suggestions regarding content as well as keeping me on the straight and narrow path in regard to the "who" and "whom." Mrs. Sharon Ishida and Mrs. Dolores Springer of Mr. Hackler's staff and Mrs. Jean Liechtenstein did the typing and preparation of the manuscript for the publisher.

Craig Wylie, head of the Trade Division of Houghton Mifflin Company, gave me encouragement from the very beginning of my writing; and Richard McAdoo, the editor whom he assigned to me, was invaluable in bringing a somewhat incoherent mass of words into publishable form. Their help and friendship has meant much to me.

However, none of it could have been done without the constant prodding, criticism, and encouragement of my wife who has put up with much to keep the typewriter clicking.

# Preface

In his preface to the first of several delightful books about book collecting, the late A. Edward Newton quoted Lord Byron as saying that "the end of all scribblement is to amuse." While I hope there are some pages of this book which will amuse the reader, its real aim is to enlighten. Since retiring from the American Foreign Service in 1960 after thirty years as a career officer, I have been questioned innumerable times as to just what the Foreign Service is and does. I have read countless articles in newspapers and magazines telling what is wrong with the Foreign Service and how it can be improved, many of them showing little real knowledge of the Foreign Service. It therefore seemed to me that there might be some virtue in recounting what an average man, without private means or public influence, did during a career of thirty years, beginning as a clerk and ending as an ambassador.

This is not a history of thirty years of American foreign policy. I hope historians will find some portions useful in their study of various aspects of American foreign policy, particularly with respect to Asia, in the affairs of which I have been chiefly concerned. They will find that much is left out, not because I didn't realize the importance of many events of the time, but because I was not intimately involved in them. It has even been necessary to omit much of what I was involved in to keep the book within manageable proportions. I have tried to tell the truth as I saw it at the time, realizing full well that my knowledge and outlook were limited.

For thirty years I was privileged to be associated with a, by and large, wonderful group of people in the Foreign Service, the State Department and other Agencies of the American Government concerned with foreign affairs. For me, there could have been no more interesting career. To the Midwesterner who became at home in Tokyo and Shanghai before he ever saw New York or Washington, the thirty years was indeed a wonderland. This book tries to tell why.

J. M. A.

Honolulu
Thanksgiving Day, 1972

# Contents

# Illustrations

*following page 192*

The author in 1929, Zone Advertising Manager for General Motors in Shanghai

The author, then Assistant Secretary for the Far East, being received by the King of Thailand

John Foster Dulles and the author at the 38th Parallel one week before the outbreak of the Korean War

August 4, 1952: Dean Acheson and the author lead the American delegation to the first ANZUS Council meeting in Kaneohe, Hawaii

The author, ready to present credentials as Ambassador to the Emperor of Japan, May 28, 1953, and Imperial Household official Goto pose before the Emperor's coach

Vice President Nixon addresses the Embassy staff in November 1953

Behind the scenes at Kabuki: the author and his wife are greeted by Ennosuke

Secretary Dulles, greeted upon arrival in Tokyo

The author and Foreign Minister Okazaki shake hands after signing an agreement giving Japan criminal jurisdiction over American troops when off duty

# Ambassador
# from the Prairie
## or Allison Wonderland

# Down the Rabbit Hole

## 1927–1932

In his unconventional biography of George Washington, W. E. Woodward points out that "in the queer mess of human destiny the determining factor is Luck." I'm not sure I would admit it is the only factor, but it certainly was luck, as far as I was concerned, that made Arthur Jorgensen, a graduate of the University of Nebraska who had spent fifteen years in Japan in the service of the YMCA, return to his alma mater to become Student YMCA Secretary during my sophomore and junior years at the university. Among other things, "Jorgie" as we all called him, told how the Japanese Government every year employed young American college graduates to come and teach English conversation in Japanese Middle Schools (roughly equivalent to an American high school). These young people were selected by the YMCA and were employed for two years by the Japanese Government at a salary of approximately $175 a month, but they had to pay their own passage to and from Japan. This was in the middle and late twenties and that seemed like a goodly sum, and it was not too difficult to borrow the necessary passage money.

I hounded Jorgie with questions and made it clear I was definitely interested. For some reason I had always had a stronger desire to go to Asia than to Europe. My major in college was political science, especially international relations, which was then being taught for the first time at Nebraska by a fulltime professor, Norman Hill. My term papers usually dealt with Asian affairs. At the end of my junior year Jorgie returned to Tokyo, and I continued with political science, receiving in my senior year the magnificent sum of $125 for grading freshman papers and being a general assistant in the department. I heard nothing from Jorgie all year and had just decided to accept a scholarship grant for a year of graduate study toward a Master of Arts degree when, during graduation week, a telegram arrived from New York saying I had been recommended for the one position open that year in Japanese Middle Schools and would I accept? It didn't take me long to reply affirmatively, although it was hard on my mother as I was an only child. My father, a good Bryan Democrat, seemed to take it more philosophically, although I knew he had hoped I would go into the family business of wholesaling furnace supplies and stove repairs.

It was the early summer of 1927. Lindbergh had just flown to Paris amid universal acclaim. When Allison got ready to leave for Tokyo the acclaim was missing. Most of my classmates thought I was crazy. I could have stayed in Lincoln and gone into business with my father or accepted the scholarship offered by the university. In either case I could have gone to the football games every Saturday afternoon. Those were the days when Nebraska always had a championship team, when Ed Weir, a fraternity brother, had gained fame by kicking off to Red Grange and then tearing down the field and tackling him just after he caught the ball. If I went to Japan, I would only be able to read about it four weeks later or maybe eight weeks. We had no air mail in those days.

But I was adamant. I had read Kipling, and I knew that I had really "heard the East a-calling." I borrowed $300 from a trustful banker and was off by rail to San Francisco, where I boarded the old *Korea Maru*. It took fifteen days to reach Yokohama, including an eight-hour stop in Honolulu. (The last time I left Tokyo it took less than thirteen hours to reach San Francisco by air.) I shared a second-class cabin with a tall, gangling, red-haired, freckled-faced young man going to teach at Yale-in-China. "Red" Hawkins became a good friend in the two weeks we spent together, but after I left the ship in Yokohama I didn't run across him again for more than twenty years by which time he had become one of our early economic development experts as well as something of an expert on Indonesian economic problems.

My two years in Japan passed quickly. Merrell Benninghoff, whose place I was taking in the Odawara and Atsugi Middle Schools, had left to take a position as a clerk in the American Consulate at Yokohama, and through him I got my first real introduction to the American Foreign Service in which I was later to spend more than thirty years.

The first three days of the week I would spend in Odawara, about an hour and a half southwest of Tokyo, and the last three days at Atsugi, where eighteen years later General MacArthur landed to begin the occupation of Japan. In Odawara I rented an upstairs room in the paper-walled home of a Japanese family, near the railway station. In the station restaurant I got my meals and the sandwiches that I took to the school for my noon lunch. In the cold winter evenings after dinner I would then go back and parboil for thirty minutes in the round, wooden, Japanese bathtub, wrap myself in a heavy winter kimono, and study or read for an hour or so before I crawled into the army cot I had been given so that I wouldn't have to sleep on the floor. The two nights in Atsugi I was put up in an inn, where I began to learn about Japanese food, and then on Saturday afternoon I would go up to Tokyo and spend the rest of the weekend with Jorgie and his family. It was a quiet but interesting life, and I began to learn a bit about the Japanese character. My first real introduction came from my students at Odawara.

One Monday morning, when I walked into the room which normally held some forty senior students, there was only one boy present. In his broken English he explained that his class was having a special emergency meeting in the gymnasium. He took me to the door, where I saw all my class seated in a circle on the floor, and one after another various members of the class would get up and make a violent speech in Japanese which I couldn't then understand. I went in to see Mr. Morinaga, the principal, as I was worried lest I had done something to offend the class. He reassured me and after talking to one of the boys he explained the crisis. On the previous Saturday afternoon there had been an intramural track meet, and this class had been defeated. This, to them, was such a serious matter that it called for prolonged "self-reflection," and they had been discussing it all Sunday and were still so chagrined they couldn't think of going to regular classes. Mr. Morinaga took no action and told me to forget the matter. The next day the boys were back in class. I began to get an inkling of how seriously Japanese took defeat of any kind. If defeat in a track meet could cause this much of a trauma, it became easier to understand what defeat in a war could mean.

During these first years I was in Japan, I also saw the beginnings of the xenophobia that eventually led to Pearl Harbor. In fact it had already started. In 1927, I was the only American teacher brought to Japan, whereas the previous annual rate had been fifteen or twenty. In April of 1928, the end of the school year, I was told that appropriations for foreign teachers had again been cut, and there was only enough to pay me for two days a week instead of six. They suggested I might get other teaching work in Yokohama or Tokyo the remaining four days, but offered, in case I wished to return to America, to pay my passage as it was through no fault of mine that there was not enough money for a fulltime teacher.

Again luck entered the picture. My predecessor at Odawara

and Atsugi, Merrell Benninghoff, had subsequently entered the American Consular Service in Yokohama. His father was a missionary teacher at Waseda University in Tokyo, and one of his former students was now an oil salesman who did a large amount of business with the Japanese Navy. Just as I learned I was practically out of a job this salesman told Dr. Benninghoff that the Naval Engineer Officers' Academy was looking for a foreign teacher of English conversation, because their regular man had been suddenly called home. I was available and I got the job. It was much better than my previous position. Instead of having to teach twenty-three hours a week, I would only have to teach twelve. My salary would be 500 yen a month instead of the 390 yen I had been receiving. I would live, for almost nothing, in the Naval Officers' Club, would be treated as a Naval officer, and would be given the commissioned officer's special discount of 50 percent on all rail journeys. This meant I could travel second class for the price of third, and first for the price of second. It seemed almost too good to be true.

The Japanese Navy at that time followed the British system of having their deck officers go to one school, their engineer officers to another, and their supply officers to still a third. The Engineer Officers' Academy was located at Naka-Maizuru in the west-central part of Japan on the coast of the Japan Sea, just across the island from Kyoto and Kobe. I was thus introduced to a very different part of Japan from the Tokyo-Yokohama area. On long weekends I explored Kyoto and made new friends among the foreign community in Kobe and Kyoto as well as many new Japanese friends. One of my shipmates on the *Korea Maru*, a young American girl of Japanese ancestry, was teaching in the Girls' College at Doshisha University in Kyoto, a famous old missionary institution. At first she undertook to guide me around the scenic spots but the xenophobic fever had already penetrated this beautiful old city, the ancient Capital of Japan, and we had to curtail these excursions. The students and townspeople looked askance at this young lady (American in everything but looks, in which she was completely Japanese), walking the streets alone with a blond foreigner. It was not only because she was being seen with a foreigner but also because she dressed and acted just like a Westerner. She told me that a few months before, she had been visiting in Tokyo and while walking down the famous Ginza with her uncle, a Japanese army officer, had been accosted and slapped by a partially intoxicated Japanese tough who had denounced her for wearing American clothes instead of a kimono.

My education in the Japanese character was further enhanced during my time at the Naval Academy. The students, who underwent a three-year course, were some of the most earnest, hard working young men I had ever known. They all had to pass an exceedingly stiff entrance examination, but once admitted they were almost certain to be graduated. One of my third-year students became ill and was in the hospital for almost half the term, but when he returned he went right on with his class, instead of being put back a term as probably would have happened in America.

If democracy means equal opportunity, it was certainly present in the prewar Japanese Navy. My students were representatives of all classes: the rich, the middle class, and the poor. One third-year student came from a farming family that was so poor there were no electric lights in the house in which he was raised. In a country where electricity was almost universal this meant his family was really poor. One of the officers whom I got to know was the son of a poor village barber, and yet he had been able to become an officer in the Imperial Navy and wear a decoration granted by the Emperor.

In many respects the students were like students anywhere, interested in athletics, especially the typical Japanese martial sports of Judo and Kendo. But they also had the curiosity of the young, and I spent almost as much time answering their questions about America and the West as I did in formal teaching. They were surprised to learn that at railway stations in large American cities we had Red Caps just as they did in Tokyo, Kyoto, and Osaka. They even accused us of stealing the name from the Japanese, for their Red Caps were called *Aka-Bo*, short for *Akai Boshi* which literally means "Red Hat." I was really stumped one day when one of my senior students came up to me and asked, "*Sensei* [Teacher], what does hinky dinky parley vous mean?"

But these young men had a serious, almost solemn side to their character. In the spring of 1928, they were invited to participate in the Coronation Ceremonies for the present Emperor. I instructed the senior class to be prepared, on their return from Kyoto, to give a three-minute talk in English about the ceremony and their impressions. Because of the intervention of field exercises following the Coronation it was not until three weeks after their return that the time came for their talks. One after another these young men got up to recite. As they did so, their faces became flushed, tears streamed down their cheeks, their voices choked up, and after looking rather wildly at me they sat down. Their task had been to guard one-half mile of the line of march that the Emperor took from the railway station to the Imperial Palace, a duty which did not permit them to see the Emperor as they faced the kneeling crowds rather than the procession. To them, this honor was so emotionally overpowering that even three weeks later they couldn't talk about it.

As the year went on I knew I didn't want to stay in Japan and teach another year, but I was undecided as to just what I did want to do. One weekend in Kobe in a local bookshop, which sold English-language as well as Japanese books, I met Frank Henry, the sales manager of Doubleday, the American publishing company, who was on his way home from a sales trip to Australia. We had a few conversations, and he told me he could probably get me a job in some branch of the publishing business when I came home the following spring. I was seriously considering going to New York when my term ended in April 1929 and taking him up on his offer, when again luck intervened.

Shortly before Christmas 1928, I was en route to Kobe for one of my regular weekend visits. It was necessary to change trains in Kyoto, and when I entered the second-class coach (for which, remember, I only paid third-class fare) there was only one seat available and I took it. My seat companion was a foreigner who looked much more American than European. I noticed he had some Chevrolet and Buick catalogs on his lap. There was a General Motors assembly plant in Osaka, and I asked him if he worked there. He replied that he was advertising manager. I confessed I had been advertising manager of my school paper and had once taken a brief academic course in advertising. My seat companion looked at me closely and asked me to come and have a drink with him the next evening. I accepted and, although I did not realize it, my future was laid out before me. I never got to be a publisher nor did I ever go back and get a graduate degree in political science which, at that time, was my second choice.

General Motors Japan was just then about to open two sales branches on the Asian continent, one in Mukden and one in Shanghai. Just because there was only one seat vacant in the train from Kyoto, I ended up as branch advertising manager of General Motors in Shanghai in June of 1929, after only two months of indoctrination at the assembly plant in Osaka. For a year I had a busy and hectic time writing advertising copy, sales manuals (I had never sold anything, but in 1929 that didn't matter), buying advertising space in newspapers and on billboards, which in Shanghai were known by the British term, *hoardings*, making an inspection trip up to Tsingtao to look over our dealer there, and at the same time trying to keep a level head in that fantastic metropolis called Shanghai. For a young man only some two years away from the plains of Nebraska it was strong wine. No one ever seemed to sleep, money was the only God, beautiful women and distinguished-looking men of every race and nationality mingled together and yet remained aloof from each other. In any hotel lobby you could hear French, German, Russian, English, and American (they're not the same) to say nothing of Chinese, Japanese, and even some Thai and Malaysian. Beggars were everywhere and on freezing winter mornings corpses were often visible in the gutters.

I lived in the downtown American Club, and for the first time in two years I had a room with a private bath, and I thought there could never be greater luxury. As the year wore on I began to wonder whether or not I really did want to be a big business-man. My superiors in General Motors, who had been with the company for some time, made high salaries, and they earned them. They had to eat, drink, and dream selling motor cars, and it seemed to me there must be something more interesting and more worthwhile to do with one's life. I was encouraged in this thought by two young friends I made shortly after my arrival. One was Arthur Ringwalt, a vice consul in the American Consulate General and a fellow Nebraskan from Omaha. The other was Edgar Snow, then a young newspaperman working for the well-known J. B. Powell, who was the *Chicago Tribune* correspondent and publisher of a weekly magazine, the *China Weekly Review*. Ed was already delving into all aspects of Chinese life as well as the role of the foreigner in the Treaty Ports. He got around and knew all sorts of interesting people: English detectives on the Shanghai Municipal Police Force, intelligence officers in the U.S. Fourth Marines, Chinese press barons, and government officials. Last, but not least, was Agnes Smedly, an American, originally from Colorado, who had lived in Germany with an Indian revolutionary after World War I, and who was now becoming more and more involved with Chinese revolutionaries. I believe she had considerable influ-ence in encouraging Ed to make his pilgrimage to Yenan to see

Mao Tse-tung which resulted in Ed's famous *Red Star Over China*, which first appeared as weekly articles in the *China Weekly Review*. These people and the work Art Ringwalt was doing at the Consulate General seemed much more interesting than trying to persuade people to buy automobiles or trucks, but I seemed to be stuck.

However, I did move out of the American Club, and Ed and I rented a small flat out on Seymour Road in a residential district. We had one large living-bed room, a dining alcove, a small kitchen, and a bath. And, far more important, we had I-Sung, a combination butler, cook, and housekeeper. I-Sung had once worked for the British Consul in Chefoo, in Northern China, and he found it difficult to reconcile himself to our small establishment. One evening when we came home the door was opened for us by a small, neatly dressed youngster who grinned at us as only Chinese children can grin. We called I-Sung and he explained that this was his nephew who would be "learn coolie" and that it was not necessary to pay him. His food would, of course, come from our supplies. I forget the young man's name, but for several months he shined our shoes, dusted the furniture, washed the dishes, made himself generally useful, and gave face to his uncle, who now had someone to order around. We finally insisted on paying him something, and I-Sung suggested that one dollar a month would be right. We agreed and everyone was happy. But I was still selling motor cars. It took an American stock-market crash, an international depression, and luck to pry me loose.

With the stock-market crash in New York in the autumn of 1929, General Motors began pulling in its horns. In December the chief officers of the Mukden and Shanghai branches, which included me, were brought back to Osaka for consultation. The main decision was to cut down staff, and several men, of far longer standing with the Company than I, were let go. It was not until the following March that my turn came and on the thirty-first of the month I was given an extra month's pay and told that General Motors would have to survive without my brilliant advertising skills. It has.

I had seen this time coming and had been in close consultation with Art Ringwalt. He had told me that it looked as if one of the clerks in the Commercial office of the Consulate was about to resign and, if I wanted it, I could probably get the job. Nothing had happened by the time I left General Motors, but Art urged me to stay on and not go home. He was sure the man was leaving, and he would introduce me to Consul General Cunningham as a possible replacement. Luck took charge and sure enough the clerk resigned and I was introduced to the Consul General. He told me if I took the job, I would have to agree to stay at least two years as it was not worthwhile taking on anyone for a shorter term. I had visions of what my mother would say when she learned her only child was staying away another two years, and I explained to Mr. Cunningham that I was an only child and had already been away three years. I went on to say I planned to take the written examinations for the career Foreign Service, which, as I was a consular clerk, could be sent to me in Shanghai the following December, and I asked if he would agree to give me leave of absence to go to Washington to take the final oral examinations if I got a high enough mark on the written part. This would mean I could go home at the end of eighteen months instead of two years. Mr. Cunningham, a huge red-faced man who looked vaguely like J. P. Morgan acting the part of a Captain of an East Indian freighter, beamed at me and commended me for my filial piety. He said he would grant me leave if I got a high enough mark on the written examination. Well, I did and he did. Not only did he grant me leave, he wrote a most flattering despatch to the Department highly recommending me for appointment as a Foreign Service Officer.

In August of 1930, I was granted leave and sailed as a Consular passenger on an American freighter. It took twenty days to reach San Francisco. Because of my Consular status I only had to pay two dollars a day. After San Francisco my transportation expenses to Washington, via Lincoln, Nebraska, where I spent a month with my family, were the same as anyone else's and made a big hole in my savings. At that time the government paid no part of a clerk's transportation expenses, although my salary did continue. I was four years out of university and was making $2000 a year which seemed then a great sufficiency. My grandson today, one year out of college, is making $8000 a year and does not consider it excessive.

In October of 1929, I arrived in Washington to take the oral examinations which would decide my fate. Again, luck was present. While I was at the Consulate General in Shanghai, before I had taken the written examination, Tom Wailes, who was to become my closest friend in the Foreign Service, had arrived as a new vice consul. He had gone to a special coaching school in Washington before he had taken the written examinations, and he had with him all his notes and texts. He lent them to me, and they played a large part in helping me pass the examinations. Tom therefore felt a certain sense of responsibility for me, and when I went to Washington he gave me a note of introduction to Cornelia Bassel, a niece of former Secretary of State Robert Lansing and a delightful all-knowning mentor and mother confessor. She was then running the Foreign Service School in the State Department, which gave newly commissioned Officers three months of rather sketchy instruction in their duties. While I was talking to Miss Bassel one day in her office, she introduced me to Thomas Wilson, a senior Foreign Service Officer who had been acting as an Inspector and was now on consultation in the department. He proved most genial and we talked at some length about my experiences. The next day when I appeared for my oral test, Tom Wilson was one of the five members of the examining panel. The Chief of Personnel, a rather frightening man who should have been on the panel, had suddenly taken sick and Tom had been substituted. A friendly and known face gave me a morale boost which I had not expected, and I managed to squeeze through the forty-five minute ordeal without complete disgrace. It is interesting to recall as we look at the current state of tension between Soviet Russia and Communist China that one of the questions asked me back in October, 1931, was whether or not I could describe the difference between communism in Russia and in China. My association with Ed Snow provided material for my answer. Apparently I didn't do too badly, for three or four days later I was notified I had passed the orals with a grade of 82.4 which, when added to the grade I had received on the written test of 79.8, brought my average just slightly over the 80 needed for admission to the Foreign Service. I was in!

Having indicated I wished to be assigned as a language student to the Embassy in Tokyo, I was first sent as a clerical vice consul to the Consulate in Kobe until I could be confirmed by the Senate as a career officer. This took place as soon as Congress convened at the end of the year. In January of 1932 I was commissioned as a Foreign Service Officer, Unclassified, a Vice Consul of Career, and a Secretary in the Diplomatic Service. The son of the Bryan Democrat from Nebraska received his first commissions, all signed by President Herbert Hoover.

# II

# The Mock Turtle's Story

## 1932–1937

ALTHOUGH I WAS now a Career Officer, it took some time for the usual bureaucratic processes to work before I could go to Tokyo and begin my Japanese studies. In the meantime, I continued to serve as sort of an all-purpose vice consul in Kobe under the general guidance of Erle Dickover, the Consul, who had been in charge of the office so long that he was looked upon by the local community as a fixture. He was a crotchety old bachelor who inspired both fear and respect in his staff. A least he seemed old to his newest vice consul; he was probably not much over forty-five.

While in Shanghai, I had worked exclusively in the Commercial office writing trade reports about the market for various American products ranging from automobiles to carbon black. Now I was in an entirely new field and under the watchful but friendly eye of Otis (Dusty) Rhoads, the senior American clerical vice consul. From him I learned the rudiments of certifying notarial documents, checking consular invoices of commercial shipments to the United States, and — most interesting of all — dealing with shipping matters. This included signing crew list visas, dealing with disputes between captains and crew, and taking care of sailors who had been having too good a time on shore and had failed to get back to their ship on time.

The days passed quickly. Kobe at that time was a bit like a small Shanghai in the variety of nationalities present and in its commercial and social atmosphere which, for the average foreigner, meant he had but little time or desire to learn anything much about Japan and the Japanese. In early February I was delighted by finally getting a cable ordering me to Tokyo.

I arrived in Tokyo on Washington's Birthday and moved in, as the first resident, to a small but most adequate apartment in one of the two new Embassy staff apartment houses just recently completed in the same compound as the new Chancery (office building to nondiplomats) and just at the foot of the hill upon which was the imposing new residence for the American Ambassador. I had a large living room, bedroom, bath, dining alcove, and kitchen. The whole compound was surrounded with a high, white wall, and we were all proud of our fine new quarters. Some penny-pinching Congressmen complained that it was a great waste of money and provided far more space than necessary. At that time the Chancery building housed not only the Embassy but the Tokyo Consulate General and the offices of the Commercial, Military, and Naval Attachés. Today the apartments in the compound have been turned into offices, an additional tall office building has been purchased and more space is still needed.

The Ambassador was W. Cameron Forbes, former Governor General of the Philippines, and on the evening of Washington's Birthday he was giving a dinner and theatre party. I had no sooner unpacked my bags than I was notified by the Ambassador's private secretary that another man was needed at the party, that I was the only available bachelor, and that I should report in black tie at the residence at 7:45, prepared to be the dinner partner of one of the daughters of the Belgian Ambassador, Baron Bassompierre. It turned out to be a most pleasant evening and as I crawled into bed about midnight, I was convinced I had chosen well; this was diplomacy as it should be, beautiful ladies, bemedaled Ambassadors, sumptuous food and drink, and a rent-free apartment to come back to. The next morning I discovered there was another side which was a bit more grim. Bill Turner, third secretary of the Embassy, and an accomplished Japanese linguist, was in charge of the training of the language attachés, and he quickly made it clear that work and more work would be the order of the day and that evenings such as the previous one would be few and far between.

Bill was right. The next two years were filled with the drudgery of learning an extremely complicated foreign language. I was not, am not, and never will be a good linguist. The mechanics of learning a foreign language bore me, and, unfortunately, too much time was spent in Tokyo where there was not much incentive to speak Japanese once the daily lessons were finished. The Japanese teachers we had, with the exception of Mr. Naganuma who had devised the course, left a great deal to be desired. The other requirements of the Embassy course, the study of Japanese history, economics, government, and culture helped to make up for the dullness of the language course. The chance to wander around Tokyo, not then the smog- and taxi-filled horror it is today, made life livable as did the many interesting friends I met from all nationalities and all walks of life.

Among the latter were some young Japanese Foreign Office attachés who have remained good friends through many difficulties and many years. One of them, Eki Sone, is a member of the Diet (the Japanese parliament) and the chief foreign policy expert of the Democratic Socialist party. Another, Ambassador Kimura, was later to be my colleague when I was American Ambassador to Prague, and a third, Eiji Wajima, who retired from the Foreign Ministry after having served as Ambassador to Brussels and Cairo and is now (1972) the executive director of the Kajima Institute of International Peace in Tokyo. Shortly after I arrived in Tokyo Ambassador Forbes departed and was replaced by Joseph Grew, one of the great figures of the prewar professional diplomatic service. He exemplified the best of the old Service and, while a hard taskmaster, he maintained a real interest in his subordinates and taught them much. At least six of the men who served under Ambassador Grew during his ten years in Japan later became Ambassadors themselves, and I believe all of them would give him much of the credit for encouraging them to make the most of their careers.

Ambassador Grew brought with him as Private Secretary J. Graham (Jeff) Parsons, a young Groton and Yale graduate, who occupied the apartment just above mine. We became the best of friends and when, some twenty years later, I came back to Tokyo as Ambassador, I persuaded Jeff to join me as Minister-Counselor and Deputy Chief of Mission. He later went on to become Assistant Secretary of State for Far Eastern Affairs and then Ambassador to Sweden. In the summer of 1971, Jeff was Deputy Head of the American Delegation to the disarmament talks with the Russians.

One of the real pleasures of Tokyo in the thirties was the large number of secondhand book shops which offered for sale books in all languages. The largest number of these shops was concentrated in a three- or four-block area in the Kanda district, near many of the universities located in Tokyo. This was a happy hunting ground on Saturday afternoons. All the classic books on Asia in English and European languages could be found, some in first editions, but the field was not limited to the Orient. On one rainy, bleak afternoon I was cheered by finding a first edition of Darwin's *Descent of Man,* for which I paid the equivalent of one dollar. I later sold it to a dealer in New York for fifty dollars.

Less than a week before Christmas 1932, I received a cable from my old roommate in Shanghai, Ed Snow. With all the confidence usually found in journalists that anything they want can be produced, Ed announced he was arriving Christmas eve with his fiancée and wanted me to produce a preacher and a wedding for them on, as the cable said, "Christ Noon." What Ed didn't realize was that no marriage is legal in Japan unless it is registered at the appropriate Ward Office which, for foreigners, would require complicated documents in Japanese and English, certified by the American Consul in the case of Americans. He also did not realize that in Japan Christmas was a holiday (not because it was Christmas, but because it was the anniversary of the death of the previous Emperor) and that the Kojimachi Ward Office, the one nearest the Embassy, would be closed as would the American Consulate. How could he get married on Christmas noon?

Because of my previous service as a YMCA teacher, I had come to know many in the missionary community, and I managed to persuade one of them, the Reverend Howard Hannaford of the Presbyterian mission, to perform a religious ceremony in my apartment at high noon on Christmas. I persuaded a young lady friend, a teacher in the American School, to come and serve as maid of honor; I would act as best man and my cook-housekeeper produced a cake. Ed and his bride-to-be appeared. She was Helen Folster who had been a secretary in the American Consulate General in Shanghai and was now, with Ed's encouragement, writing under the name Nym Wales about the trials and tribulations of the Chinese poor. Mr. Hannaford uttered the fateful words, Ed and Nym made the proper replies, and they were pronounced man and wife. I produced a bottle of champagne. It was drunk, the cake was cut, and off the happy couple went to a hotel, spiritually, but definitely not legally, married. The next day we made it all legal, complete with red seals.

Ed's example seemed to have merit and by June of the following year I had persuaded the young lady who had acted as maid of honor to take the leading role opposite me in a similar ceremony, again performed by the Reverend Hannaford. She was Jeannette Brooks who, while teaching French at the American

School, was living with her half sister, Mrs. Antonin Raymond, almost next door to the American Embassy. Antonin Raymond, who had been one of the supervising architects for the new Embassy compound, had originally come to Japan as an associate of Frank Lloyd Wright to build the famous Imperial Hotel. He was Czech by nationality and his wife, Naomi, was French, but they had become American citizens. They were both artists at heart, and Tony was also the most conceited man I had ever met at that time. Sukarno came later. The maddening thing about Tony was that he was so often right. Unfortunately, Mr. Hannaford's efforts for both Ed and myself failed to have lasting effect, and after several years both marriages ended in divorce.

The two years of study finally came to an end, and I managed to pass all my examinations and was appointed Vice Consul in Tokyo. My principal responsibility was the granting of visas to Japanese and other foreigners going to the United States, and supervising citizenship matters, including the protection of Americans who might get into trouble with the Japanese authorities. I remember one attractive young English lady who came in with her mother to get a visa to go to California. Her name was Joan de Haviland, and her older sister Olivia was already beginning to be known in Hollywood. I have never since met Joan Fontaine, as she is now known; I doubt if she would remember me.

In October of 1934, Tokyo was visited by William C. Bullitt, the first American Ambassador to the Soviet Union. I was anxious to meet him as I recalled that during my oral examinations for entry into the Foreign Service in October 1931, I had caused raised eyebrows among the examining panel when, in response to a question as to what I thought about the possible recognition of the Soviets, I had replied that I thought it was inevitable and that we might as well do it sooner instead of later. We had now done it, and here was the man who could tell me what the Communist state was really like.

Again, my luck held. When Jeannette and I were married, we were moved into a larger apartment in the same building. When Ambassador Bullitt arrived he was put up in my old apartment. One afternoon I was asked to come in at five o'clock to interpret for Mr. Bullitt who had requested a Japanese tailor to come up to see him, as he wished to order a proper ceremonial kimono. I arrived before the tailor and Ambassador Bullitt, and was met by his private secretary, Carmel Offey, who said the Ambassador would arrive shortly. Soon the door flew open and in dashed Bullitt full of enthusiasm and excitement about what he had seen in Tokyo. I was introduced, the Ambassador shed his suit coat, and called out, "You like martinis, don't you?" I agreed, and he went to work mixing one himself and handed it to me. As a young vice consul I was not accustomed to having Ambassadors personally mix my drinks, but I managed to drink it and even a second. The tailor arrived. His English was somewhat better than my Japanese, but he was an Oriental gentleman and realizing I was supposed to be the interpreter, he played up to me. Mr. Bullitt had me explain that he wanted to order two ceremonial kimonos exactly alike in all but one respect. On the sleeves and collar of such kimonos there appears in a small round circle the family crest of the wearer. In this circle Ambassador Bullitt wanted initials. On one kimono these would be WCB, his own, and on the other the initials would be FDR. I went home that evening in something of a daze. The young vice consul had not only had two martinis mixed for him personally by an Ambassador, but he had helped in picking out a Christmas present for the President of the United States. I never did find out at that time what Mr. Bullitt thought about the Communists in Russia.

A few weeks later I was to meet a man through whom I would meet still another well-known character, but one as different from Ambassador Bullitt as night is from day. One evening in the lobby of the Imperial Hotel I was introduced to Harry

Snyder who was the sales representative in Asia and the Pacific for a group of thirty or forty American publishers. All my old interest in books and publishing came flooding back, and the next night I managed to get him to our apartment for dinner. He brought me a book of essays by Christopher Morley who was one of my favorite authors. This book had been dedicated to Harry and in one section told of how Morley and Harry had come together to Honolulu, where Morley was to give lectures on Shakespeare at the University of Hawaii, and Harry was selling to the local booksellers.

As a result of this chance meeting I was to become a friend of that great, jolly and yet somewhat sad human being, Christopher Morley. Before Harry Snyder left Tokyo I had also met his partner Bill Hall, another close friend of Morley and an avid book collector, who introduced me to the works of Max Beerbohm. I took him with me one night down to the Kanda book shops, and he told me how much they resembled the shops along Charing Cross Row in London. At night some of the poorer dealers put up stalls, where all sorts of odds and ends could be found. While picking through one stall, I came upon a first edition of *The Lookout Man* by David Bone, a British sea captain and friend of Christopher Morley who had often written about him. I gave the stall keeper the thirty sen (about fifteen cents) that was marked on the back flyleaf, but he shook his head and pointed to another mark on a strip of paper inserted inside the front cover on which was marked sixty sen. He then opened the book carefully and showed me what I had overlooked, a pasted-in postcard signed by David Bone. I hastened to give him the sixty sen and went off to show my find to Bill Hall who had wandered into one of the larger shops.

Bill was delighted and later wrote a long letter to Morley which was published in his column in the *Saturday Review*, telling of my find and, with considerable exaggeration, describing me as a "bibliophile extraordinary." The next spring Jeannette and I were in New York, and I called at the old office of the *Saturday Review* on West Forty-fifth Street and asked to see Mr. Morley. A visitor just ahead of me was being turned down and was told Mr. Morley had a dental appointment he couldn't break. I diffidently handed in my card and said I would like to make an appointment to see Mr. Morley when he might be free. The young lady who took the card was Morley's secretary, and when she saw my name she told me she was sure Mr. Morley would see me right then. Apparently Harry Snyder and Bill Hall had been good advance agents, for in a moment I heard a bellow from inside, "Oh! John Allison, send him in." I was taken in and greeted with an infectious smile and an outstretched hand by this hulking figure of a man in shirt sleeves. His first words were, "You're coming to lunch with me. David Bone will be there! His ship is in."

Off we went to a delightful meal, in an upstairs room, at the old Chris Cella's restaurant on East 45th Street, which was the haunt of booksellers, publishers, and writers. Book collectors were also admitted, and here I later met Colonel Isham, the famous Boswell collector, who one noon made an entrance and exit worthy of John Barrymore. Here I also met, on still another occasion, Buckminster Fuller who was just breaking into the headlines as a result of his invention of the Dymaxion, a three-wheeled motor car. The car was parked outside, and after lunch he offered to drive Chris and me back to the *Saturday Review* office. We got in and drove up Forty-fifth Street to the amazed glances of the people on the sidewalk. At one corner we were stopped briefly by a red light. A young man came up and gazed with awe at the amazing contraption. "What in hell is that?" he exclaimed. Just then the light changed, and as we drove off Chris leaned out the window and shouted, "It's a split infinitive."

In July we returned to Tokyo, and I was again occupied with giving visas and listening to the sad tales of Americans who had suddenly found themselves without funds and had come to the Consulate confident that they would be sent home. It was my job to explain that the American Government had no funds available to take care of indigent citizens, unless they happened to be merchant seamen. In the latter case we could arrange for them to be taken back to the United States on an American vessel, and we could provide for them while they waited for a ship to become available. For other Americans there were absolutely no funds. However, there was an American Association, and in some cases it would lend funds to Americans whose cases seemed to merit it. It is sad to have to report that of the seven or eight such cases during my brief time in the Consulate in Tokyo, I only know of one where the loan was repaid.

During the latter part of the summer a young American Consul, Horace Smith, from the Consulate General in Canton, China, came to Tokyo on vacation. Horace had been a Chinese language officer just as I had been a Japanese language officer, and we often joked with each other about the respective merits of the two services. While in Tokyo Horace received word that he had been transferred to Tsinan, the capital of Shantung Province in North China. This was a one-man post in a provincial city far removed from the bright lights and conveniences of cities such as Tokyo, Shanghai, or even Canton. I commiserated with Horace and told him that the reason I had gone into the Japanese language service instead of the Chinese was because Tsinan was part of the China service.

In September I was transferred to Dairen, Manchuria, which at that time was under Japanese control. This was a small post with only two officers, and I was therefore able to engage in a much wider variety of work than in Tokyo. For the first time I had an opportunity to draft some political and economic reports and thus make use of the knowledge I had gained during my two years of study at the Embassy in Tokyo. A bit of international intrigue also enlivened the days when I received secret instructions from our Treasury Attaché in Shanghai, who was in charge of investigating narcotic smuggling, to observe discreetly the movements of the Honorary Lithuanian Consul who was sus- pected of being involved. This character was a White Russian businessman who had all the pomposity and obsequiousness of the average undertaker. My discreet surveillance, which lasted several weeks, increased our suspicions but resulted in no proof of illegal activity. When I left Dairen several months later, the Honorary Consul was still one of the pillars of the foreign community.

About the middle of the morning of February 26, 1936, one of our Japanese clerks, who had been out on an errand, returned and told us of rumors spreading through the city that there had been a revolution or an armed mutiny by army units in Tokyo and that many government and industrial leaders had been assassinated. There was nothing on the radio, and when we tried to telephone the Embassy in Tokyo we discovered all communication with the capital was cut off. The British Consul had no more news than we did, so I walked around the corner to the offices of the National City Bank to see if the manager had any information. He had a little and reported that central Tokyo was in a state of seige and that the Prime Minister, the Finance Minister, and several others had been killed.

That evening the American and European members of the Dairen Club had scheduled a dinner in honor of Yosuke Mat- suoka, the President of the South Manchurian Railway and a former high ranking Japanese official, who in 1933 after the Manchurian incident had taken Japan out of the League of Nations. We didn't know whether to go ahead with the dinner or not, but inquiries to Matsuoka's office confirmed that he wished us to. As we gathered at the Club and met in the lounge for the pre-dinner cocktails most of us were a bit embarrassed about speaking to Mr. Matsuoka about the events in Tokyo. It was something like going up to a man and saying, "I hear your brother killed your father. Tell me about it." As we got in the reception line to greet the guest of honor most members said nothing. I was standing in line just behind the Soviet Consul, and when he reached Mr. Matsuoka he exhibited no bourgeois inhibitions and, in loud tones, asked, "What can you tell us about what happened today in Tokyo?" Matsuoka didn't blink an eye but for almost twenty minutes declaimed about what he called "The Showa Restoration" and what it would mean for the future of Japan and Asia.

I had first heard of the Showa Restoration the previous autumn, when a young army Colonel named Aizawa had used it as the overall inspiration for his murder of General Nagata, Director of the Military Affairs Bureau of the Japanese War Ministry. Showa, meaning *Enlightened Peace*, had been chosen as the name of the reign of the present Emperor and upon his death he would be known as the Emperor Showa, just as his grandfather was known as Emperor Meiji. The Meiji Restoration had brought Japan into the modern world, and now young officers were talking about a Showa Restoration. At his trial, Aizawa had claimed that its purpose was to restore the Emperor to his rightful place, which the young officers believed had been usurped by capitalists and politicians. Mr. Matsuoka reaffirmed this and went on to say that the young officers who were the spearhead of the movement may have been premature in their action in Tokyo but that all right thinking Japanese would have considerable sympathy for them.

As Matsuoka stood there in his well-tailored, dark gray suit, his Dunhill pipe in his left hand, his bristling military mustache and crew cut hair, he looked every inch a member of the capitalist establishment. Yet he was backing the young soldiers in acts that were to become increasingly violent, threaten representative government, not at that time a strong reed in Japan, and eventually lead to Pearl Harbor. Mr. Matsuoka later became Foreign Minister and was one of the leaders in bringing about Japan's adherence to the Axis Pact with Hitler and Mussolini. The story was prevalent that in his youth at a school in Oregon Matsuoka had been insulted by some American calling him a "God damn Jap" and that although he spoke colloquial American and on the surface was friendly to individual Americans, he harbored a deep hatred of the people who, he believed, had looked down on him. I never found proof of the story, but one evening at a small dinner at the American Consulate a few weeks after the events of February 26, 1936, his reply to a question about what his children were doing seemed to me significant. He said that his daughter was in a girls' school in Tokyo and his oldest son in university. "My younger son," he added, "is going to the military academy to learn how to fight against the Americans!" He smiled as he said this and passed it off as a joke, but I believe he was more than half serious.

The days in Dairen went by pleasantly. The climate was invigorating and the work had sufficient variety to be interesting. Then one bright, early summer day the blow fell. I received from Washington orders to go to Tsinan and relieve Horace Smith, who was going on home leave. I was assured the assignment would only be for four months and that I would return to Dairen. As it turned out Horace never came back to Tsinan, and I never returned to Dairen. I took ship to Tsingtao and then the railway inland to what I was certain would be four months of purgatory. It turned out to be one of the most interesting assignments I ever had. I was, for the first time, in charge of a Consulate. I was the only officer, but I had two remarkable Chinese brothers to help me. The Chen brothers were jewels of great price, without whom I would have been lost.

The Consulate office was in one wing of a spacious house set in a stone-wall-enclosed compound covering an acre of ground. One half was a flower garden and one half a vegetable garden where we grew peas, radishes, lettuce, and sweet corn. In addition to the Chen brothers, who helped in the office, there was a number one boy, a cook, a *wash amah* who did the laundry, a housemaid and a coolie. Wang, the number one boy, supervised them all, did all the purchasing of food and other items needed, and received from the dealers his expected twenty percent commission which was, of course, included in our monthly bills. My wife came on to Tsinan when it was evident I was staying for a while, and we lived high on $3,500 a year, the salary of a Class VIII Foreign Service Officer. An all wise State Department did not believe it essential before World War II that Consuls should have motor cars, but I *was* provided with a private rickshaw and rickshaw puller, a relic of other times. Whenever I paid an official visit to the Governor or Mayor or other officials a taxi was hired. The rickshaw puller got fat and lazy from lack of exercise.

One of the first nonofficial Chinese friends I met was C. C. Chen, the manager of the Bank of China. "CC," as everyone called him, was a graduate of Cornell Agricultural College and had later spent time in the southern part of the United States studying the operation of cotton and tobacco cooperatives. Shantung Province, of which Tsinan was the capital, was a great cotton and tobacco growing area and the Central government in Nanking had sent CC to be in charge of the Bank of China branch there to determine what the Bank could do to help in the financing and support of cotton and tobacco cooperatives which were being set up to help the peasants. It was one of the first steps the government of Chiang Kai-shek had taken to do something definite for the people. Other measures were also under way and the people of Shantung were slowly beginning to believe that the government in Nanking was interested in them. Han Fu-chu, the tall, slender, scholarly looking Governor of the Province, had been one of the last of the war lords and for some time had been conducting the affairs of Shantung as if it were his own duchy. But he, too, was beginning to listen to Nanking and pay more than just lip service to its directions.

The Japanese militarists, who had already taken Manchuria and penetrated the Peiping-Tientsin areas in North China, saw what was happening and became fearful that their plans for the setting up and control of a puppet regime in North China might be frustrated. In an attempt to weaken the economy of the area, truck loads of armed Japanese smugglers poured into Shantung, and brazenly flaunted local laws and regulations. The efforts of the Central and local Provincial governments to do something for the people were more and more being blocked by Japanese actions, official and nonofficial. Finally in the summer of 1937, regular Japanese troops began surging into the Province after the Marco Polo Bridge incident just outside of Peiping. What the Japanese were later to call the "Special Undeclared War" had begun. The faltering steps that Chiang and his Kuomintang government had been taking to do something for the people came to a halt and were never seriously resumed.

Before all that happened, however, we were to have a glimpse of how old customs still remained in twentieth century China. One day we received an invitation to the wedding of the youngest son of Governor Han Fu-chu. The day of the wedding arrived. I put on my morning coat and high silk hat, Jeannette was in her finest, complete with long white gloves, and we hired the shiniest taxi in all Tsinan. Upon arrival at the Governor's residence we were met by a young officer in dress uniform who guided us into the mansion and through the various rooms to see all the wedding presents spread out on old, wooden tables covered with soiled white cloths. As we went into one room our guide said, "Please come over here and meet Madame Han" and led us to a rather tall, elegantly coiffured lady of indeterminate age, dressed in a bright Chinese dress with a revealing slit in its skirt, who bowed and held out a heavily bejeweled hand. We went into a second room, and the guide again said, "I want you to meet Madame Han." This time it was a young lady who at most was in her early twenties (Governor Han was in his early sixties). She was smartly, but not elaborately, dressed and seemed somewhat confused by all that was going on. We went into a third room and again were introduced to "Madame Han." This lady, obviously in her fifties, was stout and awkward in her movements, but not only was she also "Madame Han," she was, we were told, the mother of the young man who was getting married. She was the real wife who ran the home. The first lady we had met was the social wife, and we were later to meet her at social occasions that the Governor attended. The young girl was seldom seen in public with the Governor, but we were given to understand that she played a very important role in his life!

By August it was clear that the Japanese Army was really headed south and so Jeannette and our Scottie were sent back to Tokyo. In September when the Japanese had almost reached the Yellow River, some four miles north of the city, I was instructed to advise all Americans in the district to leave for Tsingtao, where, if necessary, they could get ships to Japan or Shanghai. Most, but not all, of them left. I was told to close the Consulate and go to Nanking to work in the Embassy. On a hot September day I climbed aboard a crowded, dirty, alleged express train which would take eighteen hours to reach Pukow on the Yangstze River just across from Nanking. We arrived at the Embassy compound just in time to hear the airraid sirens sound the first warning. About twenty minutes later, as I was stepping out of a most welcome shower, the alert was sounded, and we soon began to hear the rumble of the planes and then the crunch of bombs dropping on the outskirts of the city. It was the first time I had ever heard shots of any kind fired in anger, but for the next eight years I was never to be, for long, very far away from the sound of guns or bombs. Before V-J Day in August of 1945, I was bombed by the Japanese, the Chinese, the Americans (the Doolittle raid), and the Germans to say nothing of the flying bombs in London. I also went through a Japanese artillery bombardment of Tsinan, which I shall tell about shortly.

The first bombs in Nanking were not too close, but as the

Japanese became more skillful and more daring they would come right into the center of the city, fly up Chungshan Road, the main street, dropping bombs as they went and then turn off sharply just before they reached our Embassy. We were located on a hill from which we had a good view of the entire city, and when we were not at our desks we were peering out the windows and getting our first glimpse of what modern war was like. One afternoon, Ambassador Nelson Johnson and I stood at the window of his office, and watched five Japanese planes fly from across the river and head for the Nanking power plant. One after another they made sharp dives, leveled off, and dropped their bombs from not more than 500 feet. That night we used lanterns to read by.

Ambassador Johnson was outraged at the callous bombing of civilians and nonmilitary targets. He made strong pleas to Washington and to the American Embassy in Tokyo for protests to be made to the Japanese Government. All his staff shared the Ambassador's indignation. We did not forsee what total war would become. None of us could then have imagined the mass bombing of London, Coventry, Hamburg, Dresden, and Berlin. Certainly none of us foresaw the almost total devastation of central Tokyo by fire bombs or the destruction of Hiroshima and Nagasaki. When 1945 came to an end we all, Americans as well as Japanese, had unclean hands.

By the middle of November, the Japanese had not yet crossed the Yellow River into Tsinan and many of the Americans who had left the city were beginning to come back. I requested and received permission from the Ambassador to return and see what was happening. Most of the missionaries had returned and believed they could stay. The British Consulate was closed, but the German Consul, a stout, white-haired grandfatherly man, was still there. He was far from being a Nazi but was too near retirement age to make any strong protests. He told me that even if the Japanese entered the city he proposed to remain.

The Swedish Postmaster and his wife were still there, and on the first Sunday after my return they invited me to accompany them and the C. C. Chens on a picnic at an attractive spot several miles south of the city. As we were returning we suddenly heard the buzz of several small planes, and three Japanese fighters swooped down toward our car. We stopped and all dived into a ditch. We heard the rattle of machine guns, but no one was hit and the Japanese flew off. A rather sober group hastened back to the city. I walked over to the Tsinan Club, only about five minutes from the Consulate, and was having a drink with the two or three foreign businessmen who were still around, when the Club's number one boy came in and told me a strange looking foreigner was outside and wanted to see me.

I went out to discover a slender, slightly curly-haired young man in dirty khaki trousers and shirt and carrying a topee and a kit bag, standing there grinning and holding out his hand. As we shook hands he told me he was Captain Frank Dorn, Assistant Military Attaché at the American Embassy in Peiping. He had been on a walking reconnaisance tour behind the Japanese lines trying to find out what they were doing, and what the Chinese were doing in response. He needed a place to rest for a day or two and some new clothes. Dorn was a most welcome guest. Not only was he a fine soldier, but he was a great gourmet. He was later to be Chief of Staff to General Stilwell in China and Burma, and after he retired as a Brigadier General he wrote several highly praised cookbooks.

By the following Sunday it was becoming increasingly clear that the Japanese army was going to enter Tsinan. I had called a meeting of the leading Americans for Monday evening to consider what we should do when the Japanese did come in, but just before the meeting was to commence I received peremptory orders from Washington to return to Nanking via Tsingtao. The train to Pukow had been put out of commission.

Most of the missionaries decided they would stay no matter

what I did. I told the Chen brothers that I had authority to take them to Tsintao, too, but they also elected to stay. C. C. Chen, the banker, had sent his family down to Shanghai after our experience with the Japanese fighters, and when I told him I was planning to leave Wednesday evening he said he would go with me, and we secured a compartment for two on the night train. About five o'clock Wednesday afternoon the Japanese suddenly began an artillery bombardment of the city from across the Yellow River. We could hear the boom of the guns as they fired and could feel the ground shake as the shells landed. All my Chinese staff were frantic, and the Chinese managers of several American firms came rushing into what they fondly hoped was a safe refuge. The bombardment kept up for two hours and then stopped as suddenly as it had begun. I told the Chen brothers they could move their families into the Consulate and take in any Chinese who worked for American firms, but no others. I then went over to the Tsinan Club where CC was waiting for me. A Scotch and soda never tasted so good.

I finally arrived in Shanghai just before Thanksgiving and the day after the Japanese had broken through the barrier on the Yangstze that had been blocking the path to Nanking. Consul General Gauss thought it would be silly for me to try to go on to Nanking under the circumstances and wired the State Department for instructions. Back came what I have always considered a classic Department reply. "Allison should remain in Shanghai until the situation clarifies."

# III

# Pool of Tears and a Mad Tea Party

## 1937–1941

IT TOOK some time for the situation in Nanking to "clarify," and in the meantime I did odds and ends of work in the Consulate General in Shanghai. Many of the same Chinese clerks and a few of the Americans who had been there when I had been in the commercial office six years before, were still there. They seemed glad to see me, and even the American clerks, whom I now outranked, didn't seem jealous. They were content to carry out their daily routine duties, which were not too onerous, and enjoy the creature comforts of Shanghai life which still abounded. They evidently thought I was a bit of a fool for being ambitious and trying to get ahead, which would only mean assuming additional responsibilities and now and then having to make decisions, all of which they were spared.

About two weeks after my arrival in Shanghai, the Japanese finally occupied Nanking and on the same day the American gunboat *Panay* was bombed and sunk by Japanese planes as it lay at anchor in the Yangstze River near Nanking. Four persons were killed, including an Italian journalist and two American seamen. A Standard Oil employee was also killed in one of that company's small boats which was tied up near the *Panay* and sunk. Members of the American staff, who had closed the Embassy in the city and were conducting an office on board the

*Panay*, were wounded as were the ship's officers. Under the general guidance of Second Secretary of Embassy George Atcheson and Captain Frank N. Roberts, Assistant Military Attaché, who had not been injured, the wounded and other members of the ship's company were landed on shore where, with the help of friendly Chinese, they escaped further injury and eventually were all brought safely to Shanghai.

Towards the end of December, 1937, it was decided to send another gunboat, the U.S.S. *Oahu*, up the Yangstze River with divers to undertake salvage operations on the *Panay*. Inasmuch as State Department documents and codes had been lost in the sinking, I was detailed to accompany the *Oahu* to take charge of whatever State Department property was recovered. It was also decided that upon the completion of the salvage operations I would be taken to Nanking to reopen the Embassy, survey the damage to American property, and learn what had happened to the eighteen American missionaries who had refused invitations to be evacuated before the Japanese occupation. A junior vice consul, Jim Espy, and an American code clerk were assigned to help me and just after Christmas we took off from Shanghai.

What came to be known as the "Rape of Nanking" was still in progress and the Japanese authorities kept delaying agreement to our re-entering the city. When we had recovered all that seemed possible from the *Panay* and still did not have permission to land in Nanking, we steamed up the river to Wuhu to visit the Episcopal missionaries who had remained there. During a brief visit we saw what damage had been done and were able to report that the Americans were safe. On our way back to the ship a single Chinese Air Force plane appeared over the city and harbor and dropped a few bombs, apparently in the belief that Japanese troops were in the vicinity. Fortunately their aim was poor and no damage was done.

Finally, on the morning of January 6, 1938, three weeks after the occupation of Nanking and the sinking of the *Panay*, we were allowed to land. We were the first officials of any government to enter the city. The British and German consuls arrived about a week later. Downtown Nanking was a shambles, whole blocks of shops and buildings having been shelled and looted. The residential district was not so badly damaged, but there were scars and signs of wanton destruction on all sides. The Japanese had made arrangements to get us to the Embassy compound which had escaped serious damage, although we soon discovered we had no electricity or running water. There was a good well nearby, and our servants, who had remained, were able to bring us enough for drinking and shaving. Later we took turns spending a night on the gunboat in order to have a shower now and then.

The acting Japanese Consul General, who with his staff occupied the former Japanese Embassy quarters, invited us to dinner the first evening. He put on quite a show and did everything possible to try and assure us we would have his full cooperation in carrying out our duties. Immediately after dinner he had his first opportunity to do so. That same day we had met with some of the American missionaries who had been through the whole seige and occupation of the city. They had told us a frightening tale of Japanese atrocities, directed not at them or the other few Westerners in the city, but at the Chinese. We were to see much of this sort of thing before we had been there many days. We were also told that the Japanese army had confiscated practically all the motor cars they could lay their hands on. We had already discovered that the American Ambassador's car was missing. One of the staff of the Japanese Embassy was my old friend Kimura, and after dinner we strolled out on the verandah to have coffee and to talk. The Embassy compound was packed with cars of all descriptions and suddenly, under a nearby tree, I recognized Ambassador Johnson's almost new Buick. I pointed it out to Kimura and said, "Kimura-san, I want that car at the American Embassy, filled with gasoline, the first thing in the morning." Poor Kimura, who had had nothing to do with the confiscation of the car, gulped and flushed deeply. He just nodded and went inside to speak to the Consul General. At nine o'clock the next morning the car, freshly washed, was delivered to the Embassy, and Ambassador Johnson's Chinese chauffeur, who was still with us, assured me it was in good condition. Kimura was soon transferred back to Tokyo, and Japanese cooperation never seemed quite as effective after his departure.

In the Ambassador's car Jim Espy and I set off to make our first official investigation of damage to American property. Prior to the departure of the Embassy staff on the ill-fated *Panay*, official notes in Chinese, Japanese, and English had been posted on all American property in the hopes that the Japanese troops might respect them and refrain from looting. It proved a vain hope. We had heard from the missionaries that the cottage of Embassy Third Secretary Douglas Jenkins had been ransacked and his Chinese servant, who had remained in the house, killed. It was all too true. The cottage was completely wrecked. Doors hung on one hinge, windows were broken, books, papers, remnants of sheets, pillow cases, and torn rugs were strewn all over the floor. The sign stating this was American property was torn in half. The servant's body had been taken away. We found similar conditions in many American homes. One of the largest, sitting on a small hill on the edge of the city, had obviously been in the line of fire for there were huge shell holes in several of the walls and much of the roof had been burned off. But after the shelling, soldiers had swarmed through and most movable furniture had been taken away as had dishes, silverware, sheets, blankets, and anything that could be slipped into a pocket. The Chinese caretaker was still there. His torso lay in the rear garden, his head in the front.

An International News Service report dated Washington, January 8, which I have before me, gives an account of my first impressions. "Allison reported the Japanese soldiers, who went on the loose after capturing the Chinese capital, were still imperfectly controlled, but that order was gradually being restored."

While order was being restored it seemed to us in the middle of the storm that it was terribly slow in coming. I received almost daily reports of further damage to American property or assaults upon Chinese refugees and employees living on American property. As a result of the reports that the Embassy passed on to Washington and Tokyo, the Embassy in Tokyo made strong protests to the Japanese Foreign Office. The Foreign Office in turn reported these protests and their source to the Japanese military with the result that I began to be most unpopular with the Japanese army in Nanking. On January 17 the Japanese Foreign Minister told Ambassador Grew he could not understand how the "undisciplined acts by Japanese troops could have occurred because the strongest possible orders had gone out to both army and navy to avoid acts or measures which might interfere with Japan's good relations with the United States."

The very next day we sent another telegram to Washington and Tokyo reporting further raids on American property. My telegram 27 of January 18 begins with the statement:

> Between noon of January 15 and noon today there have been reported to this Embassy 15 cases of irregular entry of American property by Japanese soldiers. In addition to property of American citizens and organizations which was removed during these irregular entries, 10 Chinese women refugees residing at the properties concerned were forcibly taken away.

I went on to describe a particularly flagrant case which had taken place just that morning when "Japanese soldiers with tow trucks entered a compound belonging to the United Christian Mission and took away a piano and other property." A large section of the wall surrounding the compound was broken down during the removal of the piano. Jim Espy had seen the wall in the morning and it was intact, but when I saw it at 1:45 P.M. it had been torn down. This report was the basis of a further protest in Tokyo, and I became still more unpopular.

It was not a pleasant task having to make these adverse reports about the actions of a people I had known and liked. The grim weather, the lack of electricity, running water, and central heating in almost zero weather did not help matters. But there were lighter moments. Every other week we would send down to the Consulate General in Shanghai by radio a request for supplies which would be sent up by either the American gunboat *Oahu* or the British gunboat *Bee*.

One morning Jim Espy brought in for my approval the usual routine request. After listing the number of slabs of bacon, the several dozen eggs, the cases of Coca-Cola, and similar items, the message concluded: "one four-piece dance orchestra and three Russian dancing girls." I gasped and looked again. The message was still the same. I looked out the office window and saw that it had begun to snow; the sun had sunk behind a cloud, and my telephone began ringing with what I knew would be another report of illegal Japanese action. It was. I looked at Jim, who had kept a perfectly straight face, and decided life was too short to put up with this sort of thing. I scrawled my initials on the paper. "Now let's see what Shanghai will say!" It was Jim's turn to gasp. He had never thought I would sign the message. I knew that the answer would be cleared by my friend Dick Buttrick who was the Executive Consul and number two man in the Shanghai Consulate General. The next day the reply came. It read: "Supplies requested in your No. 12 going forward tomorrow on H.M.S. *Bee*. You will readily understand that certain of the items requested by you cannot be obtained at short notice." Life seemed a little brighter even if we didn't get the girls. The officers on the *Oahu*, through which the messages were exchanged, finally began to think of Foreign Service Officers as human beings.

My reports about the continuing Japanese violations of American property were apparently really beginning to hurt. The Japanese Consul in charge of their Embassy, Mr. Fukui, told me I was only listening to the American missionaries who were prejudiced in favor of the Chinese and that I should not place too much credence in their complaints. I told him that I had checked the missionaries' stories and that I had no reason to disbelieve them. However, in view of Mr. Fukui's statement, I said I would personally investigate the next report of Japanese illegal entry which came to me. I did not have to wait. A report had already been made that afternoon which I would investigate the next day.

I had been called on by Dr. M. S. Bates and Mr. Charles Riggs of the faculty of Nanking University, an American institution. They told me that on the previous evening armed Japanese soldiers had forced their way into the agricultural implement shop of the University and had taken a Chinese woman from the premises. She returned after about two hours and reported that she had been raped three times. Dr. Bates and Mr. Riggs had questioned the girl, who was able to identify the place where she had been taken as a former residence of Catholic priests, which had been taken over by Japanese troops. I asked them to get the girl after lunch and return to the Embassy. I made arrangements with the Japanese Embassy for Japanese Consular police and gendarmes to go with me, Mr. Riggs, and the girl to investigate the matter. We first went to the implement shop where the other Chinese workers were questioned. The woman and two Chinese were then taken by the Consular police to the building where the rape was alleged to have occurred. Mr. Riggs and I followed. The woman was taken into the building supposedly to identify her assailants, and there was a discussion before the gate as to whether Mr. Riggs and I should also enter the building. Mr. Riggs, feeling responsible for the woman, who was in his employ, decided he should follow her and he started to do so. I felt responsible for Mr. Riggs, an

American citizen, and started to follow him. Just inside the gate, which was open, I called to him to wait a moment while we discussed the matter a bit more. While we were doing so, an unusually large Japanese soldier, red faced as if he had been drinking, dashed out and in a loud, angry voice shouted in English, "Back, Back." We started slowly to do so but before we could get out of the gate he slapped me across the face, turned, and did the same to Mr. Riggs and also tore his necktie and shirt.

The Japanese gendarmes tried rather feebly to stop the soldiers, and we did get out of the gate and into the road. A Japanese officer came out and shouted at us, and several Japanese soldiers with rifles and fixed bayonets appeared. Discretion seemed the better part of valor, and I rounded up Riggs and the Japanese Consular police and went immediately to the Japanese Embassy, where I made a strong protest to Mr. Fukui. I told him I knew that the representatives of the Japanese Foreign Office did not have much power over the military and therefore I would not be satisfied with an apology from him. I told him I wanted two things. I wanted the Chinese girl released that afternoon and returned to the university. She was. I wanted an apology before noon the next day from an official representative of the Japanese military. Mr. Fukui tried to play down the incident and suggested we had no business being in the soldiers' compound. I reminded him that he had complained because I only listened to missionaries and that I had told him I would make the next investigation myself. I had done so and this is what happened. It only increased my belief that what the missionaries had told me about the actions of the Japanese soldiers had been correct. I said a full report would be made to my government, but I would not send it until noon the next day so that I could report whether or not I had received an apology from the military.

At eleven the next morning I was called upon by Major

Hongo, who was the official liaison officer from military head-quarters with the foreign consuls. He was in full uniform with medals and sword. He bowed deeply and on behalf of the Commander of the Japanese forces expressed regret for the incident and offered apologies. He told me the unit responsible had been scheduled to leave Nanking that day, but its departure had been postponed in order to complete an investigation into the matter. I thanked Major Hongo for his call and said that while I personally accepted his apology I could not say what view of the matter would be taken by my government. Upon his departure I immediately sent off my report, which I had already drafted except for the final paragraph reporting Major Hongo's call.

The following afternoon I was astounded to hear on the radio that the Japanese had announced I had refused to leave the building when the Japanese soldier challenged me and that I had insulted the Japanese army. It was less than six weeks since the *Panay* had been sunk by Japanese bombs and the Japanese military authorities apparently were worried about possible American reaction to the slapping of an American official unless they could show that it had been the official's fault. Within a few days Major Hongo told me that the question of my having insulted the Japanese army had been based upon a misunderstanding. The State Department backed me up and published large portions of my report, and Ambassador Grew in Tokyo made strong protests to the Japanese Foreign Office. Within a short time I was notified that an official representative of the Japanese Government, not just the military, was coming to Nanking to offer an apology. In a day or two Katsuo Okazaki, the Japanese Consul General in Shanghai, arrived at the Embassy in formal morning coat, striped trousers, and high silk hat with an accompanying aide. He read a formal apology from the Japanese Government, bowed, and departed.

I did not meet Mr. Okazaki again for twelve years. He was then a special assistant to Japanese Prime Minister Yoshida, who was also then acting as Foreign Minister, and I was in Tokyo with John Foster Dulles to have the first talks with Japanese officials about a possible peace treaty. When I arrived in Japan in 1953 as American Ambassador, Mr. Okazaki was Foreign Minister. We became the best of friends. He and my wife were often bridge partners at diplomatic dinners, while Mrs. Okazaki and I, neither of us being bridge players, would sit in a corner and talk about the changes in postwar Japan.

A further result of the slapping incident was that the Japanese sent a special emissary to Nanking to investigate what was really happening and to attempt to calm down the American group and our British and German colleagues who were also sending in adverse reports. The man chosen for this task was Major General Masaharu Homma, who seven years later would be executed because of war crimes committed by his troops in the Philippines. The General spoke fluent English and with his clipped brush mustache bore a striking resemblance to a British officer. My British and German colleagues and I were promptly invited to a gala dinner by the General which proved to be more like a Mad Tea Party.

We were met in the reception room of the Japanese Embassy not only by General Homma but by the general commanding troops in Nanking, several members of his staff, as well as members of the Japanese Embassy staff. A great variety of predinner drinks, including Black Label Scotch and Gordon's Gin, which General Homma had imported just for us, was passed around. While we were enjoying these reminders of a former and less arduous existence, General Homma took the floor to explain why the Japanese soldiers had behaved so badly. The three foreign diplomats listened quietly and with straight faces to an amazing tale, full of contradictions. At one point, the looting of shops and private homes was said to be due to the Japanese troops having advanced so quickly against the weak Chinese resistance that they had outdistanced their supply trucks, and the looting had really just been an attempt to obtain needed supplies to last until their own caught up with them. A few minutes later we were told that the harshness and cruelty shown the Chinese population was the result of the indignation and outrage felt by the Japanese soldiers at the unexpected strong resistance put up by the Chinese troops. Such things should not happen to the Imperial Army! Then we were told of the difficulties of imposing a uniform discipline on a large force under battle conditions. General Homma explained, in complete seriousness, that when he had been a colonel in command of a new regiment it had taken him over six months to get the soldiers to salute the way he desired. We sipped our Black Label and nodded solemnly.

Then we were led into the dining room where a really sumptuous feast awaited us. It was a mixture of Thanksgiving and Christmas; roast turkey, goose, ham, sweet potatoes, cranberry sauce, fresh celery and a green salad, and to make my British colleague happy we ended up with trifle and cheese, accompanied by a reasonably good port. With the cheese and port in pranced three little Japanese maidens in brightly colored kimonos who bowed low to the foreign guests and sang a little song of greeting. They then came to the side of each of the guests and lifting a sake cup, smirked and managed to utter in a singsong voice in English, "I like you. You like me?" Gilbert and Sullivan was never like this. Our Japanese hosts sat back and grinned broadly. Obviously their guests would not want to send to Tokyo any more bad reports about Japanese soldiers.

While conditions did improve after General Homma's visit it was well into spring before it was completely safe to walk the streets of Nanking or take hikes in the surrounding countryside. It was difficult to reconcile the behavior of the Japanese soldiers, most of whom were just country boys in uniform, with the young farmers I had met in Japan during many cross-country hikes. There, the Japanese were always polite, ready to offer tea and cakes to a tired foreigner and go miles out of their way to guide a lost American back to his inn. Here, they were bullies. Part of it was due to the harsh training they received in the old pre-Pearl Harbor Japanese army, where officers frequently slapped their men and often treated them like animals. Part of it was due to the fact that codes of conduct were created to be applied in a Japanese environment in a traditional manner applicable only to the old feudal society. They had no rules to guide them in the hurly-burly of a twentieth century industrial society imported from abroad. The Japanese ethic was essentially a situational ethic, and the situations confronting them in modern war were unprecedented.

In fairness it should also be reported that the great majority of the Japanese troops in Nanking behaved themselves. They were a bit arrogant and pushed people around, but they didn't take part in the atrocities and violations of American property which we had been reporting. However, it was still an uphill task to get the Japanese military to recognize American rights and interests in China. As the violations of American property gradually ceased, we were kept busy at the Embassy trying to get permission for American businessmen to return to Nanking to take over their property and for American missionaries and their families to come back.

As time went by, we began to get more and more back mail from the United States. In looking through a delayed copy of the *Nation* one day, I was astonished to see an editorial by Oswald Garrison Villard, the publisher, castigating me for having brought the United States and Japan close to war because I had gone to the rescue of a Chinese woman. He ignored the fact that I was investigating a violation of American property and that my entry into a Japanese military compound was in order to protect an American citizen. He merely assumed I had been overzealous and had created an incident which might have led to war. This was the same Oswald Garrison Villard who a few years earlier had strongly criticized American Foreign Service

Officers in Germany for not doing more to help the German Jews being persecuted by Hitler, none of whom were American citizens. I was reminded of this in reading the headlines and press accusations in the spring of 1971, on the publication of the *Pentagon Papers,* that the American Government had been wrong to aquiesce in the coup against Diem in Saigon, when in 1963 the same papers had been loud in their cries that the American Government had no business giving support to an undemocratic dictator like Diem.

The summer dragged on. Most of the real excitement was over. Our days were spent in making protests to the Japanese authorities about arbitrary restrictions placed upon the travel of Americans between Shanghai and Nanking. We did have our lighter moments when we spent evenings on the gunboats stationed in the river just above Nanking. The U.S.S. *Oahu* and H.M.S. *Bee* often anchored next to each other, and we here developed what might be called the beginnings of lend-lease. The American gunboat was not allowed to serve liquor aboard, the British gunboat was. The American gunboat had movies, the British gunboat didn't. The Americans would surge into the wardroom of the *Bee* for cocktails and dinner, and after dinner everyone would return to the *Oahu* for movies and coffee.

In August I was granted home leave and en route stopped in Tokyo to pick up my wife, who had been there all the time I was in Nanking. I was able to see Ambassador Grew and thank him for his support and to see my other old friends including many Japanese. Everyone was most friendly, and I began to think I could forget Nanking, although I still was not sure what the State Department really thought about my actions. It had, of course, put out press statements supporting me, but I had heard nothing direct from any officer of the Department, either commending or reprimanding me. I knew the Department didn't like its officers to get their names in the papers, and I had lost a few pounds in worry. It was not until we arrived in San Francisco on the *President Hoover* that I found out where I stood.

There, waiting for me was a letter from my old friend Jeff Parsons enclosing a copy of the latest Foreign Service promotion list. I was on it.

We spent some time in Washington, where I discovered that, in the eyes of the powers that be, I had not done too badly in Nanking. They didn't quite know what to do with me though. As a former Japanese language student I should go back to Japan, but there were doubts about how I would be received. I was instructed to book passage back to Asia, and the exact destination would be told me later. We went off to New York to spend some time with the Raymonds and then back to Lincoln, Nebraska, to spend Christmas with my family, before we took off for Asia from Seattle on the *President Pierce*, December 29. I still hadn't been told where I was going and when December 21 came, and I had heard nothing, I sent a telegram to my friend John Carter Vincent, who was Chief of the Chinese Division and technically my boss as long as I was in Nanking. My message read: "Does anyone know or care where I'm going? Merry Christmas!" It worked. The next day I got a reply saying I had been assigned as Consul in Osaka, the industrial center of prewar Japan.

The office in Osaka was a Consulate General under the leadership of Consul General George Makinson. I was the second in command and when, in the spring of 1940, Mr. Makinson was transferred to Tokyo to be Supervisory Consul General for all of Japan, I was left in charge. The work was mostly routine, although from time to time there was an opportunity to write a more than routine political or economic report. Ford and General Motors which had once had large assembly plants in Japan had been gradually forced out by an increasingly xenophobic government, and the Japanese were on their own. In 1939 they produced a total of some 25,000 passenger cars and trucks and no one expected them to produce much more in the near future. War came and their whole industry was in a shambles. Yet in 1970, Japan produced six million cars and trucks and exported over 300,000 of them to the United States.

In September of 1940, Japan signed the Axis Pact with Germany and Italy, and our government began to urge women and children and nonessential men to return to the United States. The Consulate General sent letters to all of the 188 American citizens in our Consular district, which included the ancient capital, Kyoto, and the smaller commercial city of Wakayama. By the time of Pearl Harbor there were only about twenty-five Americans remaining. The *Mariposa* and *Monterey* were chartered by the American Government and sent to Asia as evacuation ships. I thought it necessary to insist that my wife leave as an example to other American wives who hesitated to leave their husbands. In the midst of our efforts to get as many as possible to leave, I received a touching letter from the eighty-year-old Miss Florence Denton, a well-known and greatly respected missionary teacher, who for over fifty years had been in the Girls' college at Doshisha University in Kyoto. She wrote that she was a loyal American and that if I thought it would be an embarrassment to the American Government for her to stay in Japan she would reluctantly go back to America. However, she believed deeply that it was her Christian duty to stay with her Japanese students as long as possible. What was my advice? I replied that the decision must be her own but that in my judgment the American Government would not require a citizen to act against her conscience and, in my opinion, her remaining in Japan would not be a cause of embarrassment to her government. She stayed throughout the war, and a friendly Japanese businessman officially adopted her so that she would not have to be interned.

After the women left, life became very dull. Office work declined, and all of us sat around waiting for war to come. We believed it to be inevitable, but no one could guess when or how. Then it came with unexpected suddenness.

# IV

# The Lobster Quadrille

## 1941–1942

MONDAY MORNING, December 8, 1941, was a beautiful, balmy day in Osaka. Fred Mann and "Tex" Weatherby, my two vice consuls, who had arrived in Japan the previous September, were sharing my home in Shukugawa, a pleasant little suburb just about halfway between Osaka and Kobe.

As Fred and Tex and I walked down to the interurban station to catch the train for Osaka, we were wondering just when war would come. The day before, I had started out on my usual Sunday morning hike with my Dutch neighbor from across the street, but as we started up the last leg of the path leading to the Rokko hills from which we could look over Osaka and Kobe harbors, we saw at the top of the path a fierce-looking Japanese soldier complete with rifle and bayonet. We agreed that discretion was the better part of valor and turned back to our homes. As we parted, we agreed to try again the next week. Sunday evening we had been about to turn on our short-wave radio to listen to the news from Treasure Island in San Francisco, when a young Japanese couple came to see us. The wife had been born and brought up in Canada and from time to time would make use of our fairly extensive library. That night she was returning some books she had borrowed. Her husband, who worked for Mitsui, brought us a bottle of Scotch. They were good friends but whenever Japanese visited us we turned off the radio.

And so, as Tex, Fred, and I approached the station that Monday morning, we did not know of President Roosevelt's message to the Emperor of Japan, which had been carried on the Treasure Island radio Sunday night. As we reached the station, we were joined by one of our young secretaries, an American girl of Japanese descent who lived with her widowed mother in our little suburb, and she told us the Japanese radio had been blaring announcements all night telling the people to keep tuned in for important news. But nothing definite had been heard by the time she left home. With rather strange feelings just above our belts, we piled into the overcrowded electric train. As we looked around it was evident that we were the only Americans aboard, at least in our car. But none of the Japanese commuters paid any attention to us. They were all reading their morning papers, which, as I saw when I looked over their shoulders, had no startling headlines.

After leaving the interurban express, we boarded a street car for the next eight or ten blocks and then had a final block and a half walk to the Osaka Shosen Kaisha building in which our office was located on the eighth floor, along with the British and German consuls, the Indian Trade Commissioner, and the Osaka district office of Socony Vacuum. At the corner, as we left the street car, was the office of the *Asahi* newspaper, Japan's largest. As is true of newspapers around the world, the *Asahi* had large outdoor bulletin boards on which the latest news was posted. Sending my colleagues on down to the office (they couldn't read Japanese anyway), I stopped to scan the bulletins. There was news of the Combined fleet being ordered South, of fighting in Malaya, but absolutely nothing about the United States or Pearl Harbor. As I turned to go to the office, a Swedish businessman, who was a member of an informal luncheon club of Westerners who ate at the New Asaka Hotel every noon, waved and said he would see me at lunch. I haven't seen him since.

Upon reaching the office, I discovered that none of our Japanese staff had any more definite information. I went up the hall to the British Consulate to see if my friend Dermit McDermit knew anything. He lived in Kobe and had not arrived. He never did arrive, and the next time I saw him was sixteen years later, when I went to Indonesia as American Ambassador and found he was the British Ambassador. His chief clerk had slightly more news than our staff. He had seen a brief *go-gai* (an extra edition of the *Asahi*) that said war was coming but gave no details.

I returned to my office and at 9:45 on the morning of December 8, 1941 (about midafternoon, December 7, Honolulu time) I made a telephone call to Arthur Tower, the American consul in Kobe about twenty miles away. Upon hearing him tell that he had been listening to the Shanghai radio station that morning, when it had been taken over by the Japanese military, and that he was burning codes and confidential documents, I decided to do the same in spite of the fact that we had no instructions from either Washington or the Embassy in Tokyo.

Our office consisted of two rectangular general offices on either side of a hall which led in one direction to the British Consulate and in the other to Socony Vacuum. I had a small private office in one end of the larger of the two rooms. And I had a metal wastebasket in which to burn codes, blank passports, and confidential papers. Fortunately, we only had two code books and one of these, the "Gray" Code, we were sure had been broken by the Japanese, and we only used it for the sake of economy. The "Brown" Code was supposed to be safe, and we spent considerable effort and time in tearing it apart and burning it. It was a waste of time. We learned later that the Japanese had broken it too. There was a fair number of copies of reports to and from the Embassy which also needed to be burned.

We had a young American clerk at the Consulate, Bruce Rogers, who lived in a house in Osaka which boasted of a furnace. I directed him and Vice Consul Mann to take the more bulky of our confidential correspondence out to his house for burning. At ten o'clock they were able to get a taxi that took them out to Bruce's home and waited for them while they burned the papers. In the meantime, Tex and I tore up the Brown Code and lesser papers as well as blank passports and consigned them to flames in the wastebasket. My chief Japanese clerk knocked diffidently at the office door and then came in and handed me the seals used on passports, notarials, invoices, and other papers and suggested I might want to destroy them too. He was right. I had completely forgotten about them. The office was getting hot and smoky, and we opened the windows. The smoke billowed out for all to see, and I had visions of the police breaking in at any moment to put a stop to our activities. But nothing happened.

In the last six months before Pearl Harbor, we had made friends of the Foreign Section of the Prefectural Police by using the small remaining funds in our representation account to take them on beer and sukiyaki parties once or twice a month. These police were charged with watching foreign consuls and their contacts. The money couldn't be used for its normal purpose of entertaining Japanese businessmen, for in the six months before Pearl Harbor they didn't dare go out with us, lest they be taken by the police and questioned for long periods of time. So, knowing that if we didn't spend the money, we probably wouldn't get it next year, and not being certain war would come, we spent the huge sum of $75 on taking out the police, and I was soon to learn that it had been well spent.

On each floor of our office building there was a radio loudspeaker that had been sounding off from time to time. It was blaring loudly when Fred and Bruce returned at almost eleven o'clock to report their mission successfully accomplished and that our friends the police were in the hall outside. At precisely eleven o'clock Prime Minister Tojo announced over the radio that war had been declared against the United States, Great Britain, and the Netherlands. The Imperial Rescript was then read, and when it ended the police walked into our office and demanded to see me. I was still in my private office destroying as much as possible, but I wiped the perspiration from my brow, put on my jacket, and went out to be met by one of the Prefectural Policemen whom we knew well, for he had been a guest at the monthly dinners. I was told by the police I would have to obey their orders and that I must close the office as soon as possible. I said I understood but that there were routine matters to take care of which took time. (There were still about twenty-five blank passports to burn.) The head policeman was a good friend. He turned to his associate, and said, "Suzuki-san you stay here. Let no one in the office. I will go and close the British Consulate." We managed to stave off final closure until three o'clock in the afternoon, our police friends having brought us coffee and sandwiches from the restaurant that was also on the eighth floor. Then we had to go. My American clerk who lived in Osaka was told he would have to go with us to our home in the suburbs, as the police could not guard two widely separated places.

Before we left, the police told us that the officers and staff could take with them whatever personal possessions they had at the office. So we all packed up our possessions in brief cases, Japanese *furoshikis*, or just plain old newspapers. I interpreted "personal possessions" as including all the yen in the office safe, because I did not know where any more was coming from. We were not searched, and our personal belongings were not investigated. At about three-thirty I said good-by to the Japanese staff who had loyally helped in the destruction of the papers and documents. Finally, the safe was closed and locked as were all storage cabinets, and the outer doors clanged shut.

As we walked along the streets, rode in the streetcar and the interurban express, the Japanese did no more than stare and most of them didn't even do that. Our police friends were in civilian clothes and made no effort to call attention to us. Finally we were home. Our Japanese domestic staff were in tears, as they had envisioned all sorts of dire things that might have happened. The police calmed them and told them to carry on as usual but to make preparations for Bruce upstairs and to fix up a place for the police to sleep downstairs. The library was soon designated as police headquarters. It had a day bed and comfortable chairs, and the police seemed satisfied. During the next six months, we were to get to know our friends very well. Two would spend a day and night with us and then be relieved by another pair the next day. After about a week the original pair would return and so it went, week after week.

My memories of the details of that first night are blurred, but I do recall that the four of us, Fred, Tex, Bruce, and I, all had martinis before dinner and a bottle of champagne with the meal. We had no idea what was to come, nor, of course, any inkling of what had happened at Pearl Harbor, but we drank to our own armed forces and to confusion to our enemies. Our police guests remained in another room, but they must have heard us. From then on the police gave us as much freedom as was possible. They did not come into our part of the house unless it was absolutely necessary or unless we invited them, as we sometimes did.

I learned much later that our first day of war was vastly different from that experienced by other Americans in Japan. Apparently the Japanese had no nationwide program set up for handling enemy aliens when war came. In Tokyo, Ambassador Grew's telephone had been cut off as early as five o'clock in the morning, and it had to be reconnected so that he could be called to the Foreign Ministry to be told that Japanese-American negotiations had come to an end. At 7 A.M. Otto Tolischus, the *New York Times* correspondent, was roused from sleep in his home near the American Embassy in Tokyo and taken into custody by the police. The Japanese press in Tokyo seemed to have known about the war long before their colleagues in Osaka had any definite news.

Although American journalists, businessmen, and even diplomatic officials were roughly handled in Tokyo in the early hours of the morning of December 8, which was midmorning December 7 in Honolulu, none of us in the Osaka-Kobe district was disturbed until after the official declaration of war at 11 A.M.

The Osaka officials took it all casually and on the second day of the war left us entirely alone with our police guards. It was not until the afternoon of Wednesday, December 10, that the Chief of the Foreign Section of the police came out to Shukugawa and called us together to discuss the future.

The Japanese press had been reporting the results of the attack on Pearl Harbor and the airfields in Hawaii. That very morning the *Japan Times & Advertiser* had reported the sinking of the *West Virginia* and the *Oklahoma* and the heavy damage to four other capital ships and four cruisers together with the loss of between two and three hundred aircraft. Our spirits were not helped by the first announcement of the Police Chief that he had no idea whether there would be a diplomatic exchange or whether we would remain in custody throughout the war. "However," he went on, "this is not a war between individuals but one between governments." In so far as possible our reasonable desires would be met, and in this connection he asked whether we wished to stay in our present quarters or be moved into the New Osaka Hotel, adjacent to our Consular office. There was no hesitation in our answer. If at all possible we wanted to stay where we were and keep our present servants, a cook and housemaid.

We were living in a two-story, seven-room frame house that was one of three houses in a former American Board Mission compound. One of the other houses, similar to ours, was unoccupied and the third house, a small one-story dwelling, was occupied by a friendly Japanese couple and their two young children. In the rather extensive lawn between the two larger houses, we had erected a badminton net. If we could stay where we were, we would be able to get regular exercise, our books would be available, and our cook was excellent. During the six months we spent there I realized the benefits of buying more books than I could read at any one time. Among the books that I had purchased but not had time to read were Ernest Hemingway's *For Whom the Bell Tolls* and Pandit Nehru's autobiography. There was also an almost complete collection of both Sherlock Holmes and Somerset Maugham, and A. Edward Newton's charming books about book collecting, to read and reread.

When the Police Chief left that evening, we were feeling slightly more cheerful. He had agreed that we could stay in our comfortable home and had reassured our servants that they could stay and take care of us. He promised to look in on us from time to time and said that if we needed anything, to let one of our guards know and an effort would be made to supply it. As he left, he made us feel still better by explaining that while there was as yet no information about a possible diplomatic exchange, the matter was under negotiation, and we would be kept informed.

Next morning we were again sunk in gloom as we read in the Kobe *Chronicle* eight-column headlines: RISING SUN HOISTED IN PHILIPPINES   PRINCE OF WALES, REPULSE & LANGLEY SUNK. The Kobe *Chronicle*, a former British controlled paper, was to be closed down before we left Japan, but for the rest of the war the Japanese continued to publish an English edition of the *Mainichi* newspaper and the English language *Japan Times & Advertiser*, which was generally considered to be controlled by the Foreign Office. We were allowed to get these papers regularly, but of course our subscriptions to all American or European papers and magazines ceased with the beginning of the war.

As a bureaucrat of some thirty years' standing, I have often railed at the freedom and what sometimes seemed the license of the press. But since my internment experience, I have had different feelings. For only six months we were exposed to what we knew to be a controlled press, and yet, when we finally were exchanged and for the first time had access to American newspapers and magazines, both contemporary and those that had been issued during the first six months of the war, my initial reaction to the stories about the war and Japan's actions was, "It's not true." No wonder the people in Russia and in Communist China find it difficult to believe anything good about America. They have been reading a controlled press most of their lives and probably do not even realize it is controlled. No matter how much it hurts, and it often does, I am now a firm believer in a free press.

During the first few days of internment, there was little to do but read the papers, and this was not a cheerful task. On December 29, the *Japan Times & Advertiser* published a long, two-column editorial entitled "American Impudence." After predicting dire economic problems for American industry as a result of the loss of rubber, tin, and other products from Asia, the editorial went on to castigate American policy. It said:

> The Americans have accused Japan of creating "puppet" states and of limiting the freedom of action of neighboring governments. But they should look closer to home. "I practically wrote the Constitution of Haiti myself, and a very good Constitution it was," once boasted Josephus Daniels, former American Secretary of the Navy and now Ambassador to Mexico. And note how many times during the history of Haiti has that country been under the occupation of American marines who were supposedly defending that Admirable Constitution . . . What can the United States say about puppet states now in view of the enlightening spectacle of Costa Rica, Panama, Haiti, Guatemala, Honduras, El Salvador,

Nicaragua, Cuba and Santo Domingo declaring war against Japan! Are these sovereign states who can exercise their own discretion? Do the peons of those countries who hardly know where Japan is have grievances enough against Japan as to declare war? Or are they puppets dancing at the end of strings manipulated from Washington!

The very next editorial in the same paper the same morning told of "the massacre of helpless and unarmed Japanese residents by American troops at Davao" in the Philippines. We were not to learn the details of this alleged atrocity until January 25, when the same paper reported that on January 4 the Foreign Minister had received from the Japanese Consul in Davao a "graphic report" of how, when American troops realized they could not stop the Japanese tanks rolling into the city, they turned their machine guns on unarmed Japanese civilians who were interned in the Central School.

Reports of the fall of Manila and Hong Kong in the first days of January and accounts by participants of the attack on Pearl Harbor and the air bases in Hawaii were followed on January 11 by the first pictures of the attack on December 7 (Honolulu time). One photograph showed bombs exploding all around six large American warships lined up two abreast in Pearl Harbor, and the other showed huge smoke clouds billowing up from what was easily recognizable as Wheeler Field, some fifteen miles from Pearl Harbor.

On February 20 the press published pictures of the surrender of Singapore. One of these showed a group of British officers bearing a white flag approaching the Japanese lines to discuss terms of surrender. I recognized the officer carrying the white flag as a young man who had formerly been with the British oil company in Kobe and who spoke quite good Japanese. On February 26, we were told by the Osaka *Mainichi* that a Japanese submarine had bombarded an oil refinery near Santa Barbara, California, and had struck terror into the hearts of residents of Southern California. The first picture of the sunken *Arizona* with its superstructure looking as if it were about to topple into the sea appeared on March 10.

But everything in the press was not so grim. On April 13, we read in the *Mainichi* that "Filipino Women Cast Off Yankee Ways to Become True Members of East Asia." The story under that read in part:

> Down with yankeeism. The women of the Philippines no longer expound women's rights over men or dream of purely materialistic lives glittering with pianos, refrigerators, automobiles and high class radios, but are returning to the life of a pure Asian, declared the wife of the Mayor of Davao.

If only the Japanese had won, there would assuredly be no Women's Liberation Movement today! Or would there? Surely even the Japanese woman of 1970 would be loath to give up her "high class radio" or her refrigerator.

Our police friends and guards, to say nothing of the four American internees, soon became restive and bored with being confined all day to one comparatively small compound. So they suggested, and we heartily agreed, that it might be pleasant to take some hikes in the surrounding countryside. We were able to persuade them that it would be even more interesting to go into Kobe or Osaka once in a while so that Fred and Tex, who were recent arrivals in Japan, could have an opportunity to inspect some curio shops. From then on we were taken by our guards once or twice a week on trips to the city.

One dreary afternoon in February, as we were sitting around the living room grousing because a cold drizzle had ruined the prospects of a badminton game in the garden, our current police guard came in to say an officer from headquarters and the Swiss Consul, who was now in charge of American interests, were there to see us. The object of their visit was to deliver a cable from the State Department which had been despatched from Washington the previous December 5 and which was entitled,

"What to do in Case of Emergency." It had been sent, for purposes of economy, in the old Gray Code, and we were not surprised that the Japanese had been able to read it as easily as we could. They had read it, and held up its delivery so that when war came none of us had any precise instructions regarding the proper action to take.

Among other things I learned from this message that I should have cut out the first page of blank passports, which bore a serial number, and bundled them up to be taken back and given to Mrs. Shipley so that a record could be made of the destroyed passports. The rest of the passport was to be burned. I had burned the whole damned thing. Visions of being thrown into the Federal penitentiary in Atlanta as soon as I got back created a far from cheerful atmosphere.

A month later we were taken back to our office in Osaka in order to make an inventory of all official possessions before they were turned over to the Swiss Consul for safekeeping. Our Japanese staff had been assembled, and we all set to work listing official government property. As senior officer, I said I would list the various items in the one safe we had. The safe stood in the general office directly in front of the desk, where our senior police guard, whom we will call Okamoto-san, had decided to sit, while we did all the work. I opened the safe, took out various odds and ends, and then unlocked the inner compartment. To my dismay I saw about twenty or thirty blank passports which in the confusion of December 8 had been overlooked. Fortunately, I had lived several years in Japan and realized that it was the unexpected, the out of the ordinary, which disturbed the Japanese official. Anything which had not been directed by proper authority or which broke the normal routine immediately aroused suspicion. I therefore gathered up the passports as quietly as possible and calmly (on the outside) walked into my private office with them. The head policeman glanced at me as I passed and then returned to his newspaper.

As soon as I had closed the door, I grabbed a pair of large shears and began cutting out the first pages of the passports. Perhaps my sentence to Atlanta would be reduced if I came back with at least some pages with serial numbers. I had not finished with more than four or five when the door opened and in came the number two policeman. "Okamoto-san wants to know what you are doing," he said. Remembering my belief that nothing out of the ordinary or unexpected should be done, I asked if he remembered the cable from the State Department giving instructions on what to do in case of emergency. He did. I then explained in detail that I was just carrying out the instructions in that message and that I had to cut out the first pages of the passports and take them back to Washington when we were finally repatriated. I carefully pointed out the serial number on the first page and told him how it was necessary for the State Department to have a record of these numbers. I went on to say, "We are supposed to burn the rest of the passport but obviously that is now impossible. I'll put the passports back in the safe, and you can turn them over to the Swiss to burn." All the time we were talking I continued cutting out first pages. The young man looked satisfied, but he had to go and report to his superior. The pace of my cutting increased greatly while he was gone, but too soon he was back. I had only succeeded in cutting out the first pages of ten passports. There were at least twenty remaining.

"Okamoto-san says O.K." he reported. I hurried on with the cutting. My young police friend watched me a few moments. "Have you another pair of shears? Let me help you." And so Mrs. Shipley got at least half of the first pages she should have received, many of them carefully cut out and tied up by a member of the Japanese police force. I never did find out whether or not the Swiss Consul really burned the mutilated passports left for him in the safe. But in any case they would have been no use to spies, thanks to the Osaka Prefectural Police and the small entertainment allowance that had provided many pleasant evenings for them and us before the war began.

At noon that day, we were taken over to the New Osaka Hotel for lunch. We had frequently eaten there before the war, and we were pleasantly surprised by being warmly greeted by the head waiter. At a table in the corner I saw an old Japanese friend, a Mr. Harada, but I didn't know whether or not to speak to him, for I knew that at one time he had been under investigation by the police because of his friendship for the British and Americans. When our lunch was over and we had gone to the cloakroom to get our overcoats, Mr. Harada came up to the police guard who was with us and requested permission to speak to me. He gave the policeman his card so that the police would know what he had done. Fortunately the guard with us that day was one of the more intelligent and understanding officers, and he allowed Mr. Harada to approach me. As we shook hands, my Japanese friend said he was happy to see that I apparently was in good physical condition and not suffering. He went on to say that he hoped the next time we met it would be under more pleasant circumstances. I found it difficult to thank him with a steady voice, for I knew what a personal risk he had taken in asking to speak to me.

One day in early April as we were passing the Daimaru department store in Kobe, we noted in one of their display windows huge blown-up photographs of nine young men in naval officer uniforms. The Japanese ideographs surrounding them spoke of them as "Nine Human Gods." The next day we read in the papers that these were the young men who had been lost at Pearl Harbor when the five Japanese two-man submarines had invaded the harbor. But why were there only nine? Shouldn't there be ten? It wasn't until we were finally exchanged six months later at Lourenco Marques and received back numbers of American magazines that we learned that one of the young men had been thrown ashore near Kaneohe on the windward side of Oahu. He was not even listed as having participated in the invasion. Japanese soldiers and sailors were not supposed to surrender or be captured. We should have realized what had happened, for back in January a report in the *Mainichi* had spoken with disdain of American and British prisoners brought to Japan from Guam and Malaysia. The paper said:

> The American and British war prisoners who have passed six days in the internment barracks at Zentsuji are dead to all sense of shame and are enthusiastic merely in dressing smartly.

The paper described the allegedly carefree life of the prisoners and then went on to say:

> Perhaps the Yankee dictionary contains no such sayings as "Men should die for the nation's cause" or "It is most dishonorable for a Samurai to be taken prisoner" which every Japanese soldier keeps in his mind.

It is interesting to note that the Japanese contempt for prisoners did not extend to civilians, unless they were suspected of being espionage agents, or to women. Five American navy nurses were captured on Guam but, in spite of being commissioned officers in the United States Navy, they were eventually evacuated with the diplomats and other civilians. Apparently the Japanese at that time could not envisage a woman being a military officer. One of the young women, "Jo" Fogarty, was to marry Fred Mann when we reached Lourenco Marques. Pictures of American and British military prisoners were constantly being published, apparently in an effort to convince the Japanese people that the Westerners had no real courage or stamina and need not be feared.

On Saturday, April 18, our guards suggested we might like to go into Kobe after lunch, and about one o'clock we walked down to the interurban station and caught a train. At Sannomiya Station, the one nearest the old foreign settlement, we got out and started down the narrow, winding road leading to Daimaru's and the Motomachi shopping street. Everything had seemed normal when we left home, but when we left the train we noticed that the yellow air raid "precautionary alert" flags were flying. Was this the real thing or merely one of the periodic training exercises? Our police friends didn't know, and we went on to the large Daimaru department store. As we were wandering through its aisles, the radio loud speakers, which all large buildings seemed to have, began to broadcast an announcement that enemy planes had appeared over Nagoya, about halfway between Kobe and Tokyo. Our guards still claimed that they didn't know whether this was the real thing or not.

After leaving Daimaru's, we started down the narrow, crowded Motomachi with its arched street lights and its many shops known to generations of tourists. No motor traffic had ever been allowed on this street, so when a huge motor fire truck came roaring down it we began to think the alert might be real. The red "immediate alert" flags were also going up and so, while one of our guards went with us into a curio shop, the other went off to see what he could find out about the air raid. In about ten minutes he returned and said we had better be getting back to Shukugawa, as it looked as if there really had been enemy planes over Japan. As we walked back to the station and passed Daimaru's, we saw that the strong steel shutters had been pulled down over the glass display windows. We reached home without further incident and our servants, who had been listening to their radio, had already pulled the blackout curtains into place.

The next morning the papers were full of the story of what they pointed out was "the first time in history" that Tokyo had been visited by hostile planes. The brief official announcement put out by the Eastern District Army Headquarters at 2 P.M. April 18 was published in full.

Enemy planes, coming from several directions, attacked the Keihin [Tokyo-Yokohama] district at about 12:30 P.M. today. The invaders, counterattacked by our air and ground defense forces, are in gradual retreat. The enemy planes so far ascertained to have been shot down, number nine. The damage suffered by us seems to be slight. The Imperial Family is in absolute security.

Later announcements reported that planes had been over Nagoya and Kobe and that fires caused by "enemy incendiary bombs" were under control. We learned later that the one plane that had come over Kobe had hit a soap factory.

By Monday the headlines were still full of the story. One article in the *Japan Times & Advertiser* that morning was headed:

SHOT DOWN OR CRASHED IN SEA IS FATE OF ALL ENEMY PLANES WHICH RAIDED TOKYO, YOKOHAMA

Another story, also on the first page of the same paper, was headed:

AMERICANS FLEE PACIFIC COAST ON REPORT OF RAID OVER TOKYO RE-TALIATION BY JAPAN FEARED

Not until we joined Ambassador Grew and his staff on the *Asama Maru*, which was to take us to Lourenço Marques for exchange with Japanese diplomats from America, did we learn that this air raid had been led by Jimmy Doolittle, and that in fact most of the pilots had been safely recovered in China or Siberia. The Ambassador had been informed by neutral diplomats who had been listening to Treasure Island on their short-wave radios.

The Japanese official announcements that damage caused by the air raid was slight were correct as far as material damage was concerned. But the psychological damage *was* great. The people had been repeatedly told that Japan was invulnerable, that the Americans were weak and lacked courage and stamina and that there was nothing to fear. Now the people began to wonder. As far as we were concerned the immediate result of the raid was confinement to quarters. We were told there could be no more tours to Osaka or Kobe until further notice. The police claimed, and I have no reason to believe they were not sincere, that they feared we might be attacked by emotionally overwrought Japanese if we appeared on the streets. But they apparently misjudged their people; anger was directed at their own leaders, not at the Americans.

The raid had taken place on Saturday and all week we were kept at home. On the following Friday afternoon we were visited by the assistant chief of the Foreign Section, and we pleaded with him to be allowed to go out again. He was sympathetic but said we had better wait a few more days. But our guards were also getting restive. By noon on Saturday they decided that, even without official permission, we might risk going into Osaka. So off we went.

We eventually came to a small curio shop that we had not previously visited. The police always preceded us into Japanese shops and explained to the proprietors that we were from the American Consulate and should be treated politely. In this shop it did not seem to be necessary. The proprietor had cushions brought out for us to sit on, and while he showed us, one by one, some of his choice items, he told one of his assistants to prepare tea for us. Soon, an attractive, kimono-clad young maid entered with tea and cakes. She seemed to be a bit excited; perhaps the police were right, and the people had been emotionally disturbed by the air raid. As this emotionally overwrought young lady passed me a cup, she smiled and said, in Japanese, "Weren't you glad to see your boys over last week?"

One morning while we were still at breakfast we saw through the living room window four of the toughest, nastiest looking characters I had encountered since my confrontation with the Japanese military in Nanking some four years before at the time of the so-called "Rape" of that city. We heard them come to the front door and the rumblings of discussion with our police guards. However, we were not bothered until we had finished breakfast and retired to the living room. One of our guards then came in and rather apologetically informed us these visitors were members of the Kempeitai, the Secret Military Police, and that they wanted permission to search our residence for a short-wave radio. According to the police there were indications that a short-wave radio was operating somewhere in the vicinity, and it was their responsibility to find it.

We had no short-wave radio, ours having been confiscated by the police on the eighth of December. I told them to go ahead and the search began. I had never thought a short-wave radio could be concealed between the leaves of a book but every book in the house was carefully examined. When they went into the downstairs toilet, they were sure they had found something. It was directly under the upstairs bathroom, and there was a rectangular trap door on the ceiling which could be pulled down in order to get at some of the water pipes. I explained this in detail to the Kempei officer in charge and he seemed satisfied. We then went up stairs and all the bedrooms were examined and I had to explain that the foolscap-size mimeographed sheets on my bedside stand were Japanese language lessons which I was reviewing. We finally returned downstairs, and the Kempei men split up, some going into the kitchen and one of them going with me to investigate the closet in the downstairs library, where the police made their headquarters.

Most of the closet shelves were filled with old books and phonograph records, but on the top shelf I spied, with a sinking heart, about five or six thick, mimeographed copies of the monthly confidential political reports we had received before the war from the Embassy in Tokyo. I had brought them home some time before, meaning to burn them, but they were still there. The man with me, of course, saw them too and asked me what they were. I tried to fob him off with a story that they were some more of the mimeographed language lessons he had seen upstairs. He began to insist on seeing them, and I had visions of being hauled off to a Japanese jail for having tried to deceive the Kempeitai. I really didn't care about him seeing the reports for there was little of importance in them, but they were stamped "Confidential," and I felt a responsibility to protect them. Just as it looked as if I would have to hand them over, we heard a great clatter and bang outside in the hall and the sound of much laughter. We both dashed out and discovered that the Kempeitai officer had not believed my explanation about the trap door in the downstairs toilet. He was standing on the toilet seat, covered with the muck and dust of years which had showered down upon him when he jerked the trap door open. Our servants, our police guards, and Fred, Tex, and Bruce, who had been watching, were convulsed with laughter. The Kempeitai were actually blushing and apparently felt they had lost so much face that within minutes they were out of the house and down the road. The political reports were safe. We invited our police friends into the living room, and we all had a beer together. That evening the political reports were added to the blaze in the living room fireplace. The Kempeitai never visited us again.

So the days dragged on. By the beginning of May we had been assured we would be repatriated, although the timing was still uncertain. On one of our periodic hikes around the surrounding countryside our most perceptive guard, who was walking with me several feet behind the others, remarked softly, "I hope you get repatriated, Allison-san, while we are still winning." He was as certain as I that the Japanese string of victories must one day come to an end, and he feared what the emotional Japanese people might do to any representatives of the victors still in their midst.

Toward the end of May, we were told we would shortly be taken to Yokohama to await our final departure on the Japanese luxury liner *Asama Maru*. We could take two suitcases of clothes and personal effects with us. All the rest of our things would be turned over to the Swiss Consul and presumably we would regain them after the war. Surprisingly enough some four years later we did recover most of our property undamaged. The last day in Shukugawa finally came. The remaining bit of our liquor stock was just enough to make final gimlets for ourselves and our guards, before we left for the station to take the train to Yokohama. Our faithful servants were in tears when we left, as were our friendly Japanese neighbors. It was difficult to realize these were the brothers and sisters and wives of the same men who had acted so brutally in Nanking in 1938, and who, as we were to learn, had behaved so badly in the Philippines and elsewhere on their ruthless drive to the south. They have probably said the same thing about us, for war makes villains of us all.

Upon arrival in Yokohama we were taken to the New Grand Hotel, where we were to remain for another two weeks before finally boarding the *Asama Maru*. While waiting, we were taken on hikes again, and although we often passed in the street our friends from the American Consulate in Yokohama, also being taken for an airing, we were not allowed to speak. Quartered with us at the New Grand Hotel was the staff of the Kobe American Consulate as well as the Argentine and Uraguayan Consuls from Kobe. From Arthur Tower, our Consul in Kobe, I learned that when he and his staff returned to their office to make the inventory of things to be turned over to the Swiss, they found that, while all the main items were in good condition, practically all smaller items such as pencils, typewriter ribbons, erasers, blotters, rulers, and ink stamp pads had been taken by "persons unknown," presumably the police. When we had returned to our office in Osaka not a thing had been touched. The office was in exactly the same condition as when we were taken away the afternoon of December 8. That small amount of money we spent before the war in entertaining the police had certainly paid off.

The Spanish Minister in Tokyo was in charge of the interests of the Argentine and Uruguay Consuls, and it was through him we were able to have the only really lively evening of our stay. He came down to Yokohama periodically to see how his charges were getting along, and he always brought the latest news from the outside world, for, as a neutral, he still had the use of a short-wave radio, and he regularly listened to the Treasure Island station.

One afternoon our Latin American colleagues came to us filled with excitement and told us there had been a great American naval victory at Midway. They had full details as given by the American authorities, which were at considerable variance with the Japanese press accounts. However, because the Japanese, for the first time, had admitted any substantial loss, this time of two carriers, we were inclined to believe the American account of four Japanese carriers sunk and other ships sunk or damaged. From some source a store of gin and vermouth was produced, and our small group had a victory celebration. Our Japanese guards could not understand why we were so jolly, and we managed to persuade them it was because we knew we would soon be going home.

On June 17, 1942, we finally boarded the *Asama* and were reunited with many of our old friends. Among these was the late Max Hill of the Associated Press, who shortly after his return to New York produced the only book I know of recounting this weird voyage halfway around the world to meet the Swedish vessel *Gripsholm*, which carried the Japanese being repatriated from the United States. Max's book *Exchange Ship* tells the story well and gives a vivid account of the fears and hatreds of many of us at that time.

I first heard of Max when I spent a weekend in June, 1941, in Tokyo with "Chip" Bohlen, then a Second Secretary at our Embassy and later to be successively Ambassador to Russia, the Philippines, and France. On Sunday, June 22, Chip and I with Gene Dooman, Counselor of the Embassy, and Merrell Ben-ninghoff, another Second Secretary, were having lunch with

First Secretary Ned Crocker (later to be Ambassador to Iraq). Dooman and Benninghoff were Japanese experts who spoke the language fluently and had lived in the country since childhood. As we were sitting around after lunch regretting the fact that our families had all been sent back to the United States, the telephone rang, and Max Hill told us that Hitler had just invaded Russia. Dooman, the chief Japanese expert, immediately shouted that this meant our families would be back by autumn. He believed the Japanese, who not only had joined the Axis but also had recently concluded a nonaggression pact with Russia, would be so angry at Hitler for not informing Japan of his intentions, that they would get out of the Axis. He was wrong. I shall never forget Chip's immediate reaction. Seriously and almost solemnly he exclaimed, "Hitler's lost the war!" This at a time when all the Western "experts," both military and civilian, were predicting that Hitler's armies would be in Moscow in two or three months.

Max Hill tells in his book about the terrible week after the *Asama* had pulled away from the Yokohama dock and then, shortly after, dropped anchor in the harbor within easy view of the dock we had just left. A dispute over who should be included in the exchange had not been settled. Many of the American correspondents and businessmen who had been imprisoned by the Japanese threatened to jump overboard if the ship started back to the dock.

One of these, Charles E. "Chief" Meyer, had been head of Socony Vacuum for all of Japan and had only been released from prison the day before we boarded the *Asama*. Chief was an old friend, a man in his fifties, about six feet tall and normally weighing probably between 180 and 200 pounds. I had last seen him in November of 1941, about a month before Pearl Harbor. As I finished going through the boarding line on June 17 I heard someone call, "Hey, John." I looked around and at first saw no one I knew. Then I looked around a second time . . . there was Chief, but he had lost about fifty pounds, and his face was so haggard and drawn I could hardly believe it was he. He had been imprisoned from the beginning of the war, accused of being one of the principal American spies. His treatment had been shocking. Yet some twelve years later he came back to Japan to serve with me, when I was Ambassador, as head of the small economic aid mission that Harold Stassen, then head of our Mutual Security Administration, had insisted be established. Chief and his charming wife were a great addition to our Embassy family. From the way he worked with and lived among the Japanese one would never have guessed what he had gone through in the six months before we boarded the *Asama* on June 17, 1942. He was a great man.

The evening of June 24 started out like all the rest. After an early dinner (most of the American Embassy and consular officers whose families were already in the United States were quartered in steerage and ate at steerage hours), we had strolled around the deck for a bit and then settled down to bridge, poker, or just talk. Ned Crocker called me aside and said that he had managed to get hold of a bottle of Japanese Suntory whiskey. We scrounged a bit of water and then went up to a hideaway we had discovered on the top deck, where we had our drinks and began to speculate about when we might start for home. About eleven o'clock a fully lighted tug chugged out from the dock toward us, and as it drew near we heard someone on the tug shouting, "*Dempo, dempo!*" the Japanese word for telegram. Ned and I looked at each other and barely whispered, "We're going to start." We were afraid to say it aloud lest it prove untrue. A few minutes later one of the ship's officers came around and ordered us to go below. Max Hill has told in his book how about thirty of us crowded into the first-class cabin occupied by Max Stewart, "Temp" Feaver, and Herbert Norman of the Canadian Embassy, laughing and joking, hardly able to believe it, when, shortly after midnight, we felt the engines throbbing, and the *Asama* began to slide out of Yokohama harbor.

A month later we sailed into the harbor of Lourenço Marques. As we passed American freighters, the Stars and Stripes waving in the breeze and their whistles tooting a loud welcome to us, there were few dry eyes among the passengers. The next day we left the *Asama* and boarded the *Gripsholm*, where we were greeted by a tremendous smorgasbord lunch with plenty of beer for those who wanted it. Internment was over. We were free at last.

# V

# The Lion and the Unicorn

## 1942–1946

THE JOURNEY HOME from Lourenço Marques in the *Gripsholm* took another month. It was broken by a twenty-four-hour stop in Rio de Janeiro, where a reception was given for us by the American Ambassador and Mrs. Jack Simmons. After the reception a lot of us went on to a fabulous dinner at the Casino Urca, which cost almost nothing as the management expected to make their money off us in the game rooms. They did with some of my colleagues, but my Scotch ancestry came to the fore, and I left after making the magnificent sum of $25 at roulette. The gambling has now been forbidden, but my friends who know tell me Rio is still just as delightful as it seemed to us then, after six months of internment in Japan.

As we neared home, we began to wonder what our next assignment would be and whether or not we would really be able to contribute in any way to the war effort. We were told we would be given thirty days' leave before having to report for duty. I was met by Jeannette, and, through the help of some of my old friends at General Motors, we obtained a suite at Essex House with a living room looking over Central Park. I was given a twenty-five percent diplomatic discount and the whole set up cost $7.50 a day for the two of us. It was great to be home and able to relax, but I couldn't help wondering what was in store for me after the leave was over. I telephoned one of my friends in the State Department and found that I was once more in luck. An Economic Warfare Division had been set up in the Embassy in London, and an old friend, Hugh Cox, with whom I had gone to high school and college and who was a high official in the Department of Justice, had been loaned to the Board of Economic Warfare to serve as Chief of the Intelligence Section of the Division in London. He knew I was on the way back from Japan and had made arrangements for me to be assigned to London as Chief of the Far Eastern Intelligence Section of his office. Hugh had been a Rhodes Scholar and knew Europe but he was completely ignorant of Asia. Ever since our brief visit to London in 1935, I wanted to return. Now I was about to go.

While still in New York and visiting with my friends from General Motors and their friends, I was astounded to hear the men talk about what they had heard would be the first active American participation in the European phase of the war. They told me that in the following spring the Americans would stage an invasion of North Africa. They were right on everything but the date, which would be the coming November. How they got their information I don't know, but they all spent much time in Washington on war business of one sort or another and apparently the inability of Americans to keep a secret had not yet been inhibited by the war.

When leave came to an end, we moved to Washington, where for a month I was to undergo indoctrination in the Far Eastern Section of the Board of Economic Warfare (BEW). It all seemed a bit dull and theoretical to me but one evening there was a change of pace. About one hundred of us were invited to a supposedly secret meeting to hear Gardner Cowles give an account of his experiences as the chief associate of Wendell Willkie on his round the world tour. It was here I first heard of the difficulties the Allies were having with de Gaulle and his seeming tendency to think of himself as a reincarnated Jeanne d'Arc. We also heard something of the British difficulties, and I began to believe I might really find something useful to do in London.

At the end of the month, I spent a few days in the State Department just to reassure me I was still a Foreign Service Officer and not a temporary civil servant, as were most of the people I had been working with. I said good-by to my wife and was off to New York to catch a Pan American flying boat to London. It took seven days to reach our destination. Our first stop was Bermuda, where something went wrong with one of the engines, and we spent three days enjoying the sun and the blue water. When we finally took off again, our passenger list, which was limited to people on government or semigovernment business, was enlivened by the Four Jills in a Jeep, Kay Francis, Martha Raye, Carol Landis and Mitzi Mayfair. They were starting off on the USO tour that later was the basis for the famous motion picture. Kay Francis was suffering from a bad cold and kept to herself much of the time. Carol Landis was pretty and friendly and liked to read. Mitzi Mayfair, of whom I have never heard since, was just there. Martha Raye, then as now, was the extrovert who was friends with everyone and always ready to help in any disagreeable task. It was she who would get up in the middle of the night and tour the cabins to see that everyone was properly covered while he slept and who would go to the galley and make coffee whenever it was wanted.

After Bermuda we next came down in the harbor at Horta in the Azores, where we stayed for another twenty-four hours while more work was done to the engines. From Horta we headed straight for Lisbon; about twelve o'clock one night the captain told us that we were over the coast of North Africa and that he had just received word that American troops were landing some three miles below us. It was an eerie feeling to be so near and yet so far from the shooting.

Late the next afternoon we landed in Lisbon and were piled

into a bus and driven up to the Avis Hotel, where we were to have dinner. Carol Landis and I seemed the only ones interested in the war, and we shared the only copy we could find of the London *Daily Mail*, which contained stories of the North African landings. As we finished reading, I suddenly remembered that my friend Ned Crocker was at the American Embassy in Lisbon, and with considerable trouble I succeeded in reaching him on the telephone. The Crockers were giving a dinner party, but Ned said that didn't matter and for me to await him in the Avis bar, where he would shortly join me. I managed to get a sandwich or two before Ned arrived, but from then until we were taken back to the plane around eleven o'clock, Ned and I sat in the bar consuming good Scotch. Ned had been long enough in Lisbon to get the full effect of the atmosphere of the city as the battleground of the Axis and Allied intelligence networks. His stories, added to the experience of being above North Africa when the American landings took place, made me feel I was in the midst of a mighty adventure.

As we boarded the plane on the Tagus River and took off, we fondly thought we were on the last lap of our journey. We weren't. We finally reached Foynes in Ireland, and as we flew over the green fields leading to the airport the Clipper ship gave its final gasp and settled into the water at Foynes. We were told that we would be driven to Limerick to spend the night after which a land plane would fly us to Bristol, where we would board a train for the last part of our journey to London. And so we did, arriving at Paddington station at around nine o'clock at night in the middle of an air raid and the worst fog, I was to learn later, that London had had in thirty years.

Hugh was waiting on the platform and guided me through the blackout to a taxi that he had waiting. How the driver ever found his way through the darkened streets and the fog, without headlights, from Paddington to the Berkeley Hotel on Piccadilly I shall never understand. The only illumination was the explosion of antiaircraft shells and an occasional burst of flames in the distance, when a bomb thundered into a building. After a nightcap and a short conversation in which Hugh gave me an inkling of what I would be doing in London, he left me to my first night in the war torn city.

The next morning, after a fitful sleep in which were mingled the sound of sirens, the rumble of planes, the ack-ack of the antiaircraft guns, and the crunch of bombs, I was surprised to find both the hotel and myself in apparently good condition. I decided to go first to report to the main Embassy at 1 Grosvenor Square, normally only a ten minute walk from the hotel. I had reckoned without the fog, which was still with us, and after almost twenty minutes, I was completely lost. I asked directions of a passing stranger and fortunately found he was a clerk at the Embassy, and he guided me all the way. After a brief talk with the First Secretary, Waldemar Gallman, who greeted newly assigned Foreign Service Officers, I was told to retrace my steps and go back to the apartment hotel at 40 Berkeley Square, which had almost entirely been taken over by the Economic Warfare Division of the Embassy. The British Ministry of Economic Warfare, with which we worked closely, was just across the square.

The Economic Warfare Division at 40 Berkeley Square was a fearful and wonderful institution with officers and clerks running around in circles, getting in each other's way, and talking a strange mixture composed of professional economic terms, British and American officialese interlarded with descriptions of last night's air raid, and the difficulty of getting fresh eggs and anything for breakfast except kippers and strong tea. The division was under the general and genial direction of Winfield Riefler, a senior economist from the United States Federal Reserve Board, who had been given the personal rank of Minister. In his charge he had former professors, temporary Army officers (among whom was Walt Rostow, a Captain in the Air

Corps who selected economic and industrial bombing targets in Germany), a former publisher of the magazine *Yachting,* who wore a naval uniform, officials detailed from other departments of the government, including Commerce, Treasury, and Justice, and about five or six Foreign Service Officers. There was even one American banker who gave three or four afternoons a week to helping keep track of Hitler's economic condition as revealed by intelligence reports. It was a motley crew, and while you didn't have to be crazy to survive, it helped. What this disparate group of individuals was engaged in has been best described by former Secretary of State Dean Acheson in his memoirs:

> The aim of economic warfare is to cut the enemy's supplies, information and funds from foreign territory and prevent his communication with it . . . Economic warfare rested upon control of the seas but also used control of communication, commerce and finance. Intercontinental mails were routed through control points, read and stopped when desired; telephone, telegraph and wireless communications were dealt with in the same way. Through the navicert system and allied control over bunkers and ships' stores, a ship could not move without allied permission. International legal ideas about the rights of neutrals, neutral trade and the freedom of the seas became irrelevant to immovable ships. The blacklist and freezing controls stopped leaks through the blockade to the enemy by reaching enemy sympathizers' own assets, not merely shipments.

Experts or alleged experts in all these forms of economic warfare filled the offices at 40 Berkeley Square. While we seldom heard the nightingale singing, we did hear the airraid sirens, the rumble of bombers, and later the chug-chug of the buzz bombs as, fortunately for us, they soared over our heads.

One of the Foreign Service Officers, Ware Adams, was the administrative officer of the division, and it was he who helped me get more permanent and less expensive living quarters than the Berkeley provided. I think it was my second or third day in London that Ware took me to see a man who had a flat to rent above his shop and his own flat in Mount Row. The location was ideal; it was just halfway between Grosvenor Square and Berkeley Square. I would have to walk up four flights of stairs and pay seven guineas a week but that did not seem too bad for a small, furnished living room, a smaller bedroom and a bath. My landlord's housekeeper, Mrs. McKinnon, would produce breakfast for me, take care of the flat, and send out the laundry. I think the real reason I took the flat, however, was because of the cautionary note sounded by the landlord. He explained that he was a bachelor and pointed out that I was a temporary one. It sometimes happened that a young lady spent the night in his flat. If that should happen in my flat there would be no objection, but he warned me not to let it happen too often, as Mrs. McKinnon was getting along in years, and it made extra work for her in providing two breakfasts. I assured him I would bear his warning in mind. But I'm afraid I disappointed him and Mrs. McKinnon, for she didn't have to produce any extra breakfasts.

One of the advantages of working at 40 Berkeley Square I discovered was that Maggs Brothers, the rare book dealers, had their shop only about three doors down on the same side of the square. When I was in London in 1935 I had visited the former Maggs' shop on Conduit Street and on the advice of friends had asked to see Mr. Ernest Maggs, one of the partners. I explained to him that I was greatly interested in rare books and book collecting but that unfortunately the salary of an American vice consul (as I was then) did not permit me to indulge my hobby often. Mr. Maggs cared not a whit. He spent over an hour taking me all through the shop and showing me many rare editions. One of the most interesting was a copy of the first edition of the famous *Nuremburg Chronicle,* printed in the fifteenth century. He also showed me a single flyleaf, printed in Latin, that had been circulated to advertise the publication of this great work. He had a translation of the sheet which showed that some Madison Avenue techniques are at least four hundred years old. After describing in detail the many virtues of the volume, the advertisement concludes: "Not many copies of this remarkable book are being printed. They will shortly all be gone. Buy it now!" When I left, Mr. Maggs gave me copies of several of their fine catalogs, which many people had paid dearly for. Now in 1942 I was glad I could go back and in some measure repay Mr. Maggs' kindness to an impecunious young American. Before I left London at the end of four years, I had found many choice items, which are still in my library. One of the most interesting was obtained as a result of the interest I developed, while in London, in the career of Sir Robert Walpole, the first Prime Minister of Britain. One day in searching through the shelves of eighteenth century items, I found what turned out to be one of five manuscript copies of the report of the Committee of Secrecy of the House of Commons in 1742 on the impeachment of Robert Walpole. It was nicely bound in red and gold, and the manager of Maggs (Ernest Maggs had passed away) told me that it came from the library of George the Third. It seemed to me that any American should be happy to have something that had belonged to George the Third and in no time it was mine.

But book collecting was confined mostly to Saturdays. As I have said the Economic Warfare Division of the Embassy co-operated closely with the British Ministry of Economic Warfare. One of the more important of our joint enterprises was the preparation of an exhaustive report entitled: *Enemy Strategic Re-inforcement Through Biscay–Far East Blockade Running*. I was intimately involved in this, as I produced in cooperation with the British Far East staff most of the sections of the report dealing with Japan's needs that could be alleviated by imports from Germany and with Japan's capacity to furnish the Germans with vitally needed supplies. Prior to the completion of this report the Allied naval authorities had given only slight attention to the blockade running. From June, 1941, to February 25, 1943 (the date of our report), 35 known voyages with a carrying capacity of more than 200,000 tons had been attempted between German Europe and the Far East. Of this only some 40,000 tons or 18 percent had been lost through successful attack by the Allied forces. Our report stated that the continuance of this blockade running could "(a) prolong the war, (b) seriously increase Japan's war potential at its weakest point: steel capacity for shipping and machine production and (c) strengthen the German war machine at two of its weakest points of raw material supply — natural rubber, tungsten; and at the weakest point in its food supply — edible fats and oils."

It took several months of intensive work to compile all the information needed for this report, and I was continually being surprised at the amount of information we were able to get from cable, radio, and mail intercepts, reports in the newspapers of the enemy powers, which seemed comparatively easy to obtain, and information available to experts in international trade and finance, who could elicit significant facts from what seemed most esoteric material to the rest of us.

In the preparation of the report, I was able to use material from my old Shanghai roommate, Ed Snow, and from the scrapbook I had kept of Japanese press clippings while in internment in Japan. Our report raised the question of whether or not Japan would be able to get in time the machines and materials for expanding her merchant fleet so that she could transport all the oil and raw materials found in her new Co-prosperity Sphere. In the discussion of this point I quoted a paragraph from Edgar Snow's book *The Battle for Asia* written in late 1940, where he said:

> Her [Japan's] reserves of war material are estimated to be sufficient to support a war with a major power for about two years. . . . But if, in the process of war, Japan seized the total resources of Greater East Asia she might become self-sufficient in a military economy . . . It would be on the gamble of successfully grabbing these colonies before exhausting her own reserves that Japan would go to war against Britain and America.

In my scrapbooks I found a statement by Nobusuke Kishi, then Japanese Minister of Commerce and Industry, which I quoted. In a speech delivered in Osaka and reported in the *Japan Times & Advertiser* for March 10, 1942, it was stated:

> The Minister also opined that the resources in the southern regions would be supplied to this country in significant quantities in two years and disclosed that the products from these areas would not be included in the general material mobilization scheme for the 1942 fiscal year.

I concluded this section of the report with the following statement:

> The two year period is almost completed. *In her race with time Japan must count on Germany to help in supplying the machines and plants to make the steel with which to build more ships and increase her armament production.*

We managed to produce a report which so impressed our leaders that the Allied naval forces began to take the blockade running seriously and within a comparatively short time had reduced it to negligible proportions. I believe this one report contributed more to the war effort than all the rest of the things on which I spent my time while in the Economic Warfare Division.

I made many friends in England and received a good education on how to work with officials of an Allied power, particularly ones who were convinced that the accumulated international experience of the British Commonwealth was far superior to that of the rather raw, inexperienced Americans. We had our arguments and our quarrels, but they didn't last long, and in the end we both agreed that we had a lot to learn from each other. I had just begun to feel at ease with my British friends from the Ministry of Economic Warfare when I was suddenly transferred from 40 Berkeley Square to the main Embassy at 1 Grosvenor Square. I was told that my principal duty would be to maintain a close liaison with the Far Eastern Department of the British Foreign Office, but that, under the general direction of Waldemar Gallman (to whom I had reported on my first day in London), I would also be expected to be available for any special assignments which might come up. "Walde" was then still only First Secretary, but he had become the favorite of that strange, dour, almost Lincolnesque figure, John G. Winant, the Ambassador.

Ambassador Winant was a law unto himself in many things, and for some obscure reason he had taken a dislike to the man who was Counselor of the Embassy and had little to do with him. Instead of asking for the Counselor's transfer he just let him sit in his office and when the Ambassador had anything important on his mind he would call in Walde. I had been at 1 Grosvenor Square for almost two months before I met the Ambassador. In the meantime, I had renewed my acquaintance with Ashley Clark, the head of the Far Eastern Department at the Foreign Office, who had been in Tokyo briefly before the war. One day Walde called me into his office and told me that I should get ready to accompany the Ambassador on October 20, 1943, to a meeting at the Foreign Office with the Ambassadors of all the Allied Powers, who were to discuss the setting up of a United Nations Commission for the Investigation of War Crimes. I was warned that at the meeting I should be seen and not heard, and if it was necessary to impart any information or suggestions to the Ambassador, I should pass him a short note. Another officer of the Embassy who had been detailed to accompany the Ambassador to one of the initial meetings setting up the United Nations Relief and Rehabilitation Administration, had most unfortunately grown embarrassed and impatient at Ambassador Winant's slowness in taking part in the discussion and had stood up and made a statement himself. He was never forgiven. Walde told me that when he had told the Ambassador he was going to assign me to this second international meeting Mr. Winant inquired solemnly, "He won't make a speech will he?" I didn't, and from that time on I was included in the Ambassador's small group of officers with whom he would talk freely. I was even sent by the Ambassador to be the United States observer at an informal meeting on October 26.

In the late Spring of 1944, my father became seriously ill, and I applied for leave to return to the United States. This was granted, but before I was able to leave London I was called down to the Foreign Office by Ashley Clark on what he said was an important matter. An official Chinese mission from Chunking, headed by the Chinese Minister of Education, Wang Shih-jeh was in London and about to return to China via the United States. They would not be on an official mission to the United States, but Ashley Clark told me the Foreign Office believed it would be a fine thing if an American escort officer could be provided for them. Walde Gallman and the Ambassador approved of the idea, and I was instructed to draft a cable to the State Department reporting my conversation with Ashley Clark and stating that the Ambassador suggested I be detailed as escort officer. This was done and approved by the Department. I was instructed to accompany the Chinese mission as far as New York, where they would be met and taken care of from then on by the Chinese Ambassador, Hu Shih. I was then to report to the Department for consultation before going on leave. The Allison exchequer would only have to bear the roundtrip expense from Washington to Lincoln, Nebraska. I was in for another long air journey. Our first stop was in Dakar, in what was then French West Africa. For some reason, known only to Pan American, we were kept there eight hours. However, I managed to persuade the local manager that he had some VIPs aboard, and he did provide a car and guide to take the Chinese Mission and me around the city and to visit a local weekly market. We then took off, and our next stop was Natal, Brazil, where we stayed over night at the huge American wartime air base. The next morning we were off for Bermuda, where we again stayed overnight and were given an official reception at Government House by the British Governor General. My Chinese friends were greatly impressed, and no one dreamed that less than six years later Minister Wang and the government he served would be in exile from the mainland, on Formosa, and that his recent British hosts would have recognized his government's Chinese Communist enemies. We finally reached New York, and I turned over my charges to Ambassador Hu.

Before going down to Washington I took one day off in New York and had lunch with my old friends Christopher Morley and Bill Hall, the publishers' representative. I had brought with me from London a copy of the British edition of Walter Lippmann's *U.S. Foreign Policy* in order to show them what austere publishing was like. The American edition of the same book was at least an inch thick and printed on heavy book paper. The British edition was about one-quarter inch thick and produced on what looked like newsprint. While we were having cocktails before lunch, my friends examined the book closely and appeared duly impressed. After the second old fashioned, Chris reached for the book and turning to the blank endpapers took out his pencil and inscribed two verses of what up to now have been unpublished Christopher Morley.

> What's become of sonnets
> To ladies' tender parts —
> High sentiment is gone — it's
> Among the perished arts.
>
> The Varga girl — or Petty —
> Are no less chaste, perhaps,
> Than Spenser's *Amoretti*
> In praise of female paps.
>
> (Cetera desent)
> (Cetera indecent) C. M.

In celebration of my brief return from London, we had two more old fashioneds, and Chris again took my book, turned to another blank endpaper, and added three more verses.

> . . . But poets were more polished
> In days of sword and coach —
> Perhaps the lady relished
> A less abrupt approach.

> It isn't just undressing
> Gives glamor to the sex —
> To keep the reader guessing
> Is Art's withholding tax.

> And there was charm enduring
> In Lyrics of old grace —
> Progressively alluring
> Like petticoats of lace.

It wasn't only in publishing that the American standards of austerity were much less severe than the British. During the month I stayed in Lincoln, Nebraska, before my father's death, I was invited to a Ladies' Night at the Rotary Club (of which my father had once been president), and I was horrified at the amount of food served. The individual helpings of meat were equal to a week's ration in London. I was also shocked by the casual manner in which visiting Rotarians from other towns in the state bragged about how they could get extra gas coupons in order to drive to Lincoln. The war seemed very far away from Nebraska.

I returned to London just a short time before D-Day. About a week before the great day, the senior officers of the Embassy were called into a conference to listen to one of the senior military attachés tell about the forthcoming expected attack on London and southern England by what he called rocket planes, but which were later to be universally known as buzz bombs. Allied intelligence had done a remarkable job. We were told what the bombs would look like, that they would fly low (seldom more than 1,500 feet high) and that after their motors stopped you could count to 5 before they exploded. At night they would be easily visible because of the exhaust fire coming out of their tails. Various staging areas had been located in France, mostly on the Pas de Calais and they were all aimed directly at London. While attempts had been made by the air force to eliminate these launching sites, they had not had much success. It was a grim prospect, and many of those with wives in London made arrangements for them to go to the country.

Two or three nights after D-day I had dinner with some friends in a nearby restaurant, and as we were walking home the airraid sirens sounded. We had long since stopped going to airraid shelters, but we did go to the apartment of one of the ladies which was on the fifth floor of a solidly constructed eight-story building. Shortly we heard the antiaircraft guns going off in Hyde Park and soon after what sounded like a small plane seemed to skim along the top of the apartment headed north across Grosvenor Square. My friends had not been briefed on the buzz bombs so I did not voice my suspicions that the first of them had arrived. I decided to walk on home, and as I left the crowded entrance hall downstairs I heard someone say, "Well, we got that so and so. I saw the flame where we had hit him in his tail." The buzz bombs had come.

In the Mayfair district where I worked and lived we were lucky. Only two buzz bombs actually hit within the boundaries of the district and both of these on Sunday mornings when most offices were closed. One hit the top floor of Lansdowne House where Royal Air Force officers plotted bombing targets. There was just a skeleton staff present and, to the best of my recollection, only one man was killed. An old friend of mine who had been British Consul General in Osaka when I first went there in 1939, had retired because of age and returned to England. Not content to be idle during a war, he had volunteered and been commissioned a Pilot Officer (the lowest commissioned rank) in the Royal Air Force and assigned to the office in Lansdowne House where he worked on targets in Japan. He was there that Sunday and lost an eye. He didn't have to be there, but he was typical of so many of the British I saw during my four years there.

We didn't have much time to worry about the buzz bombs that summer. We tried to find some sort of shelter when their motors stopped and gradually began to ignore them unless they came too close. One midnight the door from my flat in Mount Row onto the small roof garden was blown open by a bomb that had landed in Bayswater, about a mile away. But no one was hurt. By September the British had managed to reduce the buzz bomb, or what was technically called the V-1, menace to insignificant proportions. Not only had air strikes in France knocked out many of the launching sites, but a new tactic of directing antiaircraft fire at them before they reached London had excellent results. Most of the buzz bombs were being brought down harmlessly in empty fields.

Late one early September afternoon I was sitting in my office completing a letter to my wife telling her I thought it would be all right for her to come to London. I had just finished the letter and given it to a messenger to mail, when there was a terrific explosion and a large diagonal crack suddenly appeared in my office window. By the next morning we knew that the Germans' revised version of the buzz bomb had been perfected. This was a rocket type missile called the V-2. The one that cracked the window had landed six miles away. You could at least hear the buzz bombs coming and take evasive action, but with the V-2 this was impossible. If you heard it, you knew it had landed and that you were still alive. One evening I had been to a small cocktail party given by one of the army officers attached to the Economic Warfare Division and had been asked by two other officers to come back to their flat with them after the party for a bite to eat and a talk. They lived just behind Selfridge's department store on Oxford Street, about ten minutes' walk. I was tempted; however, I knew I had a hard day coming, and so I decided to go home. I never saw my friends again. A V-2 had plunged down near their flat about an hour after I left them.

If we had allowed ourselves to brood over the fact that at any moment, without warning, we might be dead, I suppose we would have gone crazy. But we had enough work to do so we didn't have time to sit down and worry about what might happen.

In addition to my work on Far Eastern matters with the Foreign Office, I was detailed as political advisor to the American delegation to an Allied Maritime Conference, which met in London to work out an agreement on principles to govern the coordinated control of merchant shipping among the Allied Powers for, as paragraph 1 of the final agreement says:

> . . . the provision of shipping for all military and other tasks necessary for, and arising out of, the completion of the war in Europe and the Far East and for the supplying of all the liberated areas as well as of the United Nations generally and territories under their authority.

This agreement was signed in London on August 5, 1944, and it was the first time I ever signed an international agreement on behalf of my government. As usual the American Government had more delegates than the other nations, which had only one each, but I was proud as I signed, "For the Government of the United States of America," along with Philip D. Reed, head of our Lend-Lease Mission (and later Chairman of the Board of General Electric), Huntington T. Morse, of the United States Maritime Commission, and Walter Radius of the Department of State.

The working delegates in this conference, such as "Turnie" Morse of the American group, were all professional shipping men and to watch them work was an education in how to conduct international relations. All decisions in this meeting of eight nations were made by unanimous consent. There was no veto by one or two powers; every nation had the veto. There were no decisions made by majority rule; all had to agree. But these were skilled technicians who knew their jobs and knew how important it was for them all to work together for a common end. They knew and respected each other as members of the same craft or profession, hence differences of nationality were of less importance. If the United Nations could first have been based on a number of small technical or professional international groups engaged in working out solutions to mutual problems, it might in the end have proved more effective. It seems as if we started to build our international edifice from the roof down instead of beginning with the foundation. If we could have started with a number of groups, such as these shipping men working on common problems, we not only could have made progress in solving them but gradually would have built up the idea that it is a natural thing for the different nations to solve their problems over a conference table instead of a battlefield. It would then seem to be the time to set up an overall organization that would be able to discuss with some objectivity the many political and economic problems confronting the world.

Before the Shipping Conference there had been a Whaling Conference, to devise rules and regulations to limit the catch of whales so that the species would not become extinct. The American Government took a large part in the discussions, and it was my task to send telegraphic reports each evening back to the State Department recounting the day's activities. I never did fully understand why our government played such an active part in these meetings or why the other nations put up with it. The United States had long since got out of the whaling industry, and we had no ships engaged in the trade. But it was an interesting group to work with. The chief British civil service representative from the Ministry of Agriculture and Fisheries, A. T. A. Dobson, was the son of Austin Dobson, the nineteenth-century essayist who had written so charmingly about eighteenth-century personalities and literature. The chief American expert was Dr. Remington Kellogg, Curator of Mammals at the National Museum of Natural History, a part of the Smithsonian Institution. He was a big, rumpled looking figure who cared little for protocol or the normal forms of diplomacy. However, he was highly respected by the whaling experts in all the other delegations and through sheer force of character and knowledge was able to dominate many of the sessions. Mr. Dobson of the British delegation was a close second, and it was fascinating to watch and listen to the two of them when now and then they disagreed.

On October 10, 1944, there opened at Lancaster House in London the longest, and in some ways the most interesting, conference I was to be associated with. This was a conference to set up a postwar European inland transportation organization. This organization was to meet the problems expected to arise after the liberation of allied territories on the European continent as a result of the widespread shortages and poor distribution of all forms of transport equipment and materials as well as a general dislocation of all forms of transport systems. It was my introduction to dealing with the Russians, and I was to learn how Russian political or economic interests took precedence over international cooperation for unselfish ends.

The British had prepared a draft agreement which, before the convening of the formal conference, had been discussed for several weeks informally with the American and Soviet Governments. It was hoped that the organization when set up would expedite the shipment of fuel and food, as well as other supplies to the people of war-torn Europe and thus reduce their suffering. I was not in on the preliminary discussions, but I knew the Americans and some of the British who were taking leading parts in developing plans for this organization, and I know their motives were charitable. When the Russians saw the draft

agreement they immediately suggested amendments which, in
the opinion of the British and Americans, had the effect of
depriving the organization of any effective power. The Russians
contended that the powers contained in the draft constituted an
infringement on the sovereignty of the member nations and an
interference with their internal economic affairs. After considerable argument, it was agreed that this matter would be put
before the whole conference for discussion by the governments
of the European powers who would be the ones most concerned.
On October 10, therefore, the conference met under the chair-
manship of Philip Noel Baker, at that time Parliamentary Secretary of the British Ministry of War Transport.

With a few exceptions the terms of the British-American
sponsored draft agreement were favorably received by the representatives of the smaller European powers. The Russians continued to introduce amendments that would largely emasculate
the organization. On Wednesday, October 25, the main committee of the conference, consisting of representatives of all the
powers concerned, met for what was hoped would be one of the
final meetings. It was not to be.

At the beginning of the meeting, the Russian delegate made a
long statement criticizing the document before the delegates.
He declared that the European Inland Transport Organization
(EITO) should be merely "consultative and coordinating" and
that the agreement before the delegates "would interfere with
internal affairs and impair the sovereignty of the member
states." The weeks of discussion had seemingly made no impression. The Soviet stand was exactly the same as it had been
in the preliminary discussions before the conference convened.
The American delegate stated that the United States believed
EITO would be a more effective instrument to do the job the
continental countries desperately needed to have done if it were
endowed with limited, carefully safeguarded, specific powers,
but the decision must be made by the smaller powers directly

concerned, and the United States would go along with their decision. With the exception of the Yugoslav delegation, the other delegates who spoke agreed in general with the American position.

Just before the lunch hour, Jan Masaryk, the Foreign Minister of Czechoslovakia, stated that he wished to consult his government, then based in London, and said he would give the Czech position after lunch. The meeting then adjourned. Two hours later when it reconvened Masaryk made a strong defense of the British-American draft and "declared emphatically that Czechoslovakia would be willing, if necessary to the effective operation of the agreement, to give up for a temporary period any small degree of national sovereignty if by so doing lives could be saved and the rehabilitation of Europe advanced." I have quoted the report of Masaryk's statement from the cabled report sent by the Embassy to Washington immediately after the meeting. It was one of the last really free speeches of this once gay and debonair but then increasingly tragic figure, whose father had been the leading force in establishing a free and independent Czechoslovakia after the First World War.

Shortly after Masaryk's statement, the main committee adjourned to meet again on Friday, October 27. At this meeting there was practically unanimous agreement with the British-American position. The Russians were looking more and more glum when an adjournment was called until Monday, October 30. Later that afternoon, at the request of the Russians, the Monday meeting was postponed. On the same day the Soviet Ambassador in Washington, Andrei Gromyko, handed a note to the American Secretary of State. A similar note was given by the Soviet Ambassador in London to the British Foreign Secretary. These notes referred to the discussions at the EITO Conference in London and pointed out that the provisions of the draft agreement often required action in the territories of the member states. It then went on to say that the Polish National Committee (set up by Moscow as a rival to the non-Communist Polish Government in Exile in London) had called the attention of the Soviet Government to the fact that the meeting in London was being attended by representatives of the "Polish *émigré* government" which had no connection with Polish territory. The note concluded by stating:

> The Soviet Government declares that without the participation of the Polish Committee of National Liberation in the Conference on Internal European Transport, it will not find it possible to take any further part in the work of the above mentioned Conference.

And so the conference adjourned *sine die* and was not reconvened until after the Yalta Conference, which provided for the setting up of a Polish Government acceptable to the Russians. In the meantime, numerous technical discussions were held with the Russians and some of the other delegations. The conference finally reassembled in the summer of 1945 and held its final meeting September 27, 1945. Due to Soviet pressures, although EITO was formally set up, it was stillborn and never functioned.

Of course, before the EITO Agreement was signed on September 27, 1945, the war in Europe was over, and our attention was focused on postwar problems and the war in the Far East. Before V-E Day, in March of 1945, Major General Patrick J. Hurley, American Ambassador to China, descended upon London. He was en route back to Chunking via Moscow, having come from consultations in Washington. As the Embassy officer in charge of Far Eastern affairs, I was directed to meet and look after General Hurley while he was in London. We were later to find out how bitterly and unfairly the General could attack Foreign Service Officers who disagreed with him, but while he was in London he was charming and most interesting about his experiences in China and also in Washington. It was from General Hurley that I first received an inkling of how seriously ill President Roosevelt really was. The General had seen the President just before he left Washington, and he told me: "He is a very sick man. He looks terrible. I don't see how he can possibly carry on much longer. It is a great tragedy." Less than a month after Hurley left London the President was dead.

The General took me with him on his visits to various officials around London. I remember well one meeting with French Ambassador Massigli. The burden of the General's talks with British and Allied officials was to persuade them that the American strategy of bringing the war direct to Japan, instead of first trying to liberate the Asian colonies of our European Allies, was the only one which ensured success in the long run. Hurley, his eyes gleaming, his handsome white mustache bristling, strode up and down in front of the fireplace in Ambassador Massigli's office. "I love France," he almost shouted. "I have fought and bled for France, and I assure you Mr. Ambassador that our policy will benefit France in the end." I think Massigli was almost convinced, but he had heard the tales that President Roosevelt didn't want France to return to Indochina after the war, and he was skeptical.

The General was invited to a private dinner with Prime Minister Churchill, but for some reason he hesitated to accept. He discussed the invitation with me, and I urged him to meet the Prime Minister. Finally he said he would go. "But I want you here early tomorrow morning so I can tell you what happened before I forget." The next morning Hurley came into my office with a broad smile and reported that everything had turned out all right. "But I was afraid for a bit that we were going to fight. Churchill wanted me to get Washington to agree to send more troops to help in liberating Burma, and I told him we were going after Japan first. He had given me one of his big cigars, and we were both smoking. He shook his cigar at me and shouted at me. I shook my cigar at him and shouted back. Churchill stormed: 'You can't talk to me like that. I'm the

Prime Minister of Great Britain!' I shouted back, 'I'm the personal representative of the President of the United States of America, and I can talk to you as I please.' " According to Hurley, the Prime Minister began to calm down and an almost friendly conversation followed. As Hurley rose to leave, Churchill came over and put his arm around Hurley's shoulder, patted him on the back, and said: "Pat, you're the kind of man who made my mother's country great!"

Even before V-E Day, we began to get more and more concerned with the war in the Far East. In March the Embassy was informed by the State Department that Koreans claiming to represent a Korean Provisional Government had petitioned for Allied recognition. The Department, following the same policy it had maintained in its dealing with other provisional governments wanting Allied recognition before the end of the war, was reluctant to recognize any government for an occupied nation until the people of that nation had an opportunity to make a choice. The Embassy was instructed to ascertain the views of the British Government, and I was sent down to the Foreign Office to talk to my friend Sterndale Bennett, then the head of the Far Eastern Department. He asked time to consult his superiors, but by April 9 I was able to report to Washington that the British Foreign Office agreed that there was no need at that time to recognize a Korean Provisional Government. Perhaps if the Western Allies had agreed then to the request, the division of that tragic country might have been avoided and the Korean war prevented. But given the increasing Soviet intransigence and its interest in Asia, I think this most unlikely.

Upon my return from lunch about 1:30 on May 8, I found a note on my desk to report at once to Counselor Gallman's room. Walde was now the official number two officer; his office was next to the Ambassador's and there was a connecting door between. I found the other senior officers of the Embassy all assembled and was told that a telephone message had been received about twenty minutes previously from Number 10 Downing Street that Prime Minister Churchill was coming to pay a call on the Ambassador and then wished to meet and speak briefly to the senior officers of the Embassy.

As time passed we kept peering out the windows overlooking Grosvenor Square wondering where the Prime Minister could be. It normally should not take much over fifteen or twenty minutes to drive from Downing Street to the Embassy and already almost an hour had passed since the telephone call. Finally, around the far corner of the Square we saw two Metropolitan Policemen mounted on white horses advancing toward the Embassy at almost a funereal pace. About twenty yards behind came the Prime Minister in an old Rolls Royce touring car with the top down. He was sitting on top of the rear seat making the V for victory sign and bowing to the crowds, which had somehow learned of his coming and were filling the streets around the square. His daughter Sarah was sitting in the rear seat. As he drove up and stopped outside the Embassy, charwomen, doorkeepers, clerks, and hundreds of others cheered him and tried to get close enough to touch him — though two months later they would vote him out of office.

We waited patiently as Sir Winston passed into the Ambassador's office for a brief talk. In about fifteen minutes the connecting door opened and in came the Ambassador and Sir Winston. He stopped shortly after entering Walde's office, and fortunately I was standing only about three feet away. As he stood there in his striped trousers and cutaway with his famous top hat in one hand and an oversize cigar in the other, he seemed the personification of John Bull. After thanking us for our part in bringing the war in Europe to a successful close, he paused a moment, looked around the room at all of us, and then in a few words made clear why he will go down in history as *the* great man of the twentieth century. He said that now that Germany was crushed we must not think of revenge. Rather, we must consider how Germany and her people could be brought back into the European family of nations and share with all of us the hopes for a better future. It was most impressive on this day of victory to hear this great leader of the conquering powers plead for a true peace to be shared by the vanquished as well as the victors.

As the war in Asia developed after the end of the war in Europe, my thoughts began to turn back to that part of the world where I had begun my career. Ambassador Winant was apparently informed by Washington of the attempts by the Japanese to get the Soviet Union to act as an intermediary with the Allies in the interests of opening peace talks. I was asked what I knew about Naotake Sato, the Japanese Ambassador to Moscow, although I was not told why Ambassador Winant wanted to know about him. I reported that I had known Sato slightly before the war and had always considered him an honest professional diplomat but not a man of great force. I was certain that he had been against the war but had taken no active steps against it. He would always carry out his orders, but I doubted if he would take any initiative to get his orders changed to make them more realistic. I never heard any more about this matter until sometime after the war, when I was able to read the official accounts of what the Japanese had tried to persuade the Russians to do.

I had talked to some of my colleagues from the State Department who visited London before and after the Potsdam Conference, and I remember some of them agreeing that it seemed foolish for the United States to offer Russia any big concessions to get them to join in the war against Japan. It seemed to us that the Russians would be so anxious to be included in the postwar Asian settlement that they could not be kept out of the war and would come in at a time to be determined by them and not by our pleas. But we were all too junior, and our leaders paid but little attention to our views. However, as we learned later, in view of the Yalta agreements it was already too late. The deal had been made.

In the late autumn and early winter of 1945, I got involved in talks with Sterndale Bennett, head of the Far Eastern Department of the Foreign Office, about the situation in the Netherlands East Indies as a result of the Japanese surrender. I had not the remotest inkling then that twelve years later I would be the American Ambassador to what, by that time, had become Indonesia and that some of the same problems evident in 1945, would still be present in 1957.

With the war ending so suddenly in Asia, the Dutch were not prepared to go back immediately and take the Japanese surrender in the Netherlands East Indies; the task was turned over to the British. Prior to the surrender the Dutch had been optimistic about their return and were confident they would be welcomed by all but a very small minority of the natives. They had told our representatives that they believed the Japanese propaganda, advocating independence and belittling the Dutch, had influenced not more than one-tenth of one percent of the population. They were soon to be disillusioned. On August 17, 1945, Sukarno and Hatta had proclaimed the Republic of Indonesia. When Dutch officials finally got back they agreed to discuss the future with Indonesian leaders, but they refused, on instructions from The Hague, to permit Sukarno to take part in the discussions. In statements made to the British and Americans at the time the Dutch claimed that Sukarno "personifies the rebel element which had Japanese support throughout the occupation." The Dutch in The Hague just couldn't believe they were so unpopular in Indonesia. The Dutch in Indonesia were fully conscious, according to reports given us by the British, that "the old days cannot be restored," and the British anticipated a struggle between them and the home government. In 1957, a similar situation developed. The Dutch businessmen in Djakarta were bitter about the stubborn and shortsighted atti-

tude of their home government, which was to result in all the
Dutch being expelled.

In early October the situation in Indonesia became progressively worse. Admiral Mountbatten, the British Supreme Commander in Southeast Asia, informed London that if the Dutch
continued to exclude Sukarno from all meetings they had with
Indonesian leaders, civil war would be the result. On October
13, 1945, the Embassy in London received instructions from the
State Department to make representations to the Foreign Office
regarding the use of American lend-lease trucks in Indonesia
which still bore U.S. markings. Washington didn't want to have
anything officially to do with action against the Indonesian
nationalists. It did not seem right for us to be furnishing the
British with equipment with which to do a nasty job they didn't
relish while we refused to take any public responsibility. But
Sterndale Bennett was friendly and understanding when I took
the matter up with him and promised to inform the British
commanding general in Djakarta of our concern.

Conditions in Indonesia continued to deteriorate and on
November 20, 1945, the Secretary of State authorized Ambassador Winant "at your discretion" to inquire of the Foreign Office
whether the British felt it might be helpful for the American
Ambassador at The Hague to approach informally the appropriate Dutch officials and inform them of our concern that "indefinite continuation of the present dissension in Netherlands East
Indies may have widespread consequences, that a broadminded
and positive approach to the problem is essential and that we
hope the Dutch will actively continue discussions with leaders of
all Indonesian factions." Off I went to see Sterndale Bennett
who promised to take the matter up with his superiors and let
me know their reaction. His personal opinion was that it would
be helpful for the United States to approach the Dutch along
the lines indicated. He added that it had apparently been very
difficult for the Dutch to change quickly old habits of thinking

on colonial matters and to recognize changed conditions in the postwar world. On December 1, the Foreign Office gave its official reply to our inquiry. It was made in the form of an "oral communication" which Sterndale Bennett read to me. After expressing appreciation for our offer to have our Ambassador at The Hague approach the Dutch, the Foreign Office stated that the situation in Indonesia had changed considerably since Sterndale Bennett had previously talked to me. There now appeared to be no difficulty on the Dutch side in meeting with all Indonesian leaders, and the present difficulty seemed to be the reluctance of the Indonesian leaders to attend further meetings with the Dutch and their inability to control the extremists, which had led to further serious deterioration of the situation. The British, therefore, believed the proposed American approach at The Hague would no longer be appropriate.

The Foreign Office then asked whether the United States would consider making a public statement, addressed specifically neither to the Dutch or the Indonesians, expressing our concern at the cessation of talks, which had seemed to have had a good start. The Foreign Office also said it would be helpful if any such statement included an acknowledgment that British troops had gone to Java to carry out an Allied task and if it emphasized the importance of completing the Japanese surrender and ensuring the safety of the thousands of internees whose fate was a source of great anxiety.

Just after Christmas I was sent to Washington on consultation. For the life of me I cannot remember what the nature of these consultations was, but I do remember vividly a talk with Ambassador Winant just before I left for Washington. The Ambassador had the flu, and I was called to his bedroom for a private talk. He began by telling me to be sure to call on H. Freeman "Doc" Matthews who had formerly been Counselor of the Embassy in London and was now head of the European Office in the State Department. Mr. Winant had great faith in

him, as did everyone who ever worked with Doc. I was to tell
Doc that the Ambassador was greatly concerned over the proposals being made in various quarters that Trygve Lie, the
Norwegian Foreign Minister, be chosen as the first Secretary
General of the United Nations. According to Mr. Winant, Lie
was an able, honest, hard-working bureaucrat but he lacked the
broad experience and imagination needed for this extremely
important position. The only person who had all the necessary
qualifications for this position, in the Ambassador's opinion, was
John Gilbert Winant, who had been governor of an American
state, head of the International Labor Office, and American
Ambassador to the Court of St. James's! There was no doubt
that Mr. Winant was absolutely serious and that he was convinced he alone had the qualifications needed for international
leadership in the postwar world. I promised to convey his
message to Doc Matthews and the next day I was off to Washington.

When I passed the message on to Doc, he smiled ruefully and
told me he was certain that the appointment of Trygve Lie had
already been agreed upon by the British, American, and Soviet
leaders and it would be useless to attempt to get them to recon-
sider. He said that if Mr. Winant wished, he could probably be
made the United States representative to the Economic and
Social Council of the United Nations and retain his rank of
Ambassador. But that was all.

I did not get back to London for almost a month, and when I
told the Ambassador of my talk with Doc Matthews he was
obviously shaken. He was still weak from the flu, and he needed
a long rest after four years of war. He knew he would be leaving
London shortly to return to private life, but he believed he could
make an unique contribution to the future peace of the world if
the world leaders would only call on him. The realization that
he would not be given the opportunity to make this contribution
caused him great sorrow and preyed upon his mind. I am sure

that it was one of the factors that caused this gentle and kindly man to put a pistol to his head a few years later.

In the summer of 1946, Averell Harriman came to take Mr. Winant's place as Ambassador. He was a different sort of man, and I learned from him several things about running an Embassy which were to stand me in good stead in later years when I had an Embassy of my own. During that summer I had been deeply involved in negotiations with the British Foreign Office and Treasury over the disposal of Burmese tin and other mineral products. I forget the details; I only remember that our instructions from the State Department were so involved that they were almost impossible to understand. Hall-Patch of the British Treasury, the senior official with whom I had to deal, was apt to get a bit caustic at times and at one point made the almost standard British criticism that we had "got hold of the wrong end of the stick." I took all the papers home one weekend (this was before the days of strict security measures) and went through our instructions thoroughly. I concluded that the real American interests in the case could be solved if the British met our desires on only four points, which I was sure they would if all the extraneous matter in our instructions was thrown out. On Monday I took the British Foreign Office representative to lunch. He was a good friend, Colin Crow, who had an American wife he had met in Peking. (Now, in the summer of 1971, he is Sir Colin and is British Ambassador to the United Nations.) He agreed the four points could be accepted, and I dashed back to the Embassy to prepare a cable to the Department requesting authority to put them officially up to the British. When I showed the message to the Counselor of the Embassy he was reluctant to approve it, because he maintained the Embassy had no right to tell the Department what to do; we should just carry out our instructions. I suggested we refer the matter to Ambassador Harriman and he agreed. The Ambassador immediately upon reading the cable said, "This is exactly what we are paid for, to tell the Department what we think is the way to solve a sticky problem." He took his pen and initialed the cable. Within a week we had a favorable reply from Washington, the British had agreed and the matter was settled. In future years I was to follow Ambassador Harriman's example on many occasions, but not always with such success.

In August of 1946, an old friend, the late Douglas Poteat, who was then Executive Vice President of the American Red Cross, came to London en route to Germany, where he was to start on an army sponsored visit to American Red Cross installations on the continent to see which ones could be closed down now that the war was over. Doug told me the army was placing a plane at his disposal, that his party and the army colonel who would accompany them would only take up five of the ten seats on the C-47, and he suggested I come along also. Ambassador Harriman said he hoped as many of his staff as possible would have an opportunity to visit postwar Europe, and he quickly granted me leave. A week later I met Doug in Paris, and we went on together to Wiesbaden, where our official journey began. During a period of just over two weeks we visited Copenhagen, Berlin, Munich, Vienna, Prague, and Rome, with side visits to Florence and Pisa.

I was to get another valuable lesson on this trip. At every place but one where we stopped, the local Red Cross directors were either on hand personally to meet us or a special representative was there who saw that we were taken care of and given all necessary, and some unnecessary, facilities. The director in Munich was late arriving at the airport, he didn't have enough transportation available, and the quarters he had selected for us could only with a great stretch of the imagination have been deemed adequate. Doug was mad and instituted a thorough examination of the operation of the Munich station. He found that everything else was done as sloppily as the arrangements for our reception, and the director was on the next plane back to Washington. Later, when I headed Embassies where there were a large number of VIP visitors, I made it a point to see that they were properly met and treated during their stay. First impressions do not always tell the whole story, but a well-administered visitor reception staff usually indicated that the whole Embassy administration was equally efficient. And it avoided awkward investigations.

The whole trip was a wonderful sightseeing tour, but the most politically interesting stop was that in Prague and our motor journey to the summer home of President and Mrs. Beneš. Czechoslovakia was still free, and the people one saw on the streets and in the restaurants were still able to smile and laugh. Twelve years later when I was to come back as Ambassador one seldom saw a smiling face. When we arrived at the President's summer house we were first taken upstairs to his living quarters to wash up after our dusty journey.

As we came out into the large, sunny living room to have tea it was interesting to note that on the side tables were current copies of *Life, Time,* the Paris *Herald, Atlantic Monthly,* and other American magazines and papers. Mr. and Mrs. Beneš spoke fluent English, and the atmosphere was that of a middle-class American home. President Beneš had recently returned from Moscow and was hopeful that he had an understanding with the Russians which would permit Czechoslovakia to develop in peace and freedom. However, every now and then he would indicate, without actually saying so, that he still had some doubts. Less than two years later his doubts were to be fulfilled and his beautiful country was to sink behind the Iron Curtain. We didn't fully appreciate the danger at that time, and as we left Prague for Vienna and Rome, the fall of Czechoslovakia into the Communist camp was farthest from our thoughts.

# VI

# Looking Glass House

## 1946–1950

IN LONDON AGAIN about September 1, I found a cable from the State Department transferring me to Washington and instructing me to arrive by September 11. In my ignorance I thought there must be some good reason for getting back that soon, and I managed to be able to report to the Head of the Far Eastern Office by September 10. He didn't know what to do with me, and for almost two weeks I was given odd jobs that no one else wanted. Finally it was decided I should be the Far Eastern Advisor to the American delegation to the United Nations session.

Having been a somewhat naive admirer of Woodrow Wilson and the League of Nations during my high school days, I looked forward with considerable anticipation to being attached as an advisor to the American delegation to the General Assembly of the United Nations. While it soon became evident that "Open Covenants" were not always "openly arrived at" and that what Senator Vandenberg had called "The Town Meeting of the World" often generated more heat than light, I came away from the session in December with the definite conviction that the world had made a step in the right direction. Too many good people throughout the world expected too much too soon from the United Nations and were frustrated and disillusioned when their hopes were not immediately fulfilled. They forgot the old Chinese proverb that a journey of a thousand miles begins with a single step.

Each of the Geographic Divisions of the State Department had designated an advisor to the Delegation and I represented the Far Eastern Division. Our job was to get to know and keep in touch with the members of the other delegations from our particular geographic area and learn how they felt about the various problems before the committees of the General Assembly. If possible, we were to try and persuade them to take a position similar to that of the United States or at least not in direct opposition to it. During those early years we usually succeeded without too much trouble, and time and again the only votes against the position favored by the United States would be cast by the Soviet Union and its satellites: Poland, Czechoslovakia, Yugoslavia, and, of course, Byelorussia and the Ukraine. It was almost too easy, and I'm afraid it built up among many of us an unconscious arrogance, which twenty-five years later we are only beginning to discard.

Every morning in New York at the old Pennsylvania Hotel, where our delegation was quartered in 1946, former Senator Warren Austin, the permanent head of the delegation, held a staff meeting. At our staff meetings at the beginning of the UN session in September, Senator Austin would be flanked on his right by Senator Tom Connally, the Chairman of the Senate Foreign Relations Committee, and on his left by Senator Arthur Vandenberg, the senior opposition member of the committee. On a Wednesday morning in November the day after the election, Senator Vandenberg and Senator Connally exchanged seats. But the delegation continued to serve the government in the same way. It was a vivid demonstration of how, in the field of foreign policy at least, a representative government could function no matter which political party was in power in the legislative branch.

For the first time I came to know and like Adlai Stevenson, who was an alternate delegate. I didn't have much to do with him then, but he was a cheerful soul always ready to join in a friendly discussion about how we could better do our job. Congresswoman Helen Gahagan Douglas was also an alternate delegate. I don't know whether or not she was a good delegate, for she had little to do with Far Eastern matters with which I was concerned. But she was "lovely to look at, delightful to know," and I have always been sorry that President Nixon felt it necessary to run against and defeat her when he began his political career. With a white beard and only slightly padded red coat, Senator Austin would have made a perfect Santa Claus. However, he was much more than a stuffed shirt. He was sincerely anxious to see the United Nations function effectively, and he worked hard to achieve this end. While reserved and not a backslapper he was always conscious of what his staff were doing, and I still cherish his letter to me of December 14, 1946, at the end of the General Assembly Session thanking me for what he was good enough to call my "fine service."

It was at this session that I first met Carlos Romulo, the Philippine Ambassador to the United States and head of the Philippine delegation to the United Nations. He was a pocket-size ball of fire and could make a speech which in tone and delivery would be the envy of a Methodist Bishop. He was a shrewd operator and a good friend of the United States who often was able to give us suggestions on how best to approach Far Eastern issues. Some of the other delegates, because of his perfect English and friendly informality, considered him more American than Asian. This was not so. He had a real appreciation of the problems of Asia and of his own people, and if he worked closely with the Americans at that time it was because he believed this was the way to serve his people best. We became good friends, and although, as conditions changed over the years, we sometimes had our disagreements, we could always talk them over without rancor.

As Assistant Chief of the Division of Japanese Affairs I served under Hugh Borton, a Japanese scholar who later became President of Haverford College. Upon my return to Washington after the close of the UN session I took up my duties in this division. We handled all political matters dealing with Japan and Korea. I discovered there was also a Division of Japanese and Korean Economic Affairs. Why anyone ever believed political and economic affairs could be separated into what were almost watertight compartments I shall never know. Fortunately, I soon got on friendly terms with my colleagues in that division, and although we sometimes had bitter arguments, we managed on the whole to produce sensible solutions to our problems. Eventually the two divisions were replaced by a Division of Northeast Asian Affairs of which I became the Chief on October 6, 1947. There was also an Office of Occupied Areas headed by retired Major General John Hilldring who had the rank of an Assistant Secretary of State. Japan was still an occupied power, so General Hilldring along with the head of the Office of Far Eastern Affairs, at that time John Carter Vincent, both figured on the Department's organization chart as my immediate superiors. As in London, I usually ignored lines on a chart, and instead tried to find out who in any particular case had the final say and then worked closely with him. Fortunately both General Hilldring and Vincent were gifted with a large amount of common sense and a desire to get a job done without worrying too much about who got the credit, so we creaked along without much difficulty.

During the four years covered by this chapter the most internationally significant problem with which I was deeply concerned was that of Korea. But there were other minor matters that had considerable significance in connection with the internal functioning of a great bureaucracy, and it may be interesting to deal with these before discussing at some length the various ramifications of the Korean problem.

The State Department to which I returned in September

1946, was a vastly different organization from the one which I had first known in 1931, when I had passed my entrance examinations into the Foreign Service. It was even considerably different from the Department I had known when I came back from being interned in Japan at the beginning of the war. In 1931, and even to a large extent at the beginning of the war, it was possible for an officer to know, at least by name and often intimately, most of the other officers both in the Foreign Service and in the Department itself. In 1946 this was impossible. Geographic divisions with a total staff or fifteen or twenty had grown into offices with fifty to a hundred officers. Large numbers of the wartime staff of the Office of War Information and the Office of Strategic Services had been taken into the Department, and no one was yet quite sure how best to use all of them. The Foreign Service Act of 1946 had done much to improve the character of the Service and make it more nearly able to meet the demands of postwar diplomacy. But the increasing size of the Department and the Foreign Service brought with it a certain rigidity, which was sometimes interpreted by outsiders as a lack of interest in the average man and his concerns, whether they encompassed fears of a too dangerous or susceptible foreign policy, or merely the right of any individual to equal consideration for employment in this greatly enlarged and sometimes-thought-to-be glamorous Department of the government.

I was directly involved in the latter type of controversy, and I learned a valuable lesson about how to meet criticism of the Department head-on. During one of the seemingly never ending reorganizations of the State Department in the postwar years, the old Far Eastern Division had become an Office of Far Eastern Affairs, and in November of 1948 I had become its Deputy Director. In March of 1949, we received a letter from Maury Maverick, former Congressman and Mayor of San Antonio, Texas, and still a man who carried weight in the higher councils of the Democratic party.

Mr. Maverick was mad. One of his former constituents who for a time had been in our Army of Occupation in Japan had been discharged and had sought a position in the State Department which would take him back to Japan. According to Mr. Maverick he had been given the run-around; if action was not forthcoming, the ex-Congressman would take steps to see that the inefficiency of the Far Eastern Office was brought to the attention of the President and the Secretary of State.

We have been told on good authority that a soft answer turneth away wrath. Previous letters to Mr. Maverick had consisted of "soft" answers, but they had not satisfied. The latest letter from the former Congressman was turned over to me to answer. One sunny Saturday morning in April, when I would much rather have been somewhere else, I was in my office with the complete file in front of me containing all of Mr. Maverick's letters, the filled-out application of his former constituent, and the previous Departmental replies. I went through them all and then decided to write a detailed letter pointing out why the Department had not acted on the application of Mr. Maverick's friend. I wrote a two and a half page single-spaced typewritten letter, and, before I had time to regret it and without showing it to my superiors, I signed it and sent it off. I would take the responsibility for the next outburst of indignation if it came.

In my letter I pointed out that the applicant had admitted that his knowledge of Japanese was limited to a "good" speaking knowledge and a "fair" understanding knowledge. I pointed out that while his previous maximum salary had been $4,100 a year, he had said that he would be willing to accept not less than $6,000 a year, and I further stated that none of his previous experience was the sort that would be of direct use to an officer of the State Department under existing conditions. I went on to say that the record showed that when the applicant left the army he had an efficiency index of 47.1 and that while that was above the average, none of the former army officers now in the

State Department had an index of less than 50 and most of them had one even higher. After pointing out that none of the applicant's references were from former employers but were from friends such as his local pastor, I concluded by saying that the State Department had only a written record to go by and that if the applicant wished to come to Washington, we would be glad to interview him, give him a Japanese language test, and thus be in a position to make a more complete judgment of his capabilities.

In just slightly over two weeks the reply came. With a trembling hand I took it into Walt Butterworth, my immediate superior, and we opened it together. This is what it said:

DEAR MR. ALLISON:

This is a letter of personal commendation to thank you for sending a frank reply. Most of what I have gotten out of the State Department so far is that the last word on one page is the first word on the next.

It would be my pleasure to write a letter to Mr. Acheson and to the Department as a whole commending you for being frank and giving me an honest answer but this might cause you embarrassment. This sounds like an extreme statement but actually it isn't. If you think you won't get fired, please keep the duplicate for your files and send the original on to anybody that you can get to read it.

My breath is still *in absentia totalis* over your astonishing reply. This letter should at least be preserved for your grandchildren so they can show it around that grandpaw was in the State Department and wrote an honest letter.

Still trembling with utter surprise, I am

Sincerely,
MAURY MAVERICK

Walt took me and the letter up to Jim Webb, the Under Secretary of State, who joined us in an appreciative laugh. The duplicate of the letter is still with me and my grandchildren have all seen it. Didn't someone say, "Honesty is the best policy"?

I was later to have similar experiences with Congressional Committees before which I had to testify and in dealings with individual Congressmen and Senators. I found that most of these men, who were often critical of the State Department, were willing to listen to an honest presentation, backed up by facts, no matter how much it contradicted their preconceptions. Often they wanted material that they could present to critical constituents, and it has always seemed to me that government officials make a great mistake when they conceal or give only half-truths to persons asking legitimate questions. There are, of course, times when certain things cannot be made public at once and this fact, and the reasons for it, should be frankly stated.

The years from 1946 to 1950 were exciting ones and during them the State Department was to undergo a great change for the better, not only in organization but in spirit. The initiation and implementation of the Truman Doctrine and the Marshall Plan, for both of which Dean Acheson never received as much public credit as was his due, gave the men in the Department and the Foreign Service a new breath of life after too many years when all the important matters seemed to be handled by the military. As Joseph Jones says in his important study of the development of the Truman Doctrine, *The Fifteen Weeks,* "The Truman Doctrine decision unleashed for the first time the creative effort of the State Department staff."

I had no direct part in these developments, but the spirit they engendered also flowed into the Office of Far Eastern Affairs and helped all of us to become more alert and imaginative. We did get indirectly involved, for during the consideration of what could be done to aid Greece and Turkey, the probable needs of other countries had also to be considered. In telling the story, Jones points out:

> The necessity of large-scale aid to South Korea was looming at the moment. It had become clear that the Soviet Union was not going to agree to unification of the northern and southern zones, and

the American-held southern portion required vast economic re-construction and development if it was to exist as an independent country.

Not only were Korean problems coming to the fore but what was happening in China, where the Communists were driving the government of Chiang Kai-shek from the mainland to For-mosa, was giving us headaches and sleepless nights, and Senator Joe McCarthy inspiration for his ruthless and unscrupulous attacks on the State Department and its officers. Too many people who disapproved of McCarthy tried to ignore him in the hope that he would go away — but not my wife. She was an army widow when I married her in 1948, and when McCarthy burst into the limelight she still had the direct military approach to matters. (She still has.) It was not until several years later, when I was Assistant Secretary of State for Far Eastern Affairs, that she came face to face with the Wisconsin Senator, but the story might as well be told now.

It was at a Double Ten — the Tenth day of the Tenth month — reception at the Chinese Embassy in Washington that the encounter took place. The Senator was there and receiving considerable attention not only from his Chinese hosts, which was not surprising, but also from many of the guests. We were asked if we wished to be introduced and I declined. The wife of one of our navy friends was with us and she said she wanted to meet the Senator so Mrs. Allison took her along with the Chinese Embassy official who performed the introductions. He told the Senator that Mrs. Allison's husband was in the State Department, and before McCarthy had a chance to say anything my wife blurted out for all to hear: "Yes, and he is a perfectly good American!" The Senator looked a bit startled but managed to stammer, "I'm sure he is." A friend told us the next afternoon that on the radio that morning Senator McCarthy had made a point of saying that he was sure "ninety-five percent of the men in the State Department are good Americans." But he didn't stop his reckless and unsubstantiated charges of disloyalty and communism rampant in the Department. If it is a fact that the Communists, as one of their main tactics in gaining power, try to foment a people's distrust in their government, the Senator was certainly a boon to Moscow and Peking.

He was also a boon, unfortunately, to a few officers in the Department and the Foreign Service who, because of jealousy and other reasons, initiated charges against some of their colleagues. One of the most brilliant officers in the Far Eastern field was forced to appear before a Loyalty Review Board on charges of disloyalty arising from the fact that when he was attached to the Political Advisor's office in Tokyo, during the early days of the occupation, he associated with the head of the Japanese Communist Party. I was told the charges had been instigated by an officer who had worked with him in Tokyo. In fact, because the young American was fluent in Japanese, he had been assigned the task of cultivating the Communist leader in order to discover what he was thinking and planning to do. But McCarthy and the people he inspired only pointed to the fact that an American Foreign Service Officer had associated with a Communist. I spent several hours testifying on behalf of the officer, and eventually he was cleared and all charges dropped. He was restored to duty and served with distinction in various responsible posts, but the charge in the McCarthy period remained to haunt him. When the State Department wanted to promote him to an Ambassadorship several years later, certain Senatorial friends of McCarthy, who had long since died, refused to permit his confirmation. Shakespeare was right: "The evil that men do lives after them."

While McCarthy continued to be a thorn in our flesh, those of us not directly the subject of his attacks were kept too busy to think much about him. I've often wondered how I escaped his attention and what he would have said if he had known that I had once shared an apartment in Shanghai with Edgar Snow, who had helped to make Mao Tse-tung and the Chinese Communists known throughout the world through his book *Red Star Over China*. Soviet aid to the subversives in Greece and Turkey, and Soviet attempts to obstruct the Marshall Plan, the Berlin blockade, Soviet support of the Communist takeover in Czechoslovakia, the Soviets' general disregard of the Yalta pledges to set up freely elected governments in Poland and other countries of Eastern Europe — all were convincing my colleagues in the State Department's European Office of Soviet intransigence. Soviet actions in Korea were fast convincing me of their unwillingness to cooperate in building a peaceful, stable Asia unless it was completely subject to their will.

In December of 1943, at Cairo, in one of the many wartime conferences, the United States, the United Kingdom, and China agreed that "in due course Korea shall become free and independent." At Yalta, Roosevelt and Stalin agreed that Korea should be independent and that if it seemed necessary to have a transition period, a trusteeship should be set up. When the Japanese surrender came, more quickly than had been anticipated as a result of the atomic bombs, United States planning for the future of Korea was still in a state of flux. However, it was necessary to issue orders to General MacArthur as to what forces would take the surrender of Japanese troops in Korea. In his *Present at the Creation,* Dean Acheson says the line was drawn at the 38th Parallel by a young army staff colonel named Dean Rusk who had recently returned from the China-Burma theatre of operation. I heard a different story. According to this version a brilliant young West Pointer, Brigadier General George (Abe) Lincoln (now, in 1971, Director of the Office of Emergency Planning in Washington) was on duty in the Pentagon one sultry August evening in 1945 when instructions came to prepare orders for General MacArthur for the taking of the Japanese surrender. Lincoln was then supposed to be the

Korean expert. Wiping the perspiration out of his eyes, he looked at the map of Korea and then at another map to see where the nearest United States troops were. He estimated they could get about halfway up the penninsula before meeting the Russians coming down, and he scratched a line across Korea at the 38th Parallel. Perhaps both Lincoln and Rusk were in the room and made the decision together. What is certain is that there were no ulterior motives in choosing this line, as was later charged.

In any case Order No. 1 to General MacArthur provided that the United States would take the surrender of Japanese troops south of the 38th Parallel and the Russians would take the surrender north of it. The Americans considered it a purely military decision and without political significance. We were soon to learn this was not the Russian idea. At the Conference of Foreign Ministers in Moscow in December 1945, the American Secretary of State, James Byrnes, submitted a paper proposing creation of a Joint Soviet-American Commission for Korea to unify the administration of such matters as currency, trade, coastal shipping, transportation, and electric power distribution. The Americans also proposed a Four Power Trusteeship which was meant to be only temporary, to give time for the Koreans "to form an independent, representative and effective government." Several days later the Soviets countered with a similar proposal, but it said the Joint Commission should consider urgent matters of economic unification and the establishment of a provisional government. It also provided for a Four Power Trusteeship to last for a definite period of five years.

The United States, still believing an agreement on Korea possible, accepted the Soviet draft with only slight amendment, and it was included in the Protocol of the Moscow Conference. Then the trouble began. The Koreans would have nothing to do with a trusteeship. To them it was only another means of keeping them subjected to a foreign power and forty years under the Japanese had been enough. They wanted freedom and independence and wanted it right away. When I became involved in Korean affairs I found that my office was still inundated with letters, petitions, and telegrams condemning the proposal. As Secretary Byrnes reports in his *Speaking Frankly*, this Korean opposition to a trusteeship prompted him to issue a statement saying:

> The Joint Soviet-American Commission, working with the Korean provisional democratic government, may find it possible to dispense with a trusteeship. It is our goal to hasten the day when Korea will become an independent member of the society of nations.

The Koreans still weren't satisfied, and opposition to the Soviet-American plans continued.

In January of 1946, the Soviet-American Joint Commission met to carry out the mandate of the Moscow agreement. As Secretary Byrnes has said: "what seemed to us unequivocal language, once again, apparently was different in Russian." The Americans assumed the commission would consider the country as a whole and this was never agreed to by the Russians. They were only willing to arrange for exchanges between, and coordination of activities in, two entirely separate zones. With regard to consulting Korean political parties in preparation for setting up a provisional government, the Russians insisted on only consulting parties that had not opposed the idea of a trusteeship. These consisted of the Communist Party and a few minor parties of little standing. The Americans took the position that mere opposition to trusteeship should not keep anyone from being consulted. In May 1946, the commission adjourned having solved nothing and having reached no agreement.

By September of 1946, no progress had been made in bringing about the unification of Korea. In December of 1946, an interim legislative assembly consisting of 45 elected and 45 appointed members was set up in the American zone. Secretary

Byrnes declared this was to prepare the Koreans for the responsibilities of self-government and not to encourage the setting up of separate governments in the two zones. In the spring of 1947, General Marshall, who had become Secretary of State, succeeded in getting agreement to a second meeting of the Joint Commission but nothing of importance was accomplished.

The Soviets later refused to participate in a Four Power Conference in Washington to consider proposals for the early achievements of the original Moscow agreements. In the Office of Far Eastern Affairs we believed the time had come to do something. On September 15, therefore, the State Department requested the State, War, Navy Coordinating Committee (SWNCC) to obtain the views of the Joint Chiefs of Staff on the interests of the United States in continued military occupation of South Korea from the point of view of the military security of the United States. On September 26, 1947, the reply came that the United States had but little strategic interest in maintaining the existing troops and bases in South Korea. It was believed that the two divisions of approximately 45,000 men could better be used elsewhere.

The problem of the unification of Korea was put before the United Nations, and in November a Resolution of the United Nations committed the United States and the Soviet Union to withdraw troops within 90 days after the formation of a "national government" in Korea. A Temporary Commission of the United Nations was set up to go to Korea and investigate the situation and observe elections that were to be held for the purpose of setting up the "national government" provided for in the November Resolution.

The Temporary Commission went to Korea, but, while it was admitted to the American Zone and given facilities to carry out its investigations and observations wherever it wished, it was not allowed by the Russians to enter North Korea at all. In 1947, Secretary of State Byrnes had told the American people that there was evidence that the Russians had trained an army of Koreans in their zone numbering from 100,000 to 400,000 men. We wondered if this was the reason the UN Commission was not permitted in North Korea, as the Russians had never officially admitted the creation of a Korean army.

Back to the UN we went. On February 26, 1948, the Interim Committee of the General Assembly approved a resolution sponsored by the United States giving the UN Temporary Commission on Korea the right to proceed with implementing the program set forth in the November 1947 UN Resolution "in such parts of Korea as might be accessible to the Commission." This meant holding elections, setting up a National Government which would constitute its own Security Forces, and arrange for the withdrawal of the occupying powers. The Temporary Commission proceeded with its task, but still it was kept out of North Korea.

In the Office of Far Eastern Affairs we had been concerned about what the situation would be in South Korea if United States forces were withdrawn before adequate South Korean forces should be established. On March 4, 1948, we sent a memorandum to Secretary of State Marshall outlining our concern and urged that steps be taken to secure from the Defense Department high level decisions to set up adequate South Korean Security forces. On March 5, I attended a meeting in Secretary Marshall's office along with Walton Butterworth, Director of the Office of Far Eastern Affairs, Joseph E. Jacobs, and Arthur Bunce, the chief American political and economic representatives in South Korea. Walt Butterworth supplemented our March 4 memorandum by reporting that elections would be held in South Korea on May 9 and that the resulting government would then, according to the terms of the UN Resolution, be committed to arrange with us for the withdrawal of American troops. However, Butterworth went on to say that in view of the very real concern expressed privately to us by other members of the Interim Committee of the General Assembly, the United States was morally committed to withdraw our troops only after the creation of reasonably adequate Korean security forces, which would give the new government at least a 50–50 chance of survival. The Office of Far Eastern Affairs therefore contended that it was impossible at that time to set a firm timetable for withdrawal of our troops as the Pentagon had begun to urge.

The Pentagon continued to urge the setting of an early date for withdrawal, and the State Department continued to recommend flexibility and the building up of South Korean Forces. The buildup went slowly, although a Military Assistance Advisory Group for Korea was set up and a small amount of military equipment was provided. It was not nearly as much as the Koreans had wanted. The elections had been held and a government set up under Syngman Rhee as President. On December 12, 1948, the UN General Assembly adopted a Resolution declaring that a lawful government (The Republic of Korea) had been set up in that part of Korea where the UN Temporary Commission had been able to observe and consult and that "this Government is based on elections which were a valid expression of the free will of the electorate . . . and that this is the only such Government in Korea." On January 1, 1949, the United States announced that it had recognized the Republic of Korea. An old friend from my China days, John Muccio, was appointed our first Ambassador to the new Republic.

With the creation of a government in South Korea, the Pentagon increased its demands for withdrawal of American troops. The Russians withdrew their forces from North Korea after setting up a Communist controlled North Korean Government, and American forces were finally withdrawn by the end of June 1949. One year later strong North Korean troops were to surge across the 38th Parallel and with comparative ease push back the less well-equipped South Korean forces.

In January of 1948, I had been sent on a month's trip to Japan and Korea, my first visit to Asia since the end of the war. I had been flown out to Japan but had been told that in lieu of a vacation that year I could come back by ship. Arrangements were made for me to board the *President Cleveland* in Yokohama on the return portion of its maiden voyage at the end of January 1948. Not only was it a gay trip, but on it I met that most attractive army widow I mentioned previously. She was returning from seeing her first grandson in Manila, where her younger daughter was married to an officer of Standard Vacuum Oil Company. She was hastening back to Newport, Rhode Island, where her older daughter, married to a naval officer, was about to have her first child. Ten months later we were married and over the years, as we have been assigned to various posts abroad and her daughters continued to have babies, she has managed to be on hand, or only a day late, for the birth of all six of her grandchildren. Dorothy McCardle of the *Washington Post* christened her the "Galloping Grandma," and while the babies have stopped, the galloping has not. Even today, in alleged retirement, she has managed to get once to Europe and three times to Asia, with a fourth Asian trip in the offing.

During the time we were concerned with Korea, another reorganization of the State Department had taken place. The four geographic offices had become bureaus and their Directors had been designated Assistant Secretaries of State. The old divisions had been enlarged and were now offices; their Chiefs became Directors. I was assigned Director of the new Office of Northeast Asian Affairs and found myself again immersed in Korean and Japanese matters, instead of being concerned with all of Asia, as in the old Office of Far Eastern Affairs.

When the Korean matter had been taken up by the United Nations, John Foster Dulles had been the member of the American delegation who argued the American case before the General Assembly and the Interim Committee. It was here I first met Mr. Dulles who later asked me to be his special assistant and later Deputy in the negotiation of the Japanese Peace Treaty.

The State Department in these early postwar years, and in contrast to its prewar aloofness, was making a real effort to cooperate with citizen's groups and associations in educating the American public about the realities of foreign affairs. In May of 1950, I was invited along with four other Department officials to attend and address a two-day foreign policy institute held in Milwaukee. In charge of the planning and administrative details for the Department was Margaret Carter, then chief of the State Department's Division of Public Liaison. She later married a senior Foreign Service Officer, George Morgan, and both of them were with us when I was Ambassador to Japan a few years later. Other members of the group from Washington were George Kennan, Counselor of the Department and head of policy planning, Leo Pasvolsky, who had worked long and hard in helping to develop United States policy towards the United Nations, and John Abbink, a consultant on economic problems to the State Department. A copy of the *Milwaukee Journal* of May 5, 1950, reports at some length an interview I gave to one of its reporters. Looking back after more than twenty-one years, I find it interesting to discover that much of what I said then is still valid. Perhaps today I should not put quite as much stress on the dangers of communism and would stress more the need of political, social, and economic measures. But it is important to remember that Russian communism had shown no real desire to cooperate in Europe, or in Korea, as I knew from personal experience. The Chinese Communists had but recently taken over control of the mainland of China, and in February of 1950 had concluded a treaty of alliance with Russia, which was obviously directed at Japan and American military forces stationed there. Monolithic communism was a reality in 1950.

According to the *Journal*, I stated that United States policy in the Far East was directed at convincing the 500 million people who have gained freedom since the end of World War II that "we want to work with them, not use them." I went on to say: "We want to help them to maintain a free world so they can have their own type of freedom, and to make clear that communism wants to dominate them in a new kind of slavery."

I stressed some of the difficulties facing us in Asia and pointed out that the new Asian nations had no tradition of working together as had the nations of Western Europe, where the Marshall Plan was having great success. I referred to the great problems created by the many languages and dialects and by the fact that in general the economies of these nations were competitive rather than complementary. Twenty-one years later this is still largely true, although considerable progress has been made in the development of Asian cooperative organizations such as the Association of Southeast Asian Nations (ASEAN), initiated and run by Asians with no Western participation. I concluded by saying that there are four major factors underlying American policy in the Far East. According to the *Journal* these were:

> A realization that the day of paternalistic relationship between the white man and the native is over. "We must adjust everything we do to that concept," he said.
>
> The spirit of revolution — an old condition in the Far East, which has been given impetus since World War II. It is common to the whole area and demonstrates the desire of the people to raise their low standard of living.
>
> A desire to be free to "run their own show." This is true even though there is a great deficiency in know-how in government administration and in Industry.
>
> Communism. It feeds on all the other factors, especially the desire to be free from white men and the poverty of the people.

I don't think I should change that greatly if I were talking today. I am afraid that over the years we have often forgotten some of the factors I mentioned or not given them sufficient attention, particularly the first and third factors.

I see, in reading over the *Journal*'s account that I also mentioned, as demonstrating the good faith of the United States in dealing with Asians, our granting of independence to the Philippines and the withdrawal of our troops from South Korea. Slightly more than a month later the people of South Korea might have disagreed with me.

# VII

# Three Days in June

## 1950

AT SIX-THIRTY in the morning I almost got out of bed and then realized it was Sunday, and for the first time in more than a week I could relax. The boss was in Kyoto with his wife, and I had nothing to do until eleven-thirty. The boss was John Foster Dulles who had recently been appointed a Consultant to Secretary of State Dean Acheson and charged with making a preliminary investigation regarding the possibilities of negotiating a Japanese Peace Treaty. On June 14, 1950, we had left Washington for a two week visit to Korea and Japan. I was then Director of the Office of Northeast Asian Affairs in the State Department and had been asked by Mr. Dulles to assist him in his task. President Syngman Rhee had invited Mr. Dulles to Seoul, and after a three day visit there we had come to Tokyo to discuss a possible peace treaty with General MacArthur and Japanese leaders.

It was now Sunday, June 25, and I was bone tired. Mr. Dulles never stopped. There was always someone else to talk to, something else to see, somewhere else to go, and always it must be done at a gallop. The previous Sunday in Korea we had spent the morning and early afternoon going up to the 38th Parallel north of the little town of Uijongbu and inspecting the meagre South Korean defenses. While we were there a picture had been taken of us in a trench with South Korean officers and members of the United States Military Advisory Group, peering through binoculars across the Parallel. Later the Russians used this picture in the UN Security Council in an attempt to prove that the United States and South Korea were planning an invasion of the North. No sooner did we return from the Parallel than we had to get ready for a reception given by American Ambassador Muccio for all the important people in Seoul: Korean, American, and European; military men, missionaries, businessmen, diplomats, and government officials. Afterward there was an official dinner and hours of discussion. And my large suitcase with clean suits was in Seattle — the normal airline mixup.

I had survived that day and the next week and my suitcase had just caught up with me. Mr. and Mrs. Dulles had decided to go to Kyoto for the weekend and had given me the choice of accompanying them or staying in Tokyo. I elected to stay. My friend the Norwegian Minister, Christian Reusch, had invited me to lunch on Sunday. He was to call for me at the Imperial Hotel at noon. At eleven-thirty I had agreed to spend a half-hour with Frank Gibney of *Time* who wanted to talk about a peace treaty with Japan. Nothing to do for almost five hours. I turned over for another hour of sleep, then had breakfast in my room, read the *Stars and Stripes* and the *Japan Times*, had a bath, and put on my first clean suit in almost ten days.

Promptly at eleven-thirty Frank Gibney met me in the lobby, and we had a beer while talking about a peace treaty. He told me he had just come from the Public Information Section of SCAP (Supreme Command Allied Power) where he had heard the Japanese press was full of stories about Mr. Dulles and his activities. Apparently there was nothing else of equal importance. The hope for an early peace treaty and the consequent end of the Occupation was uppermost in the minds of all Japanese, and Mr. Dulles was an outward and visible sign that this hope might be realized. Pictures of him and his party filled the papers, whether they were conferring with Japanese officials or General MacArthur, or even having an informal Japanese meal and showing surprising skill in the use of chopsticks.

At twelve Reusch came for me, and we drove off to his pleasant residence about twenty minutes away. It was good to see an old friend and also to discover he had not forgotten the secret of making an outstanding gimlet, which he had first shown me some eighteen years before when he was Third Secretary of the Norwegian Legation in Tokyo, and I was a language attaché at the American Embassy.

About three o'clock Reusch drove me back to the Imperial. As I walked through the lobby to my room, I was hailed by two other friends, former Japanese Ambassador to Washington Horinouchi and Harry Kearn, Foreign News Editor of *Newsweek*, who were having tea. "Have you heard about the invasion of South Korea?" they called. I was dumbfounded, but they insisted it was true that North Korean forces had crossed the 38th Parallel early that morning. I immediately went to my room and telephoned the Political Advisor's office (the State Department representative) and was told by the Duty Officer that a brief message from the American Embassy in Seoul confirmed that hostilities were in progress. The Political Adviser, William Sebald, was in Yokohama giving the commencement address at St. Joseph's College. Mr. Dulles was in Kyoto. I then called Colonel "Larry" Bunker, one of General MacArthur's aides, who also confirmed the news. He told me the army had been in touch with Mr. Dulles, who was flying back from Kyoto, that Sebald had been reached in Yokohama, and that there would be a meeting in General MacArthur's office at six o'clock.

Shortly before six o'clock I was ushered into General Mac-Arthur's outer office on the top floor of the Dai-Ichi building just across the moat from the outer gardens of the Imperial Palace. Mr. Dulles had already arrived and was closeted with the General. In the outer office Bill Sebald was on the phone to the

State Department in Washington, talking to Dean Rusk, then Assistant Secretary of State for Far Eastern Affairs. I joined on an extension and discovered that my chief assistant, Niles Bond, a Foreign Service Officer who was specializing in Korean affairs, was also on the line. We were unable to give Washington much new information, but Rusk and Bond informed us that contact was already being made with the American Mission to the United Nations and with Trygve Lie, the Secretary-General. An urgent meeting of the Security Council was being requested for the next day, Sunday, in Washington. It was then after four o'clock Sunday morning in Washington. The men there were working all night.

Sebald and I were admitted to the General's office, and we told him and Mr. Dulles of our talk with Washington. General MacArthur was magnificent as he strode up and down his huge office, his khaki shirt open at the neck, and his famous corncob pipe gripped between his teeth. Reports from Korea had apparently been fragmentary and inconclusive, or at least the General chose to regard them as inconclusive.

"This is probably only a reconnaissance in force. If Washington only will not hobble me, I can handle it with one arm tied behind my back," he declaimed. The General then told us that President Rhee had asked for some fighter planes and that, although he was certain the Koreans would not know how to handle them properly, he was going to send a few for morale purposes. I never did find out whether this was done. The General reassured us that everything was under control and insisted that "Ambassador" Dulles would be welcome in his office at any time. We then began to depart. However, just before we left the General told us he had certain reserve powers, which he did not specify, that he could invoke in case of a serious emergency.

Feeling somewhat relieved but still concerned about the situation, Mr. Dulles told me he wanted to send a cable to Secretary

Acheson and Assistant Secretary Rusk urging help for the Koreans if it proved necessary. When I said I should like to be associated with such a message, he invited me to return to his guest quarters in the staff apartments at the American Embassy. By a strange coincidence the apartment which Mr. and Mrs. Dulles were occupying was the same one that I had moved into, as its first occupant, on Washington's Birthday 1932.

Dulles's deep concern was undoubtedly a result of his experiences in Korea the previous week. His talks with the fiery and intensely patriotic Syngman Rhee had greatly impressed him as had his visit to the 38th Parallel the previous Sunday. He also had vividly in mind the speech he had given to the Korean National Assembly the next morning, when he had assured his audience, "You are not alone. You will never be alone so long as you continue to play worthily your part in the great design of human freedom." It was the type of speech Dulles was to become noted for in later years when he was Secretary of State. But the last paragraph, quoted above, had been drafted in Washington, and Mr. Dulles considered it an expression of American policy toward Korea.

In view of the confidence that had been expressed by General MacArthur, Dulles and I hoped the Koreans might be able to hold the line; but we both agreed that the United States had a moral obligation to the Korean people who were obviously intent on maintaining their freedom from Communist rule, although there were sometimes violent disagreements among them as to how this should be done. We both also had in mind the recent Chinese Communist takeover on the mainland and the February 1950 mutual defense treaty between the Communist Chinese and the Soviet Union which seemed to be directed at Japan. Was the invasion of South Korea a first step toward the building up of a direct threat to Japan?

After fifteen or twenty minutes of discussion Mr. Dulles got out his ever-present yellow drafting pad, and the following message was agreed upon:

FOR: Acheson and Rusk
FROM: Dulles and Allison

It is possible that the South Koreans may themselves contain and repulse the attack and, if so, this is the best way. If, however, it appears that they cannot do so, then we believe that United States force should be used . . . To sit by while Korea is overrun by unprovoked armed attack would start a disastrous chain of events leading most probably to world war.

The message ended with the suggestion that the Security Council of the United Nations might call for action, although we realized steps were already being taken to accomplish this. The message was given to Sebald for transmission.

It was now almost eight o'clock, and I was due at a black-tie dinner in Yokohama given by Brigadier General and Mrs. Crump Garvin, old friends of my wife. I had telephoned them I would be late and sans black tie, but they insisted I should come whenever possible. Crump was commander of the Port of Yokohama and had previously served in Korea. As we strolled after dinner in the garden of his home on the Bluff, overlooking Yokahama harbor, the invasion of Korea was the only topic of conversation. Crump found it difficult to understand why anyone should have been surprised by the action of the North Koreans. He explained: "I don't have anything to do with Korea now, but I'm still interested in the country and I read all the intelligence messages from there. For the last two or three weeks we've had reports that the North Korean Government was moving all civilians back from the border and concentrating troops just back of the Parallel. Anyone who read the reports could see something was going to happen and soon. I don't know what G-2 in Tokyo has been doing."

The long ride back to Tokyo in the middle of the night was not a happy one. Doubts about the ease with which the South Koreans would repel the invaders had been aroused by the talk with General Garvin, and the schedule for Monday, our last full

day in Tokyo before returning to Washington, was a wicked one
to contemplate.

Monday morning was filled with meetings at the office of the
Political Advisor. At noon the British Ambassador, Sir Alvary
("Joe") Gascoigne, had invited us to lunch in honor of Mr. and
Mrs. Dulles. The invasion of South Korea was still uppermost
in Mr. Dulles's mind, and he suggested that en route to the
British Embassy we stop at General MacArthur's office and get
the latest news. Again the General was most impressive and
most cordial. More news from Korea had arrived. Ambassador
Muccio had ordered the evacuation of American women and
children and had requested air cover to protect the evacuees.
General MacArthur said that he thought Muccio was somewhat
premature and that the situation, as he saw it, did not require
such action. However, he said that he would comply with the
Ambassador's request. In MacArthur's opinion there was still
no reason to panic about Korea. Considerably relieved, we went
on to an incredibly stiff and formal luncheon at the British
Embassy attended by many of the members of the Diplomatic
Corps and their ladies. Joe Gascoigne himself was far from stiff
and formal but diplomatic luncheons too often are just that way.
I sat next to the chief Soviet representative in Tokyo, General
Derevyanko. He was a typical Russian peasant type with a
strong face who looked very military in his red-trimmed khaki
uniform. Although he spoke no known language but Russian, he
was most jovial and insisted on drinking private toasts with me as
each new course was served. I wondered how much he knew
about what was going on in Korea and what part, if any, he had
had in planning the invasion.

Lunch was finally over, and feeling much more in need of a
nap than anything else, I braced myself and accompanied Mr.
Dulles to a series of further meetings regarding the peace treaty
which culminated at four o'clock with a reception at the home
of the Political Advisor for members of the Japanese Socialist

Party, the chief opposition Party, and Japanese Trade Union leaders. What good it accomplished is uncertain, but at least it gave the Japanese in opposition to the government party an opportunity to put their views forward. Unfortunately, at that time they were not too well expressed and seemed to be quite vague. I'm afraid Mr. Dulles went away with a rather poor opinion of them.

The meeting with the Socialists and the Trade Union leaders was our last official meeting before our scheduled departure at noon Tuesday for Washington. Mr. and Mrs. Dulles were to have dinner alone with General and Mrs. MacArthur, and I had been invited by the Deputy Political Advisor, Cloyce Huston, to a black-tie dinner to meet some of the local nonofficial American community and one or two of the members of the Diplomatic Corps. Before going to this dinner, I hurried back to my room at the Imperial Hotel to try and snatch at least a half-hour nap. However, before I settled down to it, I telephoned the Political Advisor's office to inquire if there was any further news from Korea. I was told that Ambassador Muccio had telephoned from Seoul during the afternoon and after making a rather general report had asked to speak to me. I asked whether he had indicated he had some special message for me or had merely asked if I were available as we were old friends and he would like to say hello. I was told the latter seemed to be the case, so I gave a sigh of relief and shut my eyes.

Promptly at seven-thirty I arrived at Huston's house and found that, as usual, I was one of the first to arrive. Besides the host and his wife the only other couple present was George and Helen Folster. George was then the NBC correspondent, and I took the opportunity before the other guests arrived to ask him if he had heard anything new from Korea. He said he had just come from the Public Information Office of Headquarters and had been told there was absolutely nothing of significance to report. Others began to arrive and suddenly we heard a great chortle and in limped the Australian Ambassador, W. R. Hodgson, who, I had heard, had been consistently critical of the United States and all its actions in Asia.

"Well, I've just had the last conversation anyone will have with Korea," he bellowed to the whole room. "I've been talking to the Australian member of the United Nations Commission on Korea, and he says the Korean army is retreating all along the front and that the American military advisory group is getting ready to pull out." I looked at George Folster, he looked at me, and shook his head. "The P.I.O. people didn't know anything about it an hour ago," he insisted. "However, I'm to make another broadcast at 9:45, and I'll check with them again before and come back here right after the broadcast and give you the latest dope."

We went into dinner and Hodgson began regaling the table with all the faults of the Americans in Korea, in the occupation of Japan, and in Asia generally. I embarrassed our hostess a bit by talking back and referring to a few beams in the Australian eye. I had not been brought up in the more refined European brand of diplomacy, as had my host and hostess, but in the more informal and direct Far Eastern service. And Hodgson didn't really mind. He just liked to argue, and actually at bottom he was really a good friend of the United States.

George Folster had left for his broadcast, and I was anxiously awaiting his return. About ten-thirty he came back, took me aside, and reported that Headquarters had finally admitted all was not well in Korea and in substance had confirmed everything Hodgson had said about the Korean Army retreat. I immediately put in a telephone call for Ambassador Muccio, and shortly before eleven I was talking to him. He confirmed that the South Korean Army was in full retreat. The word he used was that the front was "disintegrating." I could hear the sound of artillery fire over the telephone as I asked Muccio what his plans were. He said he would stay close to President Rhee but that the Embassy staff would probably leave Seoul for the South in the morning. After cautioning him not to take unnecessary risks and telling him I would try to call him again in the morning, I hung up. Inasmuch as Mr. Dulles had been having dinner with General MacArthur, I was sure he would have been informed, but I decided to call him and see if he had any instructions.

After several attempts I finally reached him in his Embassy apartment and began by saying, "I suppose you've heard the bad news from Korea." When he said he had heard nothing I exclaimed, "But didn't you have dinner with the General?" "Yes," he replied, "but after dinner we saw a movie, and we weren't interrupted all evening. I stopped in on the way back to have a nightcap with Colonel Huff [an aid of MacArthur's] and he had heard nothing." Movies after dinner were a well-known and long-standing part of General MacArthur's life.

I then told Mr. Dulles of Hodgson's telephone conversation with the Australian member of the UN Commission, what Folster had learned at the P.I.O., and of my telephone conversation with Ambassador Muccio. I referred to General MacArthur's final word to us Sunday evening, when he said he had certain reserve powers he could use in an emergency, and I suggested now might be the time to put them into effect. Mr. Dulles said he would telephone the General immediately and would then call me back. Apparently the General's staff was reluctant to bother him after he had left the office, but Mr. Dulles never feared any man, however high in rank. In a few minutes he called to tell me he had reached the General who still had not been informed but who said he would look into the matter at once. This may be one of the few times in American history when representatives of the State Department have had to tell a high American military commander about what was happening in his own back yard. Mr. Dulles told me to be sure to call Muccio again the first thing in the morning and to put in a call to Dean Rusk in Washington so that as soon as Dulles reached the Political Adviser's office in the morning he could ask Rusk whether or not we should stay in Tokyo.

Well before eight-thirty the next morning I was in the office of the Political Adviser and arrangements had been made for Mr. Dulles to talk to Assistant Secretary Rusk as soon as Dulles reached Sebald's office. In the meantime, I was able to reach Ambassador Muccio in Seoul and had learned from him that all South Korean Government offices were being evacuated from Seoul and that he expected to accompany President Rhee later in the morning. Their destination was the city of Taejon, south of the Han River, in the center of South Korea. After again cautioning him not to take unnecessary risks, I wished him luck and told him the Dulles party was scheduled to take off for Washington via Pan American at noon.

Mr. Dulles arrived about half-past eight and was soon connected with Dean Rusk in Washington. As I had anticipated, Rusk said there was no reason for us to remain in Tokyo and that we would be more helpful back in the State Department. Mr. Dulles seemed a bit disappointed. He enjoyed being at the center of activity, and he rightly assumed that General MacArthur would soon be the dominating figure in the strategic planning of the Korean War. After cleaning up a few loose ends, we returned to our quarters to finish packing and about ten-thirty were driven down to Haneda airport, where we were ushered into the VIP room to wait for boarding time.

General and Mrs. MacArthur soon joined us as did Bill Sebald and other members of his and General MacArthur's staffs. It was a vastly different MacArthur from the jaunty, confident General who had told us Sunday night that the North Korean invasion was probably only "a reconnaissance in force" and that he could handle it "with one arm tied behind my back." It was even a different MacArthur from the one we had talked to less than twenty-four hours previously, when he had told us Ambassador Muccio had been premature in ordering the evacuation of American women and children from Seoul. Now, "All Korea is lost. The only thing we can do is get our people safely out of the country," he said bleakly. The General told us he had talked to Ambassador Muccio that morning and that all was chaos in South Korea. (I learned sometime later from Muccio that it was not General MacArthur but his Chief of Staff who had telephoned the Ambassador.) I have never seen such a dejected, completely despondent man as General MacArthur was that Tuesday morning, June 27, 1950.

As usual the plane's departure was delayed. We were told it was some small engineering problem and that it would probably be at least twelve-thirty before we could take off. As we glumly discussed the situation, we were interrupted by a messenger from Tokyo who told General MacArthur that a message from Washington had just arrived saying the Secretary of the Army wanted to have a Telecon with the General at one o'clock. "Tell them I'm engaged seeing Ambassador Dulles off. If I don't get back in time, have the Chief of Staff talk to the Secretary," was the General's instruction. Bill Sebald and I looked at each other in some dismay. This didn't seem good enough action in view of the bad news from Korea. We quietly left and found the Pan American manager who told us it would be well after one o'clock before we took off. We insisted MacArthur must get back to Tokyo in time to talk to the Secretary of the Army. After a brief discussion we devised what we hoped would be a method to ensure MacArthur's presence at the Telecon. We went back to the VIP room and managed to get Mr. Dulles aside long enough to explain what we wanted to do and to get his approval.

At approximately a quarter after twelve a voice came over the loud-speaker in the VIP room saying the plane was now ready and would the Dulles party please board. We trooped out to the plane, which in those days was able to come up just in front of the VIP room so that distinguished passengers only had a few yards to walk. General and Mrs. MacArthur walked with us to the foot of the gangplank and his shiny black official car pulled up behind them. We all said good-by, the junior members of the party led the way, shook hands with the MacArthurs, and marched up the gangplank and into the plane. Mr. and Mrs. Dulles were the last to board and after they had reached the top of the gangplank and waved to the General, the MacArthurs got in their car and sped back to Tokyo. When we were sure they were out of sight we all marched back down the gangplank and into the VIP room, where we sat around another hour before the plane was finally ready to depart.

So the General got back to Tokyo in time to take part in the Telecon with Secretary of the Army Frank Pace. We learned later that this was the all-important message which informed MacArthur of President Truman's decision to authorize the use of American air and naval power in Korea, to interpose the Seventh Fleet between Formosa and Red China, to increase military assistance to the French in Indochina, and to give further aid to the Philippine Government in its struggles with the Huks.

We knew nothing about President Truman's actions at the time and the whole Dulles party was steeped in gloom as we settled down on the plane and headed for Wake Island, our first stop. As soon as we were air-borne, we all hastened down to the cheerful, comfortable bar that the old Pan American clippers used to have. Having been warned before our departure, the bartender had Mr. Dulles's favorite Old Forester and this, together with the Scotch and martinis which the other members of the party ordered, helped to lift a bit of the gloom. But it was a sad and worried group who found little to say to each other and even found it difficult to concentrate on the latest detective stories that Mr. Dulles always seemed to have with him.

In due course we reached Wake. We left Wake. What else

is there to say about Wake? About one hour out of Wake, just as we were beginning to close our eyes and doze, the captain of the plane shocked us with an announcement over the loud speaker that we had just lost an engine and were returning to Wake. The fact that we had to jettison much of our gasoline and that this could have caught fire and blown us out of the world did not add to the gaiety of the trip back. But get back we did, and the harried Wake officials managed to find places for us all to sleep. We were told we would be delayed about fifteen hours until another engine could be flown in or the present one repaired. Mr. Dulles was frantic. If he couldn't be with Mac-Arthur in Tokyo, he wanted to be back at the State Department in the shortest possible time. The Inspector General of our air force was also a passenger, and he radioed to all possible nearby points to see if there was an air force plane that could get to Wake more quickly and take the Dulles party on to Washington. But our luck was out, and we had to spend the night.

The next morning at breakfast we had good news. We would be able to depart sooner than expected, and the radio had brought word of President Truman's decision, the same one about which General MacArthur had been informed by the Secretary of the Army after our mock departure from Tokyo the day before. Mr. Dulles completely forgot that he was a Republican. At that moment, in his mind, President Truman was the greatest President in history. The despair we had brought from Haneda vanished. There was still over an hour before we were to board our plane again. A happy and buoyant John Foster Dulles went swimming.

VIII

# The Japanese Peace Treaty

## 1950–1951

DURING THIRTY YEARS in the United States Foreign Service, the fifteen months I spent as Deputy to John Foster Dulles in the negotiation of the Japanese Peace Treaty and the security treaties connected with it were among the most interesting and satisfying. Mr. Dulles was a hard but fair taskmaster, a man of great vision, imagination, and above all, energy. When he became Secretary of State I came to disagree with him, sometimes violently, on certain policies, but I always considered him a great citizen. The negotiation of the Japanese Peace Treaty will be considered in the eyes of history, I believe, as the single most constructive act of Foster Dulles in the field of foreign relations.

There are three important ways in which the Japanese Peace Treaty was different from any previous treaties to end bitter wars to which the United States had been a party. First, there was a serious and continuous effort made to keep the members of the Senate, who would have to consent to the ratification of the treaty, and the members of the House of Representatives, who would have to pass legislation implementing the treaty, thoroughly informed of what was being done, how it was done, and the reasons therefore. Secondly, the manner of negotiating the treaty was a departure from precedent in that its substance was negotiated bilaterally, instead of by all the victorious powers sitting around a single conference table. Thirdly, from the beginning, Japan, the defeated nation, was consulted. Of course the viewpoint of the victorious powers took precedence over Japanese views, but there was no repetition of the action taken after World War I at Versailles, where the defeated German representatives were kept in an outer room until the Allied Powers had completed their work and were then brought in and told to sign on the dotted line a treaty that they had had no part in drafting.

As early as 1947, General MacArthur had recommended that an early peace treaty be concluded. The State Department agreed and in the summer of that year made an attempt to call a conference to consider procedures for concluding a treaty. This 1947 invitation was accepted by all eleven members of the Far Eastern Commission (although the British Commonwealth nations were not pleased at the timing), except the Soviet Union and the Republic of China. The Russians claimed that a peace treaty should only be considered in the first instance by the principal powers, Great Britain, the United States, France, China, and the Soviet Union. The lesser powers would be consulted after the principal powers had agreed. China agreed that all members of the Far Eastern Commission should be invited but claimed that voting should be the same as in the Far Eastern Commission, which gave the principal powers a veto. The United States would not agree to this and the matter was dropped.

From that point until the summer of 1950 there was no progress in the international field with a Japanese Peace Treaty. Many of the American officials concerned began to see that, while it was important to ensure that Japan not be in a position to repeat her military aggression and that democratic procedures be incorporated in Japan's government, it might be just as important to help Japan recover enough economically so that its people could look forward to a decent standard of living and its government achieve the stability that would enable it to stand on its own feet once the Occupation was ended. At this time I had become head of what was then called the Japan-Korean Division of the State Department, and in December of 1948 it was decided I should make my first postwar trip to those two countries and to report on current conditions.

It was on this trip that I first met General MacArthur. He seemed to have an instinctive understanding of the Japanese need for drama and aloofness on the part of people in high places. I am convinced that during the first two years of the Occupation, when the Japanese people were still stunned by their defeat, unsure of what the future held, and disillusioned with their old leaders, no one could have equaled MacArthur in giving them some one to look up to and take the place of those who had let them down. But in talking privately to some of my prewar Japanese friends (and this was not easy to do at that period in the Occupation) I found that by 1948 the magic was beginning to fade and not everything was as perfect as the Headquarters Staff would have one believe. Some Japanese and many members of the Diplomatic Corps frequently pointed out in caustic tones that when General Eisenhower was Supreme Commander in the European struggle his headquarters was known as SHAEF (Supreme Headquarters Allied Expeditionary Force) while MacArthur's headquarters was known as SCAP (Supreme Commander Allied Powers).

Unfortunately, many members of the SCAP staff did not share General MacArthur's instinctive understanding of the Japanese people.

I was appalled at the self-righteous enthusiasm with which officials of the government and economic sections of SCAP were indiscriminately purging Japanese political and economic leaders and breaking up industrial and trade organizations. The dominant philosophy of most of these officials was still that of punishing the sinners and destroying their industrial structure so that it could never again support an aggressive militarism. Bill Sebald, who did know Japan well, tried as State Department representative to ameliorate some of the more glaring faults of other sections of SCAP, but the voice of the State Department carried but slight weight in that military headquarters.

I returned to Washington convinced that many of the Occupation reforms would be discarded as soon as possible after a peace treaty, unless they could be softened and administered in a more understanding manner, and unless our policy could be changed to one of stimulating economic and political recovery, rather than continuing a policy of punishment and repression.

Prior to my return to Washington I had spent a week in Korea. Although Korea was a liberated country and Japan an occupied ex-enemy country, the atmosphere in Seoul was much more restrictive than in Tokyo. This was partly due to the continued division of the country at the 38th Parallel insisted on by the Russians, who were building a Communist regime in the North, and partly due to the difficulties of working with the obstreperous Koreans who have often been called the Irish of the Orient. Also the top American military commander in Korea, General Hodge, a fine combat officer, did not have the political sensitivity of General MacArthur, and this was reflected in the harsher attitude toward the Koreans by his command than was taken toward the Japanese by the troops under MacArthur.

In addition to consulting with the State Department and economic aid officials in Korea, one of my principal tasks was trying to get that great Korean patriot Syngman Rhee to be more cooperative. Rhee had been exiled from Korea for many years and had only returned after the Japanese surrender. He had spent most of his exile in the United States, where he had gone to Princeton, and called himself a Wilsonian Democrat. Because of his long record of opposition to Japan, he considered himself the natural leader of any free Korea and was furious with the American authorities because they would not declare him President of liberated Korea. I spent at least two hours one cold winter night trying to explain to Rhee why the Americans could not do as he wished. We believed free elections were the sign of a democratic nation, and I told Rhee that we hoped soon to have elections. Rhee argued that the Korean people all wanted him as their leader and that we should understand this and place him in his rightful position. I countered with the argument that the Americans could not choose the President of Korea, that it should be done by the Korean people, and if he was right in his estimate of their feelings for him, he had nothing to fear. He went away unconvinced and grumbling about the stupid, technical Americans. Elections were held later, and Rhee was elected first President of Korea, but not without charges of police coercion, stuffed ballot boxes, and outright bribery. I have since come to question seriously whether an American style election can have any validity when forced upon an Eastern people who have long lived under an authoritarian rule and who have only the most rudimentary understanding of Western democratic ways.

From the spring of 1948 until the spring of 1950 there was continual discussion of a possible peace treaty with Japan and what its character should be. As the Russians became more intransigent, and as the Communists increased their hold on the mainland of China, there was increasing agreement that any treaty with Japan should restore complete sovereignty and place no artificial restrictions on Japan's economic and political rehabilitation. The timing of the treaty came to be the chief point of dissension. George Kennan and others in the State Department argued that a treaty should not be concluded until Japan had made sufficient economic and political progress to stand on its own feet after the Occupation had been withdrawn. The Pentagon argued that no treaty should be concluded unless the Russians agreed, for otherwise they would still be at war with Japan and could send in occupation troops.

While these discussions were going on, I continued to preside over what came to be known as the Office of Northeast Asian Affairs, dealing with day-to-day problems concerning Japan and Korea. I also served as Far Eastern Advisor to the American delegation to the sessions of the United Nations in 1949, and it was there I first met Mr. Dulles. He was an Alternate American Delegate and had been given the responsibility of arguing the case for the political unification of Korea before the Political Committee of the General Assembly. Dulles was an indefatigable worker and after spending all day at the sessions at Lake Success would often have his advisors meet him after dinner at his home. At one of these sessions we were to discuss the speech Mr. Dulles was to deliver the next morning in the Political Committee. I had been asked to prepare the first draft. This I had done and had given a copy to Mr. Dulles early in the afternoon. Sometime before our evening meeting he had found time to read it, and when he showed us his revised version of the text I was dismayed. Not more than twenty percent of my original draft had been retained. Mr. Dulles looked at me, smiled, and said, "Don't look so distressed. I've used more of your draft than I have of any other speech ever written for me." From that moment on I was his man.

Around the middle of May 1950 he was asked by Secretary Acheson to take charge of the Department's Japanese treaty responsibilities. Shortly after he had accepted this task, he invited all of us in the Department who had anything to do with Japan or treaty matters to meet in his office. Here we were told of his assignment and his general ideas of how he should go about it, and we were asked for any comments we might want to make. I expressed a long held opinion that if we expected any of the Occupation reforms to last, it would be necessary to have a liberal treaty that would encourage the Japanese and make them desire, of their own volition and not by force, to be decent members of the family of nations.

As the meeting broke up, and while most of those attending were still in the room, Mr. Dulles beckoned to me and asked me to walk down the hall with him. He said he had received approval from the Secretary to make a brief trip to Japan to consult General MacArthur and Japanese leaders about a treaty and asked if I would go with him. I expressed my personal pleasure at his request and my willingness to go but pointed out I was a career officer and had definite responsibilities in the Department which I could not relinquish without the approval of my superiors. I also pointed out that Max Hamilton, American Chairman of the Far Eastern Commission, was senior to me, and I knew he had hoped to be associated with work on the treaty. Mr. Dulles said he understood and that Hamilton's position on the Far Eastern Commission was importantly concerned with the treaty but that my job would be to act as his personal associate and advisor. He wanted to have a small staff, not more than three or four persons, who would work closely with him and have no other responsibilities.

The next few weeks were spent in divesting myself of most of my current responsibilities and studying all that had been done about a treaty with Japan in the past two years and the various points of view expressed by the State Department's offices concerned with the matter, the members of the Far Eastern Commission, and the Pentagon. Mr. Dulles took time to explain his own views. They were generally in accord with those expressed in the most recent treaty drafts prepared in the Department, although he thought them too involved in detail. He had been a junior member of the American delegation at the peace conference at Versailles at the end of World War I, and he was convinced that a punitive treaty only contained the seeds of future wars and that expectations of getting huge amounts of reparations payments from a defeated power were not realistic.

He also believed firmly that the Japanese should be consulted from the beginning, although their opinions could not be considered necessarily decisive.

Because of his work at the United Nations in arguing for the recognition of the Republic of Korea (the government headed by Syngman Rhee in Seoul) as the only legitimate government in Korea, and because he wished to reassure the Koreans that their views about a peace treaty with Japan would be taken into account, Mr. Dulles sought and received approval from the Department to visit Seoul prior to his talks in Japan.

On Sunday, June 18, we visited the Korean troops just behind the 38th Parallel. While there, as I have told elsewhere, we had our picture taken in a trench surrounded by Korean officers and a few members of the American military advisory group. Mr. Dulles, wearing his formal Homburg, was seen peering intently at military maps of the region. I was just behind him, my bald head concealed under a borrowed hat, and because I was peering across the 38th Parallel through huge binoculars I was practically unrecognizable. Just a week later, at almost the exact spot where we had been, the troops of the North Korean Communist regime poured across the border headed for Seoul. A few weeks later in the United Nations the photograph taken that Sunday was passed around by the Russians as proof that America, under the guidance of Mr. Dulles, had plotted to invade North Korea.

The next morning Mr. Dulles gave a speech before the Korean Parliament in which he went far to assure the Koreans that if they persisted in the development of a democratic government, they would have the support of the United States. The Russians later cited this speech, in connection with the photograph of Mr. Dulles at the 38th Parallel, as additional proof that the United States was responsible for the war in Korea.

Returning to Tokyo we found General MacArthur in accord with our conception of a nonpunitive treaty that would restore complete sovereignty to Japan and encourage it to become a responsible, peaceful member of the family of nations. The General also believed we should go ahead with the treaty as soon as possible and was a strong ally in our continuing dispute with the Pentagon, which urged indefinite delay. Secretary of Defense Louis Johnson and General Omar Bradley, Chairman of the Joint Chiefs of Staff, had been in Tokyo while we were in Korea and were still there vainly trying to get MacArthur's support for delay. But the General remained firm. His support was of great assistance to Dulles and the State Department in finally getting approval to go ahead with the treaty.

After General MacArthur, the single most important person with whom Dulles talked was the Japanese Prime Minister, Shigeru Yoshida. Their first meeting was a dismal failure. Mr. Dulles, full of enthusiasm for pushing forward, was met by a cautious, seemingly evasive Yoshida who was particularly reluctant to make any commitment on security matters. The problem of Japanese security and how it would be maintained after the end of the Occupation was one of the chief bones of contention between the State Department and the Pentagon, and Mr. Dulles had hoped to get from Mr. Yoshida some suggestions as to how this problem might be solved. But the Prime Minister on a first meeting confined himself to generalities and refused to get involved in details. When I saw Mr. Dulles after the meeting he was completely frustrated and almost bitter. It took the combined efforts of Bill Sebald and myself to calm him down and get him to agree to show a little patience. Later, of course, after Yoshida and Dulles had come to know each other better they worked with considerable harmony.

In addition to General MacArthur and Prime Minister Yoshida, the Dulles party talked with members of the Diplomatic Corps, particularly the representatives of the British Commonwealth nations, leading American and European businessmen, missionaries, newspaper correspondents, and many officials of the Occupation. Among the Japanese, not only did we talk to members of the government, but to leaders of the opposition parties, to trade union leaders, educators, publishers, religious leaders, and a cross section of Japanese businessmen and industrialists. When we left to return to Washington on June 27 we had, we believed, a comprehensive idea of how these diverse groups felt about a treaty and what it should contain.

The Korean war broke out while we were in Tokyo, and at first we wondered whether or not this would delay our work on a treaty. However, by the time we left Tokyo Mr. Dulles was convinced that, if anything, the work on the treaty should be expedited. We again received support for this position from General MacArthur and Bill Sebald.

Throughout the summer the argument with the Pentagon continued. In addition to worrying about how the security of Japan could be maintained after a peace treaty, the military argued that any treaty concluded without the participation of the Soviet Union would give that nation the right, being still at war with Japan, to take any action it wished against the Japanese including the introduction of Russian troops into the country. They brought down to Washington a distinguished New York lawyer, Goldthwaite Dorr, to argue with Mr. Dulles about the necessity of not doing anything without the Russians. Mr. Dulles took the position that if the Russians really wanted to intervene militarily in Japan, they would do so and find an excuse to justify their action. They might claim that a peace treaty without Russian participation was sufficient justification, or any other excuse, if that was not available. Mr. Dulles was supported by the State Department in his views, and as the summer wore on the Pentagon began to be more flexible. A small Defense-State Department committee was set up to discuss points at issue and suggest possible solutions. Major General Carter B. Magruder was the chief Defense representative, and I was the chief State Department member. General Magruder had a good, if slow moving, mind, and he was extremely hard to convince, but once his agreement had been obtained he lived up to it wholeheartedly.

By September 4 General Magruder and I had worked out a joint memorandum to be signed by the Secretaries of State and Defense and presented to the President. This memorandum spelled out security objectives which the Defense Department believed essential and the manner in which Mr. Dulles proposed to secure them. The two Secretaries signed the memorandum, and it was approved by the President. The way had been cleared within the United States Government, and the treaty negotiations could go ahead. On September 8, 1950, President Truman authorized the State Department to undertake negotiations looking toward a treaty, and Mr. Dulles was placed in charge under the guidance of Secretary Acheson.

Having succeeded in persuading the Pentagon to concur in going ahead with a treaty and in agreeing to the general principles that should govern it, the next task was to approach the principal nations involved in the war against Japan and ascertain whether or not they were in sufficient agreement with us to justify going ahead. These were the nations on the Far Eastern Commission. In addition the Republics of Korea and Indonesia, which had obtained independence since the end of the war, were consulted. The Foreign Ministers of most of these nations were to attend the Fifth Session of the General Assembly of the United Nations at Lake Success, and it was decided the first approach to them would be made at that time. Mr. Dulles was a member of the United States delegation, and I was an advisor. In addition to believing in a nonpunitive treaty and one which would place no restrictions on the sovereignty of a post-treaty Japan, Mr. Dulles wanted a brief treaty which would not be filled with complicated detail. He prepared a two-page memorandum setting forth seven principles that should govern the treaty, and this he presented to the foreign ministers and other representatives of the concerned governments. These seven points can be briefly summarized as follows:

1. Parties to the treaty should be "any or all nations at war with Japan which are willing to make peace on the basis proposed and as may be agreed."

2. Japan will apply for membership in the United Nations.

3. Japan will agree to a United Nation Trusteeship, with the United States as administering authority, for the Ryukyus and Bonin Islands. Japan will recognize the independence of Korea and accept "the future decision of the United Kingdom, the USSR, China, and the United States with reference to the status of Formosa, the Pescadores, South Sakhalin and the Kuriles" and Japan will renounce all special rights and interests in China.

4. Japan will agree to the retention of United States forces "and perhaps other forces" in Japan pending effective security arrangements within the United Nations.

5. Japan will adhere to treaties dealing with narcotics, fisheries, and international trade.

6. There will be a mutual waiver of claims.

7. Disputes will be referred to the International Court of Justice.

The memorandum was not designed, of course, to do more than initiate discussion, but some of the persons to whom it was shown seemed to think it was our idea of a complete treaty, and their reaction was vigorous to say the least.

Mr. Dulles and I met with Australian Foreign Minister Percy Spender and David McNicol, from the Australian Embassy in Washington, in a small private room just off the Delegates' Lounge at Lake Success. Sir Percy (as he is now) is a rather short, reddish-haired man with a florid complexion. As he read the memorandum his face grew more and more suffused with color, and at one point I thought he would burst a blood vessel.

Japanese troops had come close to Australia and the bitterness caused by the war was still intense among his people. And here was their ally, the United States, proposing a peace treaty with no restrictions on the remilitarization of Japan and no provision for reparations of any kind. Sir Percy did not hesitate to express his opinion in colorful and uninhibited language. Mr. Dulles fortunately did not respond in kind and patiently explained his ideas and the reasons for them. Sir Percy eventually calmed down, and by the time we all reached San Francisco, a year later, he was one of the principal aides to the United States delegation in making the conference a success.

Other delegations were also disturbed, but by the end of the session we believed we had sufficient agreement to enable us to go ahead with a first draft of a complete treaty. The only nation which withheld any substantive comment at that time was the Soviet Union. Later the Russians claimed they had not participated in any discussions, but on three separate occasions, October 6, 1950, November 20, 1950, and January 13, 1951, the chief Soviet delegate at the United Nations, Deputy Minister of Foreign Affairs Malik, had talks with Mr. Dulles about the treaty. Mr. Malik would not meet with Mr. Dulles at Lake Success, where he might be observed, but insisted on coming at night to Mr. Dulles's home.

These meetings with Malik provided an interesting education in the difference between the official and public Russian and the nonofficial and private one. When Malik and his interpreter sat down in Mr. Dulles's library to discuss the peace treaty with our small group they were relaxed and smiling. They accepted the fine Scotch and soda provided by their host, and, secure in the knowledge that no television cameras would reveal their actions to a waiting public, they would even joke and laugh from time to time. Malik really needed no interpreter, as his command of English was quite good, but no Soviet diplomat would ever be caught alone in the company of his non-Communist colleagues.

So young Mr. Troyanovski was brought along. His father had been the Soviet Ambassador to Tokyo in the late twenties and early thirties, and the young man had attended the American school there. His English was perfect. He later followed in his father's footsteps and also served as Soviet Ambassador to Tokyo. Most of the time at these meetings was spent in answering Malik's questions and explaining in detail the principles that governed the United States's conception of the treaty. The Russians seldom volunteered any information at that time as to their conception of a treaty. After an hour or so the two Russians would depart, after cordially shaking hands all around and profusely thanking Mr. Dulles for his hospitality. The next morning in the Political Committee at Lake Success Malik would glare across the table at Dulles, shake his finger at him, and shout to the world that he was a "Fascist beast." The public and official Russian was in command, the friendly drinking companion was forgotten.

Mr. Dulles and I had no decisive part to play in the discussions that raged back and forth that autumn and winter from Washington to Tokyo, to London and Lake Success about whether General MacArthur should let his forces cross the 38th Parallel into North Korea. At one point I was asked my opinion, as a former head of the Japan-Korean Division of the State Department, and I took the position that such a crossing should not arbitrarily be precluded, in which opinion I was joined by Dean Rusk, then Assistant Secretary of State for Far Eastern Affairs. However, neither of us contemplated that the General would go all the way to the Yalu and attempt to unify Korea by force, nor did we believe this was contemplated by the pertinent United Nations Resolutions. But General MacArthur took matters into his own hands with the result that in December we were faced at the United Nations with the necessity to consider possible evacuation of our troops.

After the United Nations session ended, we returned to

Washington and reviewed our position with regard to the Japanese treaty. The warriors at the Pentagon were at least partially satisfied and had agreed we could go ahead. The talks with our allies at the United Nations had, on the whole, been encouraging.

Back in 1947 the State Department had contemplated a peace treaty conference made up, in the first instance, of all members of the Far Eastern Commission, but because of Chinese and Soviet objections to the procedure proposed, the idea was dropped. Now that we were again ready to go ahead with treaty discussions the question had been raised as to what kind of a peace conference we should have. The world, and particularly the Pacific political situation, had completely changed. The members of the Far Eastern Commission had been increased from 11 to 13. Of the 12 members of the commission other than Nationalist China, half recognized as the legitimate government of China the Communist regime which had driven the Nationalists to Formosa from the mainland. It would obviously be impossible to reach agreement on which Chinese government should be invited to a conference. If we were to wait for agreement, it might be years before we had a treaty. Mr. Dulles had become more and more convinced that an early treaty was essential if Japan was to be kept as a voluntary member of the non-Communist world. If normal treaty making procedures could not be used and a general conference convened, why not discard precedent and talk with the concerned nations individually?

Mr. Dulles decided to take with him on a trip to Japan a representative group not restricted to the State Department. From the Pentagon there were Earl Johnson, Assistant Secretary of the Army, Major General Carter Magruder and Colonel C. Stanton Babcock, who had been an Assistant Military Attaché in Tokyo at the time of Pearl Harbor. From the Department of State there was just myself and Robert Fearey, a junior

Foreign Service Officer who had made a special study of the postwar Japanese economic situation. John D. Rockefeller III, who had developed a deep interest in Asian art, was invited to join us as a cultural representative.

The main problem in the back of all our minds at that time was security. How was a completely disarmed Japan to be defended? Critics will probably say this was not the most constructive way to approach peace making, but it is only necessary to consider the international environment at that time to understand our concern. The Chinese Communists had conquered the mainland and almost driven the United Nations forces out of Korea. In addition, they had but recently concluded a treaty with the Soviet Union which was plainly directed against a revived Japan, and Japan had no military forces of any kind of her own. A monolithic communism was a fact of life in 1951, and those who had any sort of responsibility for maintaining peace and stability in the world could not ignore it. Before leaving Washington, our mission had been charged not only with exploring the possibility of retaining American troops and bases in Japan after a peace treaty, but also with looking into the possibility of some sort of Pacific Security Pact of which Japan could be a member.

This latter idea appealed strongly to Mr. Dulles. He was adamant in his determination that a peace treaty should not include any provisions that would forbid Japan to rebuild its own defense forces, but he understood the fear in the minds of our Philippine, Australian, and New Zealand friends which would arise from lack of such provisions. Mr. Dulles hoped it might be possible to include a Japanese defense force in an international organization where it would be used for the benefit, and under the direction, of all members of the organization and not just for the national purposes of Japan. In the end this was not to prove possible. In a speech before the Japan-America Society of Tokyo on February 2, he brought the problem publicly to the attention of the Japanese people. In this speech Mr. Dulles pointed out the dangers of an unarmed Japan and said that if Japan wished it could share collective protection against direct aggression. He then added, in order to make clear, as he explained later at the San Francisco Peace Conference, the position of the United States Government:

> That, however, is not a choice which the United States is going to impose upon Japan. It is an invitation. The United States is not interested in slavish conduct . . . We are concerned only with the brave and the free. The choice must be Japan's own choice.

The afternoon before Mr. Dulles's speech to the Japan-America Society, he had been visited by the Socialist Chairman, Mr. Suzuki, and the late Inejiro Asanuma, Secretary-General of the Socialist Party Executive Committee. It was therefore no surprise to us that Mr. Suzuki should take exception to Dulles's public invitation to Japan to share collective security. The Socialists had left with us a long memorandum setting forth their policies and had talked at length about their belief that unarmed neutrality was the answer to Japan's security problem. In light of Communist actions in Czechoslovakia, China and Korea, Mr. Dulles found the Socialist viewpoint completely unrealistic, and I believe he then decided to make his next day's speech a little stronger in order to impress the Japanese public with the dangers, as he saw them, of an unarmed Japan. The Socialists also expressed concern about possible restrictions on Japanese emigration in view of the constantly increasing Japanese population and the restriction of Japanese territory to the four main islands. We were able to reassure them on this point, and, in a press statement later, I pointed out that there was nothing in the seven-point peace proposal that would prohibit Japanese emigration.

During this second visit to Tokyo Mr. Dulles had, at first, again found Prime Minister Yoshida reluctant to discuss the security problem in detail. While Mr. Yoshida was a firm anti-

Communist and was much more realistic than the Socialists, he nevertheless had a genuine fear of re-establishing a Japanese military machine. He had been imprisoned for a time by the Japanese army during the war. Later, when I was Ambassador to Japan and got to know Mr. Yoshida well, I often would discuss this problem with him. I pointed out that in the new Japan the military had none of the special powers they had in prewar Japan and that with civilian control the military could be the servant, not the master of Japan. Mr. Yoshida would look up at me with twinkling eyes and an impish grin and say, "Yes, but they have guns, haven't they?"

In addition to discussing security matters during our two weeks in Japan, we were besieged by representatives of all sorts of special interests, such as the shipping industry, who maintained it was vital to Japan's economic recovery to rebuild a strong merchant marine and a ship-building industry. Mr. Dulles and I agreed, and although we were to have considerable trouble with our British allies over this matter, we were in the end able to maintain our position of no invidious restrictions in the treaty. We were also deeply impressed by the Japanese plea for the restoration of the Ryukyus and the Bonin Islands. While we could not grant their wishes at that time, I believe it was then that Mr. Dulles conceived the idea, which he later announced at the San Francisco Peace Conference, that Japan should retain residual sovereignty over the islands but that they would be administered by the United States. The Bonin Islands were returned to Japan in 1968 and the Ryukyus in 1972.

We took off from Haneda Airport on a cold, blustery Sunday morning and some eight hours later landed in Manila and walked out of the plane into what seemed a burning furnace. Ambassador and Mrs. Myron Cowan took the Dulleses and me to their air-conditioned residence, where we just had time to have a snack, a shower, and prepare for a formal black-tie reception to meet official and unofficial Manila. As I was coming out of the shower, Ambassador Cowan came into my room with a stocky, handsome young Filipino who seemed a bit nervous. It was the late Defense Minister Magsaysay, the hero of the people and the scourge of the corrupt politicians, who wanted to talk privately with Mr. Dulles. At that time, because of threats on his life, Magsaysay was staying in a different place every night and appeared in public as little as possible. Slipping into a bathrobe, I went to fetch Mr. Dulles and managed to get him back to my bedroom, also in underwear and bathrobe. There, for fifteen minutes we had a weird conversation in which Magsaysay told of his hopes for his country and of his fears of the politicians on one side and the Huks (Communist guerillas) on the other. He made an eloquent plea for patience, understanding, and help. Mr. Dulles was impressed. Ambassador Cowan had a great admiration for the young man which was apparently recipro- cated. As Magsaysay got up to leave, he put his arm around the Ambassador's shoulders and said, "Thanks, Myron, go to your party, I'll slip out the side door." We finished dressing and went down to meet smartly dressed men and beautiful ladies among whom were many who would have been delighted to get their hands on the young man we had been talking with upstairs.

On the morning after our arrival Mr. Dulles and I had break- fast at Malacanan Palace with President Quirino and Foreign Minister Romulo to begin our discussions.

Mr. Dulles outlined his views on the necessity of a nonpuni- tive treaty to an unsympathetic but polite audience. He must have made some impression, however, for as the meal and the discussion drew to a close, President Quirino voiced a most statesmanlike view. It was so at variance from Quirino's normal parochial outbursts that it still remains vivid in my memory. After pointing out that he had every reason to hate the Japa- nese, who had murdered his wife and one daughter, he went on, "but God put Japan and the Philippines in the same ocean, and we must learn to get along together."

The President's sentiments were not embraced by many of

the Philippine bureaucrats or legislators with whom we later talked, who, although they were consistantly pleasant and friendly, did not yield much in their demands. It was obvious that some sort of reassurance was necessary that the Philippines would not stand alone if again menaced by an aggressive Japan. Informal discussions were therefore held which laid the basis for the Philippine-United States Mutual Defense Treaty which was later signed in Washington on August 30, 1951, by Secretary of State Acheson and Foreign Minister Romulo, just before they left for the Japanese Peace Treaty Conference in San Francisco. It was this defense treaty which made it possible for the Philippines to sign the peace treaty at San Francisco, although they did not ratify it until after an agreement had been reached with Japan under the treaty clauses providing for reparations in kind to countries which had been occupied by Japanese forces.

From Manila we flew to Canberra, first landing briefly in Darwin. The Australians were not slow to point out that Darwin had been bombed by the Japanese during the war. A more dismal spot would be difficult to find. We were met in Canberra by Foreign Minister and Mrs. Spender, the American Ambassador, Pete Jarman, and members of his staff, as well as by representatives from the Ministry of External Affairs with whom we soon became good friends. With two of these men I was later to serve: Sir Alan Watt and I were Ambassadors in Tokyo at the same time, and Sir Lawrence McIntyre and I were Ambassadors in Indonesia together.

Foreign Minister Doidge of New Zealand and some of his staff came over to Canberra and took part in our talks. Here again reassurance against a revived Japanese militarism was necessary and the main accomplishment of our visit was the completion of the first draft of what later became the ANZUS Treaty of Mutual Security between Australia, New Zealand, and the United States. Mr. Dulles made public speeches expounding our views about a nonpunitive treaty and these had some effect, but it was the ANZUS Treaty which made it possible for the Australian and New Zealand government leaders to get the agreement of their parliaments to sign a treaty of reconciliation with Japan.

The six days in Canberra passed quickly. The only real stumbling block in the whole period was encountered when Bob Fearey and I went to the front desk (rooms had no telephones then) to inquire how we could get our suits pressed. The lady receptionist was most cordial and with an air of great accomplishment reached under the counter, pulled out an ironing board and an electric iron, and said, "Here you are, chaps, go to it." I think Bob did. I settled for putting my trousers under the mattress.

From Australia we went to New Zealand, first to the capital, Wellington, and then up to Aukland. During the three days we spent in Wellington, Mr. Dulles made more speeches, we talked individually to many people, and we had the rare privilege of being invited to a meeting of the New Zealand Cabinet. Mr. Dulles sat at the long table next to Prime Minister Holland and after the Cabinet had listened to a report from Foreign Minister Doidge of what we had accomplished in Canberra, Mr. Dulles was invited to address the Cabinet. He obviously made a good impression, and the members almost gave an audible sigh of relief when it was made clear that the United States would not leave New Zealand and Australia alone to face a possible renewed Japanese aggression. We received a most favorable impression of the seriousness and understanding with which these New Zealand political leaders went about their work. Almost all members of the Cabinet had questions to ask Mr. Dulles about his conception of a treaty, whether or not their immediate responsibilities had anything to do with foreign affairs, international trade, or defense. Like the British Cabinet in London, the Commonwealth Cabinets feel and exercise a joint responsibility for all major government policies in a manner not found in Washington.

We flew up to Aukland for a night before heading back for

Washington via Samoa and Honolulu. The Mayor of Aukland gave a large luncheon for us attended by leaders of the local community. Before luncheon a tall, robust gentleman came up and asked me if I had served in the American Embassy in London during the war, and he reminded me of briefing a group of Australian and New Zealand journalists and publishers about the American views on the war in the Pacific. He was Leslie Munro (now Sir Leslie) who later became New Zealand Ambassador to the United States and to the United Nations and was elected President of the General Assembly in 1957.

When we had returned to Washington in March, I was invited to talk to the members of the Far Eastern Commission about our visit to Japan. I pointed out that this had been my third postwar visit to Japan and that, as I had spent about ten years there before the war, I had some basis for comparing the Japan of 1951 with that of 1940. One of the things that had most impressed me was that the Japanese had begun to be much more frank in their talks with foreigners. Of course many of the Japanese we saw did attempt to flatter us and tell us what they thought we wanted to hear, but there was a goodly number who, as I told the commission, "were not at all hesitant in saying what they thought was wrong with the Occupation, what they thought was wrong with the way we had done things, what they thought should be done in the future, whether they thought we would like it or not." I added that I considered this a "healthy development." I also said:

> One of the most prevalent criticisms which was made about what the occupation had done was what it had done to the family system . . . the reforms had come too quickly . . . and the result was one of confusing the young people and taking away their discipline and family controls and not yet giving them anything in their place resulting in a considerable increase in juvenile delinquency.

I went on to say that some of our reforms, which we had insisted upon from the best of motives, had not sufficiently taken into account Japanese customs and tradition and the fact that people can't be changed overnight. After telling of the great interest of the Japanese in the United Nations and their somewhat naive faith that it is the answer to all their problems and will enable Japan eventually to get back into the world on a peaceful basis without rearming, I said:

> We were all disturbed I think by the implication and the emphasis the press had given in some places that we had gone out to rearm Japan. There was nothing further from the truth, and if it had been true, we would have found that it would have been very, very difficult in view of the public opinion in Japan . . . we got thousands of letters, some of them individual letters, some of them petitions by various groups and . . . at least 95 percent of the letters stressed the fact that the Japanese people do not wish to see the revival of militarism in Japan.

I pointed out that even those Japanese who recognized that Japan might eventually have to depend upon itself for its own defense wanted any defense force to be brought about in a limited way and in a manner that would make it impossible for a military caste to regain control of the government. I stressed that no one could be sure how long this feeling would last and that there was probably some of the reformed-drunk attitude which could disappear when the patient felt better; but I added that there was "a very sincere desire to build up a peaceful Japan that will not have to depend on military strength to be accepted in the world on an equal basis." I believe this desire still dominates the great majority of the Japanese people.

I reported to the members of the Far Eastern Commission that there were those in Tokyo so concerned about the future of their economy that they tried to persuade Mr. Dulles to give a written agreement to underwrite Japan for an indefinite period. But, as I told the commission, "Mr. Dulles made it very clear both privately to government officials and publicly in speeches that . . . Japan would have to stand on its own feet. It could not expect an indefinite continuance of any American subsidy

. . . If they used ingenuity in the abilities they had shown in the past, imagination in developing new products and new uses for some of their old products, we felt there was a good chance that Japan could be self-supporting in the future at a decent standard of living."

During all of March, after our return, in addition to talking to our friends on the Far Eastern Commission, Mr. Dulles and his staff were busy preparing a draft treaty for the consideration of our allies. By the end of the month a first draft was completed and circulated. This was still a brief document and consisted of only eight mimeographed foolscap pages. It is important to point out that when at last we reached San Francisco, the final treaty signed there consisted of twenty-one pages of similar size. As I later told the members of the American Society of International Law, at their 1952 annual meeting, "The change from a document of eight pages to a document of twenty-one pages is evidence of the fruitfulness of the discussions which took place among all the Powers concerned, and effectively disposes of the charge made by the Soviet Union and its satellites that the treaty signed at San Francisco was merely an American document forced upon a reluctant conference."

It is time now to look briefly at the way in which Mr. Dulles ensured that the Legislative and Executive branches of the government were in accord regarding the peace treaty and that ratification would not be denied. He had vivid recollections of how the Versailles Treaty ending World War I had been rejected by the United States Senate, and he was determined that the Japanese Treaty would not suffer a similar fate. From the time he was designated by President Truman as chief United States negotiator on September 8, 1950, until the treaty was signed in San Francisco just one year later on September 8, 1951, a consistent effort was made by Mr. Dulles and his associates to keep the members of the Senate Foreign Relations Committee informed of what was being done and why. During this period there were nine formal meetings between the Dulles team and the members of the consultative Subcommittee on Far Eastern Affairs of the Senate Foreign Relations Committee. On several occasions as specific problems arose the whole committee was consulted. In addition, Mr. Dulles also consulted influential members of the Senate who were not members of the Foreign Relations Committee but who would be called upon to pass final judgment on the treaty. There were also several meetings with members of the Foreign Affairs Committee of the House of Representatives. Although they would have no direct part in the ratification of the treaty, they would have a part in passing legislation to implement its provisions. When the time came to send a delegation to San Francisco, members of both the Senate and the House of Representatives were included in the delegation. This continuous consultation with members of the Congress proved to be justified when the treaty came before the Senate. It was approved unanimously by the Foreign Relations Committee and was then approved by the whole Senate by a vote of 65 to 11.

While we had been busy in Washington developing our March treaty draft, the British government had been consulting other members of the Commonwealth and had produced a draft of their own. Mr. Dulles hinted that that U.S. and British drafts might be merged into one, and the British sent over to Washington a small team of experts who worked with us to see if this could be accomplished. By early May a joint draft had been completed, but there were still outstanding problems which were to require a journey to London by Mr. Dulles and his team before a final draft was ready for circulation to the other Allies. The late Frederick S. Dunn's book *Peace-Making and the Settlement with Japan*, published by Princeton University Press in 1963, gives the best detailed account of the trials and tribulations we went through in producing an agreed text. Although we accepted much of the more detailed British drafting, we were able to maintain our position that there should be no invidious post-treaty controls on rearmament or economic development, and reparations should be kept to a minimum and restricted to those countries that had suffered from direct Japanese occupation.

As Professor Dunn points out in his thoughtful book, one of the chief problems that remained for Mr. Dulles to discuss with the British in London concerned China. The United Kingdom Government recognized the Communist regime in Peking as the government of China, while the United States continued to recognize the regime of Chiang Kai-shek on Formosa as the legitimate government of China. The British Labour Government wanted to have Communist China sign the peace treaty, but Mr. Dulles knew that if this came to pass, it would be impossible to get the treaty accepted by the United States Senate, at that time largely under the spell of Senator Joseph McCarthy and his Republican allies, aided and abetted by a vigorous and ruthless China Lobby. Mr. Dulles therefore took the position that the question as to which of the Chinas Japan should sign a treaty with, should be left up to the Japanese upon their regaining their sovereign status as contemplated in the treaty. At the time he talked to the British in June 1951, Mr. Dulles had an oral understanding with Mr. Yoshida, the Japanese Prime Minister, that gave him confidence the Japanese would not make a deal with the Chinese Communists. This was not communicated to the British at that time. Moral purists will accuse Mr. Dulles of sharp practice, but in his own mind he was certain he was acting in the interests of peace and justice by making certain a treaty would be approved which would restore Japan to a position of equality in the family of nations. His reading of the Senate mind was vindicated when, in September, fifty-six Senators signed and sent to the President a warning that if Japan recognized Communist China or negotiated a treaty with it, they would consider this "to be adverse to the best interests of the people of both Japan and the United States."

Had Mr. Dulles not succeeded in persuading the British to

leave to the Japanese the problem, there would undoubtedly have been no San Francisco Conference. In December of the same year, Mr. Dulles together with Senators John Sparkman and H. Alexander Smith of the Far East Subcommittee of the Senate Foreign Relations Committee visited Japan, and Mr. Yoshida gave Mr. Dulles an official letter which made clear the Japanese intention to negotiate a treaty with the regime on Formosa and not with the Communists in Peking. This was before the treaty had been ratified, and when the British learned of it there was considerable criticism, and questions were asked in Parliament.

However, this was in the future and did not spoil our London visit. Before we left Washington we had been informed that President Truman's daughter, Margaret, would be paying her first visit to London while we were there and that we should take with us white tie and tails in order to attend a formal ball to be given by the American Ambassador. This was the only real social event the men of our party attended, although our wives had been entertained at formal luncheons for Miss Truman and invited to a Trooping of the Colors on the Horse Guards Parade, a splendid spectacle. At the Embassy ball we had the pleasure of meeting Princess Elizabeth, the present Queen, and her younger sister Princess Margaret. It was one of the six times in thirty years in the Foreign Service that official functions have required me to wear a white tie. Yet in only six years of residence in Washington, I have been required three times to wear similar regalia when attending Gridiron dinners given by members of the Washington Press Corps who often delight in referring to the "effete, white spat diplomats."

After London, we went briefly to Paris for talks with the French Government, and then I was off to Tokyo once more, via Karachi, New Delhi, and Manila, where I had discussions with local officials about the treaty. The people in Karachi were friendly, in New Delhi correct, and in Manila vigorous in their criticism of what we were doing. Carlos Romulo was still Foreign Minister and he greeted me warmly, grinned his infectious grin, and said: "John, we're going to give you a bad time. Can you take it?" I assured him I could, and he told me he had arranged a luncheon in a private room at the Manila Hotel where my fellow guests would be twenty Philippine Senators, all of whom were angry at us for advocating a treaty with no restrictions against Japanese rearmament and provision for only a minimum of reparations.

The luncheon and the discussion lasted more than two hours, and, in spite of the air conditioning, I came out of the meeting wet with perspiration and completely exhausted. I doubt if I persuaded anyone, but I was able to correct some misunderstandings; I did my best to reassure them that the United States had no intention of sacrificing the true interests of the Philippines, and that in case of renewed aggression we would be at their side. The Senators were personally polite, and we all shook hands before the meeting broke up, but I noticed that most of them departed in twos and threes still shaking their heads.

The next day I left for Tokyo and final talks with the Japanese about provisions of the treaty that worried them. After my experience in Manila the talks with the Japanese were almost relaxing. The two chief Japanese negotiators were Sadao Iguchi, already mentioned, and Kumao Nishimura, head of the Treaty Bureau of the Foreign Ministry. They were forthright in their expression of the Japanese point of view, but they were also realists. They recognized that even in a treaty of reconciliation some of the demands of those countries which had suffered most at the hands of the Japanese militarists would have to be met. But we were able to iron out many points, and when I returned to Washington in early July it was possible to put the finishing touches on the joint British-American draft. This draft was circulated to all the Allied Powers by the middle of July and was kept open for further changes until the middle of August.

However, all was not work while in Tokyo. On my last Saturday night there, I was invited to a dinner given by General and Mrs. Matthew Ridgway at the American Embassy residence. I had no idea then that just about two years later I would be occupying the same residence. General Ridgway had replaced General MacArthur since my last visit to Tokyo, and the change in atmosphere was startling. General MacArthur rarely entertained at night, his large official functions always taking place at noon. No alcoholic beverages had been served at the two luncheons I had attended, and the guests gathered in the large drawing room with Mrs. MacArthur and sipped orange juice. When everyone was assembled the General would sweep into the room with a grand flourish, kiss his wife as if he hadn't seen her for years, and then proceed to greet each guest individually. If you had been there before and were an American, you were called by your first name and given a warm pat on the shoulder. When you entered the dining room there was the General, already at the head of the table. It was most impressive the first time, but later it did seem a bit staged.

I doubt if any of us, British or American, who had worked on the draft circulated to the Allies was completely satisfied with it. We all had our own ideas of how it could have been improved, but we all agreed it was a good treaty if not perfect. One of Mr. Dulles's favorite axioms was "The perfect is the enemy of the good." The Japanese Peace Treaty was an example. If we had waited to get a perfect treaty, we would never have had a treaty, and so we were content with a good one.

When this draft was circulated it was accompanied by an invitation to attend a conference in San Francisco for the purpose of signing a treaty of peace with Japan. An oral statement made at the same time to each recipient made crystal clear that the only purpose of the conference was to sign the treaty which had been negotiated over a period of almost eleven months through diplomatic channels instead of around a single conference table. In response to a request made by several of the

Allies, it was agreed that the delegation of each nation that attended the conference would be given an opportunity, if it so desired, to make a statement setting forth its views on the treaty and the reasons for its action in signing it. But negotiations would not be reopened.

To the surprise of almost everyone the Soviet Union accepted the invitation. In view of the many public and private objections the Soviets had made during the eleven months, not only to the content but also to the method of negotiating the treaty, it was easy to foresee stormy weather ahead. The Soviet attempt to undermine American policy in Japan was no new thing. Herbert Feis, the former State Department official and Pulitzer Prize-winning historian points out in his intriguing book *Contest Over Japan*, this attempt began even before the Japanese had accepted the Potsdam Declaration, and when the Russians were suggesting the possibility of joint U.S.-U.S.S.R. control over a defeated Japan. Most of us would have agreed with Feis's contention that the Soviet support of the North Korean invasion of South Korea was inspired by the hope that an encirclement of Japan by Communist power would make impossible American plans to bring Japan as an ally into the non-Communist world.

In order to ensure that the peace conference could proceed expeditiously with its work and not be subjected to disruptive and delaying tactics, strict rules of procedure were drafted under the personal direction of Secretary Acheson. I had but little part in this, and my principal task from the time the final draft was circulated until the treaty was signed was to meet with, and explain to, our allies the grim necessity of first supporting the adoption of these rules of procedure, and then of supporting the Chairman of the conference in enforcing them. As Professor Dunn says in his book:

> It was obvious to everybody that the major purpose of the Russians and the satellite countries was to delay the proceedings indefinitely and to block the settlement altogether if that were possible. The tactics of the Communists, which were a repetition of their action

in other conferences, merely tended to exasperate the other delegations and to make them more favorably inclined toward the settlement worked out by the United States.

In keeping the Communists under control Secretary Acheson,
who was President of the conference, was the chief actor, but he
was ably supported by Percy Spender, the Australian Foreign
Minister, who had been elected Vice President. This was the
same Percy Spender who had reacted so violently when he first
learned of the type of treaty Mr. Dulles was contemplating.

In accord with Mr. Dulles's belief that the Japanese should
not be treated the way the Germans were at Versailles after
World War I, the Japanese Government had been invited to
San Francisco as participants without vote, but with the right to
make a statement the same as every other nation. Prime Minister Yoshida headed a distinguished Japanese delegation which
sat through all sessions of the conference and was included in all
social events on the same footing as other delegations. After all
the Allied nations had made their statements, Mr. Yoshida was
called upon. His statement was brief but well received. He
expressed appreciation for the generous terms of the treaty,
frankly explained some of Japan's concerns caused by the treaty,
but emphasized his country's determination to live by the spirit
of the United Nations Charter, and its complete willingness to
sign and be bound by the terms of the treaty. He also spoke of
Japan's completely defenseless position and announced its intention of signing a security treaty with the United States.

An almost religious emotion pervaded the San Francisco
Opera House as we listened during four days to the speeches of
the various delegates. Some of the most moving statements
were made by the representatives of nations that had only
recently achieved independence. The spirit prevailing was well
expressed by the delegate from Ceylon, Finance Minister J. R.
Jayewardene, who pointed out that his country had suffered
damages and was entitled to ask for reparations, but then went
on to say:

We do not intend to do so, for we believe in the words of the great
Teacher whose message has ennobled the lives of countless millions
in Asia, that *"hatred ceases not by hatred, but by love."* It is the
message of Buddha . . . which bound us together for hundreds of
years with a common culture and heritage. This common culture
still exists, as I found on my visit to Japan last week on my way to
attend this conference; and from the leaders of Japan, Ministers
of State as well as private citizens, from their priests in the temples,
I gathered the impression that the common people of Japan are
still influenced by the shadow of that great Teacher of peace, and
wish to follow it. We must give them that opportunity.

Zafrullah Khan, the Foreign Minister of Pakistan, said of the
treaty:

> It opens to Japan the door passing through which it may take up
> among its fellow sovereign nations a position of dignity, honor
> and equality . . . It is evidence of a new departure in the relations
> of the East and West as they have subsisted during the last few
> centuries. We welcome it as a harbinger of even happier con-
> summations.

Several of the Asian delegates quoted four sentences from the
statement of Mr. Dulles when he was explaining why it was
necessary to proceed at once to conclude a treaty with Japan.

> Dignity cannot be developed by those who are subject to alien
> control, however benign.
> Self-respect is not felt by those who have no rights of their own
> in the world, who live on charity and trade on sufferance.
> Regard for justice rarely animates those who are subjected to
> such grave injustices as would be the denial of the present peace.
> Fellowship is not the mood of peoples who are denied fellowship.

The Syrian delegate characterized these statements of Mr.
Dulles as a golden rule, "especially in dealing with smaller
nations," and expressed the hope that these principles, "which
are the basis of the draft treaty with Japan, will also be the
guiding principles in the policies of the United States and the
United Kingdom and all other big powers dealing with other

nations which are still denied the elementary rights of justice and fellowship."

After the delegates had signed the treaty on the final Saturday morning (the Soviet, Polish, and Czechoslovak delegations did not attend the final session and have never signed the treaty) Dean Acheson, as President of the conference, made an eloquent closing statement. He pointed out that what had been accomplished could only have been brought about "because all of us, in the words of Benjamin Franklin, 'doubted something of our infallibility' . . . and we were able to do that because we were doing something which lifted our spirits, something of which we were proud."

All of us who had worked on the treaty *were* proud. And as we look at Japan today, twenty years later, and see what it has accomplished, we can, I believe, justly say we have had a part in that amazing development. Of course, most of what Japan has done is due to the skill and hard work of the Japanese people, but without the kind of treaty which was signed at San Francisco on September 8, 1951, the skill and hard work of the Japanese people would have availed but little.

# IX

# Wool and Water

## 1951–1953

AT THE END of the San Francisco Conference, I had almost two months' leave coming before it would be time to pack up and head for Tokyo, where I had been assigned as Deputy Chief of Mission with the rank of Minister. One Friday morning toward the end of November, the telephone rang and Dean Rusk, then the Assistant Secretary of State for Far Eastern Affairs, asked me if I could come down to the Department and see him at eleven o'clock that morning. I put on a necktie and started out wondering what Dean could want. He knew that we were to leave for Tokyo in about ten days, and I knew that all my responsibilities at the Department had been terminated.

At precisely eleven I was ushered into Dean's office. He greeted me with a broad grin and asked, "Have you sold your house yet?" I told him we hadn't and when he said fine, I retorted, "Why, are you going to fire me?" "Much worse than that," replied Dean grinning, "You're going to have to take my job!" He then told me that he was going to Tokyo to negotiate the Administrative Agreement implementing the Security Treaty with Japan, which had been signed in San Francisco the afternoon after the peace treaty had been signed. He would not come back to the State Department. While it would not be announced for several days, he had been elected President of the

Rockefeller Foundation, and as soon as he completed his negotiations in Tokyo, he would take up his new position in New
York. Dean said I would only be appointed Acting Assistant
Secretary and after two or three months, when a permanent successor had been found, I could go on to Tokyo with increased
prestige.

Dean left for Tokyo and on the morning of December 8, 1951,
the *New York Times* announced that on the previous day I had
been appointed Acting Assistant Secretary of State. Just ten
years earlier the Japanese police had entered my office in Osaka
and told me our countries were at war. It had been an exciting ten years, but when it began I did not dream that when
it ended I would be helping to make policy not only for Japan
but for all of Asia as well.

Toward the middle of January my friend Carlisle Hummel-
sine, then Deputy Under Secretary for Administration and now
head of Colonial Williamsburg, began asking me whether I
would consider accepting, if it were offered me, a permanent
appointment as Assistant Secretary. I needed time to consider
this. I was a career officer, not quite 47 years old. The position of
Assistant Secretary was a political appointment, and it was
obvious that the chances of the Democrats being returned to
power the following November were slim. I didn't want to be
turned out to pasture at 48; and yet the job fascinated me.

While I was considering what to do, my old chief, John Foster
Dulles, came down from New York and dropped into my office
for a chat. He was not only a good Republican but was generally
considered the most likely Secretary of State if the Republicans
came to power. I put the problem up to him. After only a
moment's thought he advised me to take the job if it was offered
to me. He said I was known to be a career officer who had not
participated in partisan politics, that the Far East was my field,
and that it was important for the country to have someone in
that position who knew the area and its problems. He went on

to say that if the Republicans did win the election, he thought he would have some influence in the party councils. While he obviously could make me no promises, he did believe I would not suffer if I accepted the appointment.

For about a week I heard nothing and began to wonder whether I was going to be offered the chance to test Mr. Dulles's ideas. Finally one morning I was called up to Secretary Acheson's office and asked whether I was willing to take on the slings and arrows which always seemed to be part of the job of a permanent Assistant Secretary. I said if he was willing to take the risk of appointing me, I was willing to take the risks that went with the job. The Senate confirmed my appointment and, on February 7, 1952, I took the oath of office in the presence of my wife and Secretary Acheson, along with a few friends from the Department and others. In looking at a photograph taken as I was reciting the oath of office, I note that while my wife is looking quite pleased, Secretary Acheson is staring intently at me with a rather grim expression as if to say, "You damn well better make good, young man!"

I have never regretted taking Mr. Dulles's advice. Not only was the work continually absorbing, but it gave me an opportunity for closer association with Dean Acheson, one of the outstanding men of our time, and in my opinion the greatest postwar Secretary of State. I also had the opportunity to meet and know slightly President Truman, who in comparison with those who have succeeded him in the White House, will, I believe, go down in history as one of our great Presidents.

Writing in late 1971 and early 1972, just twenty years after I took over the responsibility for dealing with Far Eastern affairs, it is amazing to see how greatly, in some ways, our attitudes toward problems of that area have changed. Even the name of the game has changed. The man now occupying the desk where I once sat is called the Assistant Secretary for East Asian and Pacific Affairs. We are now looking directly at Asia and the

Pacific and no longer peering the long way around through Europe and the Middle East. It is also interesting to note how many things have not changed and how many of the problems with which I was concerned are still bothering my friend Marshall Green, who is sitting at my old desk.

A speech I made only a few months after I took office, on April 17, 1952, at the fourteenth annual Public Affairs Conference at Principia College, just outside St. Louis, illustrates what I have said above, that much has changed but that much is still the same.

I began by stating that "the basic fact which we must always keep in mind is that today the nations of the Far East are united in at least one thing, if nothing else, and that is their desire for national freedom and independence." That is certainly still true. I went on to point out that while we still heard criticism of Western imperialism and colonialism and while there remained much to be done in this field we should not ignore what had been done. In just seven years since the end of the most destructive war in history, over 600 million people in seven nations had attained independence, and I claimed this was "by no means a negligible achievement." I stressed the importance of remembering that these new nations often lacked a sufficient number of trained leaders, administrators, and technicians, and I said it would be unrealistic to expect that in the short period of seven years "there would arise strong and stable countries who could expect to carry on their activities in the same manner and with the same degree of success as the older countries of the Western world with their long experience of independent activity." Twenty years later we can see much progress, but we must admit there is still a long way to go.

I stated that the peace treaty with Japan would go into effect the following week and "this nation of almost 85 million vigorous, intelligent, and industrially trained people will once again be a factor to be reckoned with whenever we think of Asia."

Today this sentence might almost be a candidate for *The New Yorker*'s department of understatement. I referred to the then completely unarmed position of Japan and to our belief that the Communist aggression in Korea "was at least partially due to the unarmed condition of Japan and the belief of the aggressors that domination of the Korean peninsula would make more easy the ultimate domination of Japan with its great industrial base and industrially trained population."

I note that in speaking of the rest of Asia I referred to the "enslavement of 400 million Chinese by a ruthless, Soviet-dominated Communist Government." It would be difficult to say the same thing today, and yet it is important to remember that in 1952 we still had good reason to believe in a monolithic communism and in its threat to the real independence of the young nations just emerging from colonialism. Today, with 20/20 hindsight we can admit that perhaps our fears were somewhat exaggerated, and certainly a monolithic communism no longer exists. But that was not the world I saw in 1951 and 1952, nor was it the world our friends in Asia saw. And so we had a Security Treaty with Japan, a Mutual Defense Treaty with the Philippines, and the ANZUS Pact with Australia and New Zealand which President Truman had referred to at the San Francisco Conference for the signing of the Japanese Peace Treaty as "initial steps" in the formation of an eventual Pacific security system.

In view of the situation as we understood it at the time, I am not surprised to find, in going over my notes, that in the early months of 1952, I spent some time in considering our policy with regard to China and particularly our policy concerning the government of Chiang Kai-shek, which had been driven from the mainland by the Chinese Communists and was now established on Formosa. Various elements in our government, both civilian and military, were considering the possibility of using Chinese Nationalist forces in Korea or on the mainland in connection with United States Pacific policy. On January 3, 1952, I sent a long memorandum to the Secretary of State commenting on some of these proposals.

One of the more interesting of these proposals pointed out that military and economic programs for the support of Formosa had had only limited success due, at least in part, to the Nationalists' refusal to effect political reforms and their failure to eliminate corruption among their officials. This proposal stated that if the Nationalist forces were to be made more effective as defense forces for Formosa or as guerrilla units on the mainland, it would be necessary to bring about (1) a change in United States policy respecting the use of Nationalist forces and a more aggressive approach to the use of guerrillas and (2) political reform of the Nationalist Government. The proposal recommended that the United States decide upon a positive policy of aid to the Nationalists which would only be forthcoming if that government gave proof by action of its fitness to again become the government of the mainland. This program would need, to carry it out, a senior overall United States representative, which we did not then have.

In commenting on this proposal, I stated that before any decisive action be taken, the United States should decide whether its policies toward China should be based on the assumption that (1) the Communist regime was here to stay and, therefore, the only hope was to wean it away from subservience to the Soviet Union or (2) that the Communist regime could in due course be liquidated through a positive United States policy in cooperation with a *reformed* Nationalist Government of China. I pointed out that the proposal before us did not give adequate attention to the effect on Japan and Southeast Asia of what we do or don't do with respect to China. I stated that there was considerable agitation in Japan to resume relations with mainland China, and I predicted that in the long run this could not be prevented. I said that it was in the interest of the United States to see to it that conditions on mainland China were so changed that Japan could resume close relations with it, without this constituting a threat to the United States. I also referred to the obvious importance of mainland China to the nations of Southeast Asia and stated that in view of the alarming reports recently received concerning the possibility of Communist Chinese intervention in Indochina, there was urgent need of action that would keep the Chinese Communists so occupied within their own country that they would have neither the ability nor the desire to spread out into Southeast Asia.

I went on to make the further point that our major ally, the United Kingdom, was convinced that our China policy was purely negative and that the Japanese, who wished to remain on good terms with both the United Kingdom and the United States, were concerned over these differences between the British and the Americans. I argued that if the United States could adopt some positive policy that envisioned the eventual return to the mainland of a *truly* reformed Nationalist Government, the British might well take a more favorable view of our policy. I added that Japan would then be able to increase its trade with the mainland which, to some degree, would reduce its competition with the British in Southeast Asia. I continued by stating that while Chiang Kai-shek and his government were the only non-Communist elements with which the United States could work in the beginning, serious consideration should be given to persuading Chiang, at an appropriate time, to remove himself from the scene and thus make it possible for younger and more liberal elements on Formosa to take control. I recognized the difficulties in adopting any such policy, particularly in an election year, but I maintained that the dangers of continuing our present policy were even greater. I concluded by strongly recommending that every effort be made to develop a policy along the lines of the proposal submitted to us and that the Policy Planning Staff be directed to study as a matter of urgency, in cooperation with the Bureau of Far Eastern Affairs, all of the possibilities and implications of the proposed policy.

I have discussed this matter at some length, because I think it brings out certain things we have often tended to forget. One of these is the obvious implication in both the proposal and my comments on it that the Chiang regime was driven from the mainland not only because of Communist strength but also because of its own weaknesses, principally the corruption of its officials and its inability to do enough for the Chinese peasant and laboring man. Few of us in responsible places in either the military or civilian side of the government believed there was any hope of Chiang returning to the mainland and being welcomed there unless his government was completely reformed. It is also important to realize that the influence of mainland China on Japanese public opinion was even then great and this should not be ignored. Too often it has been — most recently in President Nixon's dramatic decision to visit mainland China without in any way consulting our Japanese friends.

Just two days after my memorandum had been forwarded to the Secretary, he was at the airport welcoming Prime Minister Churchill, Foreign Minister Eden, and a group of important British officials for talks which would cover the whole gamut of British-American relations, including China and the Far East in general. Mr. Churchill had but recently been returned to power, and he thought it essential to exchange views with the United States and wherever possible bring our policies closer together. Most of the early stages of the visit were confined to informal discussions between Mr. Churchill and President Truman and their most senior advisers. Secretary Acheson in *Present at the Creation* has told us that during these talks the problem of China was discussed, and he says that the new British Government "viewed the Far Eastern questions much more as we did than had their predecessors, and discussion in all respects but one brought us closer together." The one question in dispute at the time was with which China the Japanese should conclude a peace treaty. I have told in my chapter on the Japanese Peace Treaty how important Mr. Dulles believed it was to have the Japanese make a treaty with Nationalist China, as otherwise he was certain the United States Senate would not consent to the ratification of the treaty. The British still believed that if the Japanese signed a treaty with Nationalist China, it would prejudice their future relations with China, and Mr. Eden stressed this in the private meetings. Twenty years later it is not at all certain that Mr. Eden was wrong.

In addition to the meetings between the smaller group of most senior officials, there were several formal meetings in the Cabinet Room of the White House which were attended by the Chiefs of Staff and high Foreign Office and State Department officials. At one of these, where Far Eastern matters were to be discussed, I was present. I remember little of the discussion, which dealt mostly with the Korean armistice negotiations, but I have a vivid recollection of the general atmosphere of the meeting and the impression made on me by Mr. Churchill and Foreign Minister Eden. I sat just behind President Truman and directly opposite Mr. Churchill. I had not seen him since his appearance at the American Embassy in London on V-E Day, and I was shocked at the change that had taken place in this great man. His face was puffier than it had been, his eyes were often clouded over, and at times during the discussions he seemed almost in a semistupor. Mr. Eden sat next to him and from time to time would nudge him and whisper what apparently was advice as to what to say. Then, just as you began to think the old gentleman should be put to bed, he would straighten up, his eyes would have the old sparkle, and a few cogent and beautifully phrased sentences would make the perfect comment on the discussion and once again the greatest world figure of the twentieth century was in our midst.

After lunch on January 29, my secretary came in and told me I had really attained everlasting fame. She handed me a copy of that morning's New York Times, turned to the crossword puzzle, and pointed out that I was the answer to line forty going down — the clue being "Dulles's co-worker on the Japanese Treaty."

Toward the end of March the China problem again came to the fore. Nothing of importance had been done as the result of the proposal put forward in January and my memorandum to Secretary Acheson. The military were beginning to get restive and put forward some proposals which, because of their far reaching significance, I believed should receive the most thorough consideration before being approved by the Department of State. On March 24, 1952, I sent a memorandum to the Secretary outlining my views on the military proposal. In essence, this proposal seemed to imply that the United States should decide "at this moment" on all-out support of the government of Chiang and that it should do all in its power to increase the military potential of that government with a view to its eventual use on the mainland of China. The military also recommended that that portion of the mission of the Seventh Fleet which was to prevent Chinese Nationalist incursions onto the mainland should be eliminated. This would meet the demands of the Republicans and the China Lobby that Chiang Kai-shek should be "unleashed." The military said that the provision of material assistance to the Nationalists should be continued with a view to (1) maintaining the internal security of Formosa, (2) providing for the external security of the island, and (3) eventually establishing ready units in the Chinese Nationalist forces capable of overt military action outside Formosa.

The military still maintained that positive aid to Nationalist China should only be given if that government instituted political reforms, including positive action to reduce, if not eliminate, corruption. However, the Pentagon made clear that in its opinion all these matters lay within the purview of the military chiefs and should be handled by them "with due regard to other commitments, budgeting, and funding limitations." I told Secretary Acheson that "in my mind it is not at all certain these matters are only for consideration by the Joint Chiefs of Staff, as they involve certain fundamental political decisions which would seem to be the responsibility of the Department of State." In view of the prime importance of these matters, I again recommended that the Policy Planning Staff undertake an urgent study of the problem in cooperation with the Bureau of Far Eastern Affairs and the office of the State Department Counselor, which was then occupied by my friend Chip Bohlen.

It was an election year. The Korean armistice talks and the increasing difficulties of the French in Indochina seemed at the time more urgent than the problem of what to do about Chiang Kai-shek. And then, as in the past and as is still true today, the most senior of our officials were more concerned and more knowledgeable about Europe and its problems than about Asia. Even Mr. Acheson, for whom I always had the highest regard, looked first to Europe. His attitude is well expressed in *Present at the Creation,* when he is discussing the problem of putting pressure on the French to grant greater independence to the states of Indochina. He did not believe withholding help to the French would be effective in this regard, and he adds: "Furthermore, the result of withholding help to France would, at the most, have removed the colonial power. It could not have made the resulting situation a beneficial one either for Indochina or Southeast Asia, *or in the more important effort of furthering the stability and defense of Europe*" (italics added).

Little was done, therefore, to determine an overall United States policy toward the government on Formosa. Things were allowed to drift and problems were met on an ad hoc basis. What might have happened if the United States had undertaken, by a positive policy, to bring about reforms in the Nationalist Government which would have justified helping it to return to the mainland? Would the Chinese Communists have been seated sooner in the United Nations? Probably. If I have learned anything in thirty years of diplomatic service, it is the futility of one government and people attempting to impose its methods and standards on another. But I do believe that more might have been done to keep the military from dominating our Far Eastern policy if it had not been an election year and if European problems had not seemed so pressing. Without any overall policy or direction, the military seemed to occupy a more and more important place in our consideration of Asian matters. When a new administration came into power the following year, they made no great effort to dislodge the military but, instead, tended to encourage them. The activism and anti-Communist zeal of Mr. Dulles, although inspired by the highest motives, encouraged the military rather than the slower, patient methods of traditional diplomacy.

When I was not worrying about China or Japan or the Korean armistice negotiations, I had to worry about our budget for the next fiscal year and whether or not Congress would agree to our requests. The hearings before the House of Representatives had been concluded before I took over the Bureau of Far Eastern Affairs, but just about two weeks after I had taken the oath of office as Assistant Secretary of State, I had to appear before the Subcommittee of the Committee on Appropriations of the Senate. The Chairman of the Subcommittee was Pat McCarran of Nevada, and the two members who sat with him were Senator Ellender of Louisiana and Senator Ferguson of Michigan. All three of these gentlemen were highly suspicious of the State Department, and all three were inclined to agree with Senator Joseph McCarthy that the State Department, and particularly the Bureau of Far Eastern Affairs, was responsible for the United States "losing" China.

Before I went up to the Hill to testify, I had made up my mind to be as frank and straightforward with the Senators as I had been in my letter to former Congressman Maverick, mentioned in the last chapter. Perhaps the Senators would react as he had. It wouldn't hurt to try.

Nearly all the need for the increase that we were requesting was due to the projected cost of setting up and staffing an Embassy and consular offices in Japan, when the peace treaty signed at San Francisco came into effect. It was like pulling teeth to get the Senators to realize that upon the treaty coming into effect, Japan would no longer be an occupied country, and the facilities which we had been getting previously from the army at little or no cost, would no longer be available. Again patience and willingness to go over and over the same point in great detail paid dividends. It is interesting to note that the testimony before the subcommittee showed that prior to World War II the State Department had 82 Americans in all of Japan and that it was estimated that the new setup after the war would require 214 Americans. Some of the reasons I gave for this staff increase are interesting to look back on after twenty years. Our main justification was that the Japan that had come out of the war and the Occupation was a new Japan and that the United States would have "to take a much more active part for a year or two in advising and assisting this new Japan . . . than we ever did before or ever had any opportunity or reason to before." I went on to say that the Japanese were coming to us for advice and assistance in many fields and that we would need many more officers to meet the need. I am glad to note that I limited this active intervention in Japanese affairs to a period of only one or two years. This proved to be optimistic, and several years later we were still trying, with only fair success, to mold the Japanese into an American image. I am more happy with what I said a little later in the hearings, but it must be remembered that this was said at a time when we had what appeared to be good reason to believe in an aggressive Chinese and Russian communism in Asia. I told the subcommittee:

We have, sir, I think, in Japan, over the next year or year and a half, probably the greatest single opportunity to prove to Asia that an Asiatic nation can cooperate on a basis of equality with a Western nation and still maintain its independence. India, Burma and Indonesia are doubtful whether our intentions are honorable, you might say; whether we might want to take over Japan, and they are beginning to believe Communist propaganda that says we are imperialists. In this close relationship in Japan, under the security treaty . . . I am sure that if we use our heads we can show the Asiatic people that we can operate on a basis of equality with an Asiatic government. I think we will then have done more than any other one single thing to cut out the ground from under Communist propaganda there and we will be able to get the other people of Asia on our side.

Senator McCarran nodded and then began to question me about Formosa and what we were doing there. This was his real interest as it was of Senator Ferguson. In discussing Formosa and China I learned that these men, who asked sharp and difficult questions, would listen to a detailed answer. I shall give only two examples. At one point Senator Ferguson charged that we were dragging our feet in providing aid to Formosa. He stated that of the previous year's appropriation of aid "to the soldiers of Nationalist China" only 38 percent had been delivered and asked if I didn't think he was justified in saying we were dragging our feet. I took a deep breath, gave a silent prayer, and said I did not agree with him. I then went on to point out that there was a shooting war in Korea which had first priority on our supplies and that we were helping the French who were engaged in a shooting war in Indochina and that this had second priority. There was no shooting war in Formosa. Our supplies were limited, and we were doing the best we could with what we had. The Senator moved on to another subject.

While we were discussing the Chinese Communists and Formosa, we went off the record and Senator McCarran asked if I didn't agree with him that the United States should unleash

Chiang Kai-shek and let him go back to the mainland if he wished. Again I expressed disagreement. I said that, according to the best information available, it did not appear that Chiang could successfully invade mainland China without massive American help. If he decided on an invasion and we gave him the necessary help, we would be at war with Communist China. I said: "There may be good reasons why we should go to war with the Chinese Communists, but I should like to see the decision on that matter made by the President of the United States and you gentlemen of the Congress and not by Chiang Kai-shek." The Senator gave me a stern look but said nothing. We went on to other matters. Having gone that far, I continued during the rest of the hearing to speak as frankly. None of the Senators showed any great friendliness, but on the other hand they didn't bite my head off as had happened to some of my colleagues from other bureaus of the Department. As the hearing drew to a close, I almost fell out of my chair when I heard Senator McCarran say: "Before we recess, I want to express my appreciation for the manner in which you have handled this subject, Mr. Allison. It is really refreshing. You seem to know your subject and you have been very candid and frank with us."

I could only stammer "Thank you very much, sir," and stagger out of the room. I collected a couple of my efficient staff who had helped me in preparing my testimony and dashed off to the Metropolitan Club to have a much needed very dry martini.

During the first six months of 1952, I had my first direct contact with the problems connected with what we then thought of as the French war in Indochina but which has turned into the present war in Vietnam. Fortunately, I had in the Office of Southeast Asian Affairs, which was under my jurisdiction, an able group of officers who had considerable experience in dealing with these problems. In February they prepared a memorandum, which I forwarded to Secretary Acheson, that discussed the possible courses of action, political, economic, and military, that the United States could take in the event there was no overt Chinese Communist aggression but that Chinese technical and material assistance to the Viet Minh rebels should increase. We were already contributing approximately $200 million to the French effort in Indochina and were being urged to give more. This memorandum was designed to consider some of the factors involved in deciding whether or not to accede to the French request.

Although this memorandum was prepared by the staff of the Office of Southeast Asian Affairs, I signed it and sent it forward to the Secretary of State. I must therefore assume some of the responsibility for our early involvement in what twenty years later seemed to so many Americans a tragic error. I still believe our original intervention was justified, given the situation which then existed, but I have long had doubts about the form our intervention took and the way we let the French call the tune during the early years with only the most rudimentary consultation, although we were bearing almost forty percent of the financial burden.

The February memorandum stated that the United States objectives were to prevent Indochina, and hence Southeast Asia as a whole, from passing into the Communist orbit. The Communist domination of Southeast Asia would seriously endanger in the short run, and critically endanger in the long run, United States security interests, because it would render the United States position in the Pacific offshore island chain precarious and could result in such economic and political pressures in Japan as to make it extremely difficult to prevent Japan's eventual accommodation to communism. The memorandum also stressed the critical effect the spread of communism would have in Southeast Asia, which was a principal world source of rubber and tin, and a large producer of oil.

The memorandum then went on to state, correctly I believe,

that the long run security of Indochina against communism would depend upon the development of native governments having the support of the masses and national armed forces and therefore capable of relieving the French of the major burden of maintaining internal security. After twenty years, progress in this line is still limited. The memorandum recognized the weaknesses existing at that time, particularly the Vietnamese suspicion of any French supported regime, such as the Bao Dai government in Vietnam, and the fence-sitting attitude of the bulk of the people. While believing that under the conditions then existing it was unlikely the French would suffer a military defeat, there was a distinct possibility the French Government might soon conclude it could not continue indefinitely to carry the burden of its military commitments. In such a case, it was pointed out, the French might (1) seek a settlement with the Communists, (2) seek agreement to internationalize the action in Indochina, or (3) reduce the French NATO obligations.

After considerable discussion of various alternatives, the memorandum concluded that if the French showed any signs of withdrawal, the United States should consult with the United Kingdom. It went on to say that the most effective way to proceed was to support the expansion and use of national armies, press Bao Dai to take a more active part, and broaden the representation in his government. The memorandum also suggested that we should publicize in Indochina and Southeast Asia the extent and character of French concessions to Indochinese nationalism. We said United States financial assistance on a large scale would be needed and should be given. Apparently we failed at that time to mention what we would require of the French if we gave the necessary aid. I do recall that in our discussions of what we should do, within the department, we agreed that aid to the national armies was most likely to ensure that in the long run the French would have to grant effective independence to the Indochinese states.

In May of 1952, the problems of Indochina were still being debated within the American government. A letter from Secretary of Defense Lovett to Secretary Acheson, dated May 1, set forth in several enclosures the views of the military and civilian leaders in the Pentagon. They contended that a State Department paper on Indochina had not been positive enough. The Pentagon believed that efforts to promote international support for the three associated states should be intensified, and if possible a United Nations flavor should be added. They agreed that the introduction of United States ground forces into Indochina might inspire overt Chinese Communist intervention but pointed out that air and naval power could be employed without having the same disadvantage. The Pentagon paper accepted the premise that Indochina was the key to Southeast Asia and must be kept secure from Communist influence. The Defense Department, therefore, believed that consideration of future United States policy should include consideration "of a dynamic program geared to produce positive improvement in the military and political situation." The Defense Department position strongly implied that the United States should put pressure upon the French to grant more real independence to the three associated states as well as agree to increase funds, equipment, and training for the Indochinese troops in the national armies.

On May 6, I again signed and forwarded to the Secretary a memorandum prepared in the Office of Southeast Asian Affairs, commenting on the Defense papers. We took the position that, while we agreed with much of the Defense position, we believed it went too far in pressing the French to grant independence too quickly. We believed that this might well result in the French withdrawing from the area and leaving the United States with the sole responsibility. However, we did agree with the Defense Department that United States policy "must be designed not to keep the French committed indefinitely in Indochina but to facilitate the transition from colonialism to self-government in such a way that there is no opportunity for Communism to flow into a power vacuum." We also agreed we should seek to obtain the fullest measure of international support, including as many Asian nations as possible. Finally, we recommended that in the course of the 1953 fiscal year the United States provide $250 million, mainly to finance the national armies, and that this financial assistance be in addition to that already allocated.

On May 19, shortly before leaving for a meeting in Bonn with the British and French Foreign Ministers to discuss German matters, Secretary Acheson was called to a meeting at the White House with Secretary of Defense Lovett and General Omar Bradley, Chairman of the Joint Chiefs of Staff, to discuss the Indochina problem. As a result of this meeting Mr. Acheson was instructed to discuss the matter with Eden and Schuman. There is evidence that our memorandum of May 6 may have had some influence in the White House discussions, for among the points that the Secretary was to make were two that had been included in our memorandum. One of these was our willingness to give additional aid to the national armies, although specific amounts of aid were not to be mentioned. The Secretary was also instructed to avoid suggesting internal changes in Indochina other than the beefing up of the national armies. In addition, the Secretary was to discuss a possible tripartite warning to Peking against aggression in Indochina as well as the courses of action open and acceptable to the three powers should Peking ignore the warning. As Mr. Acheson has told us in *Present at the Creation*, "It was thought that such an agenda would keep the French to the points of immediate practical importance and avoid irritation on secondary and peripheral matters."

After the talks in Bonn were concluded, Mr. Acheson tells of the discussions held in Paris with the British and the French concerning Indochina. He made clear that the United States would not contribute ground forces to the war in Indochina but said we would consider with our allies contributing air and sea power if it was considered necessary to cut communications between China and Indochina. The Secretary says significantly: "The prerequisite to planning was a French political and military policy that her allies could help toward success. None was ever provided."

The chief result of the Paris discussions, as far as I was concerned, was the agreement to hold talks in Washington with Jean Letourneau, the French Minister for the Associated States, upon the conclusion of an inspection trip he was making to Indochina. These talks were held around the middle of June with officials from not only the State Department but also from the Department of Defense, the office of the Director of Mutual Security, the Mutual Security Agency, and the Department of the Treasury. As Assistant Secretary of State for Far Eastern Affairs, I acted as Chairman of the American delegation.

After several days of discussion, a communiqué was issued which pleased Letourneau and enabled him to return to Paris sure of continued, and even increased, American help to the French in Indochina. The communiqué recognized that the French effort in Indochina "is an integral part of the worldwide resistance by the Free Nations to Communist attempts at conquest and subversion." It was also stated that "success in this continuing struggle would entail an increase in the common effort and that the United States for its part will, therefore, within the limitations set by Congress, take steps to expand its aid to the French Union." Then came the only part of the communiqué which some of us really approved. It said: "It was further agreed that this increased assistance over and above present U.S. aid for Indochina, which now approximates one third of the total cost of Indochina operations, would be especially devoted to assisting France in the building of the national armies of the Associated States."

During the course of the talks, we had made a real effort to

Shortly after this picture was taken in Shanghai in 1929, when the author was Zone Advertising Manager, he and General Motors happily parted company and he joined the Foreign Service.

The author, when Assistant Secretary for the Far East, being received by the King of Thailand in October 1952. American Ambassador Edwin Stanton is seated on His Majesty's right.

John Foster Dulles and the author, concealed by binoculars with a hat hiding his bald head, at the 38th Parallel just one week before the outbreak of the Korean War.

August 4, 1952: Dean Acheson and the author lead the American delegation to the first ANZUS Council meeting at the Marine base in Kaneohe, Hawaii. Security Agent Frank Madden precedes them.

The author, ready to present credentials as Ambassador to the Emperor of Japan, May 28, 1953, and Imperial Household official Goto pose before the Emperor's coach.

Vice President Nixon addresses the Tokyo Embassy staff in front of the Chancery in November 1953. The author is to the left of the Vice President.

U.S.I.S. Photograph

Behind the scenes at Kabuki: the author and his wife are greeted by Ennosuke, one of Kabuki's most famous actors. Mrs. Okazaki, wife of the Foreign Minister, is at Mrs. Allison's left.

Secretary Dulles, greeted upon arrival in Tokyo in the autumn of 1955 by Foreign Minister Shigemitsu and his daughter while the author casts an appreciative glance at Miss Shigemitsu.

U.S. Army Photograph by M/Sgt. Al Chang

September 1953: The author and Foreign Minister Okazaki, surrounded by their associates, shake hands after signing an agreement giving Japan criminal jurisdiction over American troops when off duty.

Doughty hunters watch for ducks at an Imperial Duck Netting Party. The author and Prince Takamatsu, brother of the Japanese Emperor, face the camera; Princess Takamatsu and Embassy Minister Parsons are facing them.

A friendly President Sukarno jokes with the author after presentation of credentials at Merdeka Palace in Djakarta in February 1957.

A Christmas party at the Embassy residence in Djakarta for the children of Embassy servants. The author and Mrs. Allison are at the center of the mob.

The author and the late President Sukarno at the dedication of a new cement plant near Surabaya in eastern Java.

Mrs. Allison signs certificates of accomplishment for students from University of Indonesia who, as initiation rites into a student club, had to clean up the Embassy residence.

The author and his senior staff are greeted by former President Novotny of Czechoslovakia on the presentation of his credentials in April 1958. Foreign Minister David and a protocol officer stand behind the President.

This cartoon in an Indonesian Communist paper depicts the author and Secretary Dulles, along with the Dutch, instigating revolt against the Indonesian Government.

Another sarcastic cartoon shows the author giving hand grenades as Christmas presents to Indonesian rebels. The caption says, "Peace on Earth," in Indonesian.

Damai di Dunia
Merry Christmas

get from Letourneau precise information about French plans for Indochina but without much success. One of my associates, who has recently carefully read the record of the discussions, has pointed out that during the political parts of the discussions, Letourneau spoke in what my associate calls "waffly" English, but that during the financial discussion when the question of what the United States would do came up, he spoke in precise French. The political questions were all answered in English which, as Letourneau used it, served to keep the answers general and imprecise. He gave the appearance of doing his utmost to give responsive answers and, in fact, said practically nothing. For example, I asked him what could be done to make the governments of the Associated States more obviously responsive to the needs and desires of the people so that they would look upon them as "their governments" which were "working for them," and I added: "our whole effort is to work with you on that." Letourneau's reply was that it was up to the governments of the Associated States themselves to provide better service for their people and to convince them they were working for their interests. France was posing no obstacles in this regard. Nothing was said about the meagre training France had given the local government officials in the art of self-government. In fact, when, during the course of the talks, I suggested it would be helpful in explaining the war effort to world and American opinion if Letourneau would draw up a "balance sheet" type of presentation of what France had done in the way of preparing the Associated States of Indochina for independence, he virtually ignored the suggestion. Unfortunately, he was a minister in the French Cabinet, whereas the Americans sitting opposite him were at the most members of what has come to be known as the President's Little Cabinet. We neither thought we could put more pressure on him nor believed our superiors would approve further pressure at that time.

In his memoirs, *Full Circle*, Anthony Eden tells how Secretary Acheson had complained to him in Paris before our meetings with Letourneau of the French refusal to provide needed information and their attitude that, although we were providing one third of the financial outlay in Indochina, we had no right to ask inconvenient questions. Eden says that after Acheson's departure he had told the French they were going about it in the wrong way if they wanted to get more money out of the Americans. He then tells how surprised he was when, after our meetings with Letourneau, he was told by Secretary Acheson that the United States was going to provide an additional $150 million to the French.

The State Department feared that if we pressed the French too hard they would withdraw and leave us holding the baby. While this may well have been true, I believe it would have been better to have forced the issue then and found out just how much we could count on the French in helping us to build a stable world having the political, economic, and social strength to stand up to Communist subversion without which no amount of military action could be successful. Eventually the French did pull out anyway and left practically nothing behind in the shape of native governments trained to function efficiently or conscious of the vital necessity of earning the support of the masses by meeting their needs.

Summer in Washington is said to be the "silly season" as it is in many places and the summer of 1952 was no exception. In late May I received a letter from Edwin Reischauer, then a professor at Harvard, asking if I could help his colleague, John Fairbank, obtain a passport so that he could study in Japan. Professor Fairbank had been with the Office of War Information in China during World War II and had caused some raised eyebrows because of his sometimes extreme liberal views and his skepticism about the "democratic" government of Chiang Kaishek. He was an acknowledged scholar, and the purpose of his visit was to supplement his knowledge of China by a study of the language and history of Japan. I forwarded a copy of Ed Reischauer's letter to the Passport Office and stated in a covering memorandum that, while I had been in almost complete disagreement with many of Mr. Fairbank's views, I believed him to be an honest man, and I believed it would be helpful, rather than otherwise, to issue him the requested passport.

About ten days later I received a memorandum signed by Mrs. Shipley, the head of the Passport Office, referring to my memorandum and informing me that during the previous year, while our military occupation of Japan was still in existence, Mr. Fairbank had been refused military permission to go to Japan. The whole army file together with all information in the possession of the Passport Office, including an FBI report, was therefore being sent to the Security Division for its comments. One could almost see Mrs. Shipley looking over her shoulder to see if Senator Joe McCarthy was watching.

In due course the Security Division replied, and I was asked to give an official statement as to whether or not the Bureau of Far Eastern Affairs had any objection to issuing Mr. Fairbank a passport. In my reply to Mrs. Shipley I pointed out that the Security Division had raised no objection to granting the passport. It had pointed out that the FBI investigation of Mr. Fairbank had been directed toward the question of whether or not he was a suitable person for employment by the State Department. While the general conclusion was that he should not be employed by the Department, this had no bearing on his passport application. No evidence existed that Mr. Fairbank was or ever had been a Communist, although there were such allegations. There was considerable evidence in the file that he was well thought of by his professional colleagues, that he was a serious student of Far Eastern affairs, and that his professional career would be adversely affected if he was not permitted to travel and carry on further studies in Asia. I therefore stated in my memorandum that the Bureau of Far Eastern Affairs had no objection to giving Mr. Fairbank a passport.

Mr. Fairbank has written extensively on China and Asia in general and is today considered one of the leading American, if not world, scholars in his field. At least in one case Joe McCarthy and an oversensitive military failed to block the advancement of learning.

During the late spring and summer of 1952 we were engaged in preparation for the first meeting of the ANZUS Council — composed of the Foreign Ministers or their deputies from Australia, New Zealand, and the United States — which we hoped could be held before the first anniversary of the signing of the Pact.

As our plans progressed, two main problems arose which occupied our minds when we weren't worrying about Communist China, Indochina, or Joe McCarthy. The first problem was where the Council should meet, in Australia or the United States? The second was the desire of the United Kingdom to have observer status at the meeting. A third problem, the necessity of reassuring our Philippine and Korean friends as well as the American public that a meeting of the three ANZUS Pact members did not mean that we were setting up a "white man's pact" from which Asians would be excluded, came to plague us after we returned from the meeting.

Shortly after the middle of May, I received a memorandum from the Secretary's office requesting comments on the suggestion that the first meeting of the Council should be in Australia. In my reply I pointed out that if the Secretary went to Australia for the meeting, it would probably be necessary for him to visit other countries in the Pacific area and that this would be very time consuming. However, I added that "it would be of the greatest value to United States policy in the Far East if the Secretary could find it possible to make such a trip." No Secretary of State, while in office, had ever made a visit to any of the countries of the Far East, and there was a definite feeling in the area that the United States considered them in a second-class category as compared with Europe and Latin America. I concluded: "Should the Secretary believe it impossible for him to make a trip to all of the areas of the Far East, I would strongly urge that the initial meeting of the Pacific Council be held in Honolulu and that the Secretary plan to attend. This has the additional advantage of being the headquarters of Admiral Radford who would be the United States military representative on the Council." The Secretary agreed with my final paragraph, and on July 3 I was informed that Admiral Radford had agreed to having the meeting in Honolulu beginning on August 4. I was later to regret my use of the term "Pacific Council."

At the end of the first week in June I received from the Secretary's office a copy of a memorandum of a conversation between the Secretary and Sir Oliver Franks, the British Ambassador. Sir Oliver had called, on instructions from Foreign Minister Eden, to raise the question of the desirability of having an observer from the United Kingdom at the meetings of the Pacific Council. The British from the beginning had shown signs of some resentment at not being included in our Pact with Australia and New Zealand and were apparently attempting to come in through the back door. There was considerable feeling in the American Government that to let the British in would open the door for other Western powers with interests in Asia, and if we were not careful, we would soon find ourselves in an alliance with the colonial powers with consequent alienation of Asian friends. Secretary Acheson avoided a direct answer but said we would discuss the matter with the Pentagon and the other ANZUS Pact members. When the Council meeting finally took place, Mr. Acheson, through private informal discussions with the heads of the other delegations, managed to keep the subject from being officially considered, and in due course it died a natural death.

The Council meeting duly convened on August 4, at the Marine Air Force base at Kaneohe, just across the island of Oahu from Honolulu. It was good to meet my friends Alan Watt and Jim McIntyre from Australia and Foss Shanahan from New Zealand, all of whom had worked with us at Canberra in the drafting of the ANZUS Pact. The New Zealand Ambassador to Washington, who was also present, was my friend Leslie Munro, whom I had first met in London during the war. In addition to the problem of whether or not to have a British observer, the Australians in particular, and the New Zealanders to somewhat lesser extent, hoped to get agreement to some sort of arrangement for their Chiefs of Staff to have a definite relationship with the American Joint Chiefs. With the able assistance of Admiral Radford, Mr. Acheson also handled this problem. Our friends from the South Pacific were far from the center of world activity and felt out of things. They longed for a larger role.

Secretary Acheson understood their longing, but he knew the American Chiefs believed they had enough problems with NATO and didn't want to add anything to them. He therefore spent the first two days of the meeting on a detailed *tour d'horizon* which brought the Australian and New Zealand delegations completely up to the minute on the chief world problems with which we were concerned. Then, with Admiral Radford, the Commander-in-Chief, Pacific, arrangements were made for the Australian and New Zealand military to have special liaison with the Pacific Command and everyone was happy.

At the end of four days we returned to Washington. During our trip home a radio news bulletin was brought to Mr. Acheson who read it, bristled, got red in the face, handed it to me, and growled, "See what your friend Dulles has done now!" Mr. Dulles had left the State Department after the Japanese Peace Treaty had been ratified and was now busily engaged in campaigning for the Republican party in New York State. In what can only be described as an excess of partisan zeal he charged that the Democratic Administration was treating Asians as "second-class expendables." As the officer directly charged with dealing with Asians, I was just as angry as Mr. Acheson, and I determined to do something about it, although I didn't know just what it would be. However, the problem of explaining that the ANZUS Treaty was not a "Pacific Pact" was waiting for me, and I had to postpone answering Mr. Dulles.

Why we ever used the term "Pacific Council" to describe what later came to be called the "ANZUS Council" I can't remember.

On August 11, after our return from Honolulu, I was invited to lunch by Carlos Romulo who had become the Philippine Ambassador to Washington. He had an appointment with Secretary Acheson the next day, and he wanted to explain to me what he was going to take up with Mr. Acheson. President Quirino of the Philippines had become concerned at reports of the Pacific Council meeting and at charges by opposition elements in the Philippine Congress that the ANZUS Pact was a white man's pact which excluded Asians. Romulo said he had told Quirino that the Council meeting was a perfectly normal and natural consequence of the treaty signed in San Francisco. He had reminded Quirino that the Philippine-United States Mutual Defense Treaty had previously been signed in Washington in the presence of the Presidents of the two countries and that, in fact, the ANZUS Treaty merely brought Australia and New Zealand up to equality with the Philippines in their relations with the United States. Romulo went on to express the opinion that it was unfortunate the ANZUS Council meeting could not have been held quietly in Washington as this would have obviated considerable misunderstanding among Oriental nations. He then went on to refer to an editorial in the *New York Times* which had tried to account for the lack of Asian representation in Honolulu and had suggested the formation of some sort of "general consultative Pacific body." Romulo thought this idea had great merit and could not do any harm. He said such a council would have no military functions whatever nor would it be in any way a policy-making body. It would exist solely for the purpose of exchanging ideas on broad Pacific matters: cultural, economic, and social. Romulo said that if some such body could be set up, and if Asian nations, including Japan, which to my surprise he specifically mentioned, could be brought in, it would go far toward reassuring Asian nations that they were not being forgotten. Being nonmilitary it might also attract Burma and Indonesia.

I sent a memorandum to the Secretary reporting what Romulo had said and saying that I believed his idea had some merit, and I recommended the Secretary tell Romulo, when he saw him the next day, that, while we could make no commitments to any form of organization we would be receptive to any further concrete suggestions he might make and would give them serious consideration.

Ten days after my lunch with Romulo, Ambassador Yang of Korea called at my office and, among other things, brought up the subject of a "Pacific Pact." He said his government attached great importance to the formation of a Pacific Pact which would embrace all the nations of the Far East and expressed his government's regret that the American Government apparently was only willing to ally itself in such a pact with Australia and New Zealand. He went on to say he had heard comments that this was a "white alliance" and would never include the yellow race. Ambassador Yang really knew better, I was sure, but he was acting under instructions from a new and extremely sensitive government, so I went into considerable detail to reassure him.

I told Dr. Yang that we would continue to support the idea of a Pacific Pact but that I believed the Asian nations themselves must get together to initiate it. The Ambassador said he recognized the difficulties but strongly urged, still apparently under instructions, that the United States take action to form an all-embracive alliance. He said his government believed that given the opportunity, all the Asian nations would gradually participate. My talk with Ambassador Yang reminded me of my talk almost four years earlier with Syngman Rhee, who had wanted the United States to make him President of Korea without waiting for a decision by the Korean people.

About this time the late Bill Costello, then a CBS news correspondent and later Ambassador to Trinidad, came to me and suggested I do a radio program which, among other things, would clear up the problem of the alleged white man's pact in the Pacific. I agreed and in turn suggested the program be enlarged to include comments about the present situation in Asia and give me an opportunity to answer Foster Dulles's charge that we were treating the Asians as second-class expendables. Bill readily agreed, and we worked out a series of questions and answers which was broadcast over CBS at 12 noon on Sunday, September 14, 1952.

Toward the end of the program, Bill Costello asked me, "Would you say it is fair to conclude that it is our policy to treat Asians as second-class expendables?" During my long answer to this question my only mention of Mr. Dulles was to refer to his "energetic and imaginative guidance" in the negotiation of the treaty which gave the Japanese the opportunity "to take their place in the world community as equal partners." I spoke of the American blood and treasure that had been poured out in Korea, the money being given to an aid program in the Philippines, and the money being spent in Indochina, Formosa, and the economic aid programs in Thailand, Burma, and Indonesia. I asked, "Would these more than 100,000 American casualties and billions of American dollars have been sacrificed for people whom we considered second-class expendables?" I then concluded:

"But what of Russia? What is its ultimate purpose in Asia? To make the nations of Asia free? No. Remember, Stalin said the

East was the road to victory in the West — that is what they are interested in. They are attempting to use the people of Asia to achieve that victory. It is the Soviets — it is the Communists — who really believe the people of Asia are second-class expendables. There have not been 100,000 Soviet casualties on behalf of their North Korean and Chinese Communist friends. No — they let them spend their own blood."

A few days later Mr. Dulles telephoned me from his New York office. After some preliminary remarks he said, "I hear you've been criticizing me on the radio." I admitted the charge and said I would send him the text of what I had said. I did, with a brief covering letter which read:

> DEAR FOSTER:
> Herewith the complete text of my statement proving you were absolutely wrong. All the best to you and Janet.

I never received a reply, but when he became Secretary of State the following year, he recommended to President Eisenhower that I go to Japan as Ambassador.

Before we went to Honolulu to the ANZUS meeting, it had been decided that toward the end of September I should make a trip to Asia and visit all the countries which then came under the purview of the Bureau of Far Eastern Affairs. Australia and New Zealand at that time were still listed under the Division of British Commonwealth Affairs in the European Bureau. Our territory went from Japan and Korea in the north to Indonesia in the south. While still in Hawaii, at an after-luncheon talk with Secretary Acheson, I raised the question of whether or not I should take Mrs. Allison with me. I believed she could be most useful in talking to the wives of our officers as well as the women members of our Embassy staffs. There was no incipient women's liberation movement at that time, but we did realize that the ladies often got restive, and if they had an opportunity to talk to someone from Washington, who might be able to do something about their problems, I was certain it would be a big morale booster. I told the Secretary I hoped to take my wife along, but if I had to pay the whole expense, it would be something of a wrench to my finances. Mr. Acheson agreed that my wife should go and also agreed that I should not have to bear all the expense. I am sure he was sincere and that when we returned to Washington he did his best to help. But to no avail. So we both went anyway, and, while the family finances suffered, the morale of the Foreign Service in Asia did go up. A shortsighted Congress still refuses to appropriate funds for the travel of wives on such visits, although it would not be difficult to ensure that such funds were not misused.

One morning shortly before taking off for Asia I was at the White House attending a meeting, about Korea I believe, and as the meeting adjourned, just before a regular Cabinet meeting, President Truman came into the room and took his seat at the table. There were a few minutes remaining before the Cabinet was to meet, and I asked Mr. Acheson if he would take me over to the President as I should like to get a statement from him which I could use on my trip. The Secretary immediately took me over and told the President I was shortly going to the Far East and that it would be helpful if I could have a statement from him to use in talks with the Asians. Mr. Truman looked up, smiled, and asked: "What do you want me to say, young man?" I told him I was to be the first senior State Department official to visit these nations which were just coming out of colonialism and that they were extremely sensitive about maintaining their independence. I said this was particularly true of Burma and Indonesia which were fearful the United States was going to try to force them into a Pacific Pact. They only wanted to be neutral and tend to their own affairs. Could the President reassure them that we had no such intentions? The President at once said, "Certainly. We had the same attitude when we were a young nation. You tell them we understand their problem and have great sympathy for their point of view."

When I got to Asia, Mr. Truman's statement was well received. I used it wherever I could in press conferences and in private talks. The following translation from the Rangoon newspaper, *New Light of Burma*, of October 14, 1952, shows what the Burmese thought.

> We are much heartened because of the statement made by the U.S. Assistant Secretary of State clarifying the U.S. Government's attitude in regard to the neutral policy adopted by most Asian nations.
>
> It is evident from his statement that the U.S. Government is anxious to allay any fear on the part of the Asian nations by making known its true attitude.
>
> We are much encouraged because the Americans now seem to understand more of the real aspirations of the Asian peoples . . . we pray that the Americans will back up their words with deeds.

For a time it did seem easier to talk to the new nations of Asia without their seeming to discount ninety percent of what you said. But this was not to last. A year later a new administration was in power in Washington, and the new Secretary of State had proclaimed that neutrality was "immoral." I believe this single statement did as much as anything to cause the Asian peoples to begin to question whether the United States was really on the side of anticolonialism. From then on they looked at everything we did with a wary eye. Several years later, when I went to Indonesia as Ambassador, this statement was still to cause trouble, although by that time it was no longer being shouted from the roof tops.

After selling some stock and borrowing from a trustful friend to finance my wife's ticket, we took off toward the end of September for Manila which was to be our first stop.

We had to stop for refueling at Wake Island about two o'clock in the morning. It was September 27. As we trudged down the gangway and drowsily wended our way to the restaurant for a cup of coffee, the loudspeaker on the control tower started blaring out: "Message for Assistant Secretary of State and Mrs. Allison. You have a new granddaughter waiting for you in Manila. Baby and Mother doing fine. Congratulations!" Of all six grandchildren this was the only one at whose birth my wife was not present, and she only missed this by twenty-four hours.

My trip to Asia lasted from the end of September until the sixteenth of November. I returned from my circuit of East Asia with what I described to my staff as a feeling of "cautious optimism." I reported that in general the political, economic, and social stability of the various countries was better than a year before. I said there was also a better appreciation of "the true nature of the Chinese Communist menace" among the leaders of the different governments. This was true as well of the British officials that I met in Southeast Asia and Hong Kong. We must remember that the Chinese Communists had but recently almost driven the United Nations forces out of Korea and were making threatening noises about other areas of Asia. There still was a monolithic communism, and because of our experience with it in Europe and Korea, we were perhaps overly suspicious of it in Southeast Asia. I didn't see a Communist under every bed, but I probably did see one under every other bed.

With regard to the Philippines, I said it was difficult to make up one's mind. On the surface things seemed good and certainly the security situation was better, but when you began to dig a bit the outlook became murky. The leaders, from President Quirino down, tended to shrug off their economic problems and failed to get down to fundamentals. An election was in the offing, and the first priority of President Quirino and his Party was to get re-elected.

Quirino was greatly interested in promoting a Pacific Pact and hoped I would further his ideas. I visited Manila twice, and between the visits I did talk about a Pacific Pact wherever I went, but upon my return to Manila I told Quirino the prospects were not good, at least for the near future. In large part to reassure the Filipinos that they were not being forgotten by the United States, we held a political-military conference in Manila during my second visit. From the United States Defense Department came William Foster, Under Secretary, and Frank Nash, Assistant Secretary. Admiral Radford was the chief military delegate, and Ambassador Spruance and I represented the State Department. On the Philippine side were President Quirino, Foreign Minister Elizalde, Defense Minister Magsaysay, the Speaker of the House of Representatives, and the President of the Senate. We got lots of publicity in the Philippine press, and I believed the conference did succeed in assuaging the feelings of the Filipinos. It had other good results also. We made clear that all thought of a Pacific Pact might as well be thrown out until the Philippines ratified the Japanese Peace Treaty, and we also said it would be much easier for them if they regularized their relations with the Associated States of Indochina. On the other hand, it became evident that the Japanese, on their part, would have to be more forthcoming on the reparations issue if any progress was to be made, and I was later able to report this to the leaders in Tokyo.

From Manila we went to Bangkok and Rangoon. I told my staff that after visiting both countries I believed Burma was by far the more important place to concentrate our efforts. I said the Thais would do what everyone else does; they would rather be on our side, but if it proved dangerous, they would swing the other way. The Burmese appeared to be definitely non-Communist but just as definitely wanted to develop their own strength before they got involved in foreign adventures. I was more encouraged about Burma than any other place in Southeast Asia. Within a few years I was proved wrong, and Burma

had retreated into a self-imposed isolation and a neo-Marxian
dictatorship under Ne Win, from which it is only just now
slowly beginning to emerge.

From Rangoon we flew to Djakarta for a hectic two days. I
reported to my staff that President Sukarno was by far the most
impressive Asian I met on my whole trip. I said, "He has great
ability, is frank, amusing, personally magnetic and could be
dangerous." I told how Sukarno had stressed the importance of
regaining West New Guinea, which the Dutch had retained
when they gave the rest of the Netherland East Indies independence and it became Indonesia. Sukarno said that if the United
States would only recognize, in principle, that the sovereignty of
West New Guinea rested in Indonesia, he could get his country
to do anything we wanted it to.

I told how I had met Vice President Hatta and how he and
Sukarno made a good team. Hatta was quiet, comparatively
conservative, and economically literate. Sukarno was a dynamic,
colorful leader who could have easily sold Hatta's policies to the
people. At that time I was still hopeful the partnership would
work. It didn't. The Indonesian press was suspicious of the
reasons for my visit and charged I was there to force Indonesia
into a Pacific Pact. I strongly recommended that the United
States should not press these new countries too hard but that
from time to time we give them a gentle push.

Malaya was different. The Communist insurrection was still
in full force. We spent a day and night in Kuala Lumpur, and I
had an opportunity for a long talk with General Sir Gerald
Templer, the High Commissioner. He talked with me for over
an hour in the late afternoon and after telling me of the origins
of the Communist trouble and its present extent, he emphasized
that the problem was twenty-five percent military and seventy-
five percent political, social, and economic. How different from
the outlook of the American military leaders in Vietnam fifteen
years later! In the evening the General gave a black-tie dinner

for me at which was present a representative group of leaders of the country. There was the Deputy High Commissioner, a civilian, the Attorney General, the military commanders, the Minister of Education, a Ceylonese, two or three leading Malayans, two of the leading Chinese residents, and two Indian labor leaders who came in business suits and showed no evidence of being embarrassed. After the toast to the Queen at the end of the meal, I was taken into a small study, where all those present who wished to came in individually to talk and let me question them. Sir Gerald remained in another room and neither he nor any members of his staff made any attempt to listen to these discussions.

The American representative in Kuala Lumpur was a relatively junior Foreign Service Officer, and I recommended that we send a more senior officer. I told my staff that I thought that Kuala Lumpur was destined to be more important than Singapore, where we did have one of our senior officers. None of us then foresaw an independent Singapore and what Lee Kwan-yew would make of it.

A week in Indochina was interesting, but I reported that my talks with the French in Saigon were not very profitable. I was more impressed by the young King of Cambodia, Norodom Sihanouk, now in exile in Peking. Sihanouk did not spend all his time sitting on his throne but went into the country and talked with his people. In 1952, he was popular and respected and presented a sharp contrast to Bao Dai, whom the French had set up as King in Vietnam. The latter was more interested in the French Riviera than in the problems of his people.

We next went to Taipei. Many of the old faults we had known on the mainland before the war were still there, but in some fields considerable progress had been made. This was most evident in rural reconstruction, land reform, and public health activity. If as much had been done on the mainland by the Chiang government, I believe it might have been able to resist the Communist attacks. In an interview with Generalissimo Chiang, I urged the withdrawal of his troops from Northern Burma, where they had gone to escape the Communists. This was a sore point with all elements in Burma, and instead of helping the anti-Communist cause, as was being claimed, they only provided fuel for Communist propaganda. The Generalissimo listened politely and did nothing. It was several years before this sore spot was removed from Burma, and, in the meantime, it did much to increase Burmese suspicion of the United States, as they believed we were supporting Chiang's troops.

Our next stop was Tokyo. General Mark Clark, our military commander, surprised me by exhibiting a political sensitivity not always found in our military leaders. His close friendship with Ambassador Robert Murphy was proving most helpful in coordinating our political and military problems. The Japanese people appeared to have more spirit and life and seemed healthier than when I had been in Japan a year previously. They were making tremendous progress in reconstruction, but there were disturbing signs that the government and people were assuming that their comparative prosperity, based at that time primarily upon UN and United States procurement for the Korean War, would last indefinitely without the Japanese having to take any steps themselves to shore up the economic situation.

The mass of the Japanese people were still reluctant to rearm because of the economic burden, and also because they feared the resurgence of a military caste which would dominate the country. I tried to point out to them that because the postwar Japanese Constitution did not give the military the preferred position they had previously had, it should be possible to build up a defense force that would be the servant rather than the master of the people. Some agreed with me, but the majority were not convinced.

Japanese relations with Korea and the reparations problem were the two principal matters of concern besides those connected with the setting up of some sort of a defense force. These problems were still unresolved when I arrived in Tokyo as Ambassador some six months later.

While in Tokyo, I was informed by Ambassador Murphy and General Clark of their worry about a recent flurry of flights of Soviet planes over Hokkaido. They said that over the past six months Russian activity over northern Japan and the Kuriles had increased tremendously. Although diplomatic and trade relations between Japan and Russia steadily improved over the years, the Russians gave no sign of intending to return to Japan the southern Kurile islands, which they had occupied upon Japan's surrender.

I concluded my report by recounting a conversation with a professor at Tokyo University which seemed to me to illustrate rather graphically an Oriental trait that Americans often ignore or seem unwilling to believe in. This man told me that a year previously all of his students were going Communist. The professor said that he was anti-Communist but despite his teachings the students were taking the opposite line. However, this year (1952) the situation was different, and the students had become anti-Communist. He said that this was due to the fact that the Communist forces had not been able to push the Americans out of Korea, but had been thrown back, and that the United States was more active in supporting the Chinese Nationalists on Formosa. In Asia, nothing succeeds like success.

While we were in Hong Kong, we spent one Saturday afternoon on the famous Cat Street, where Mrs. Allison indulged her hobby of looking for early Chinese blue and white ceramics. As I remember she found a few, but the finest acquisition was a Chinese bamboo birdcage, which was to become famous and be written about not only in the press of Taipei but in society columns of the *Washington Post*. When we reached Taipei, we were put up in the Government Guest House, and when we were not in the friendly hands of Karl Rankin, the American Chargé d'Affaires and his wife, we were taken care of by Major General Huang, the Grover Whalen of Formosa, and his wife. Americans probably get on a first name basis with Chinese more quickly than with any other Oriental race, and it was not long before our Chinese hosts discovered that my wife's nickname, by which she was known by all her family and friends, was "Toots." General Huang quickly pointed out that Toots, if spelled in the Chinese style, *Tu'tz*, meant rabbit. At a farewell luncheon given us we were served dumplings in the shape of rabbits and at the close of the luncheon Toots was presented with a beautiful agate rabbit by General and Mrs. Huang. When we got ready to go to the airport, the agate rabbit was placed in the birdcage purchased in Hong Kong, which my wife clutched in her hands. The local press was at the airport in strength to see us off, and they were much intrigued by the birdcage. My wife, with her usual lack of inhibitions, told them the whole story of the cage and its passenger, the agate rabbit. When we reached Washington we discovered what the result of her frankness had been. Karl Rankin had sent on copies of the Taipei newspapers that had come out the morning after our departure. There was a four column headline: "Assistant Secretary of State Allison and Toots Leave for Tokyo." By the time we went back to Japan, when I became Ambassador, we found the tale had spread and gifts of stone, silver, porcelain, and wooden rabbits began to fill the house. Fortunately no live rabbits were included, but the inanimate ones were almost as prolific.

It was election day, 1952, when we left Taipei for Tokyo, and when the Japanese Press met me in Tokyo, they bombarded me with questions about what effect the elections would have on American policy in Asia and particularly in Japan. The results of the election were not yet final, but I was able to tell them that I believed whichever party won the election, American policy toward Japan would be much the same as at present. I pointed out that if the Democrats won, they would retain much of the present policy and that if the Republicans won, John Foster Dulles, the man who had been chiefly responsible for the negotiation of the Japanese Peace Treaty, would undoubtedly have considerable influence, and I knew he had a true appreciation of the importance of Japan. I said they need not worry about being forgotten.

While in Japan I was asked to give a talk before the members of the America-Japan Society and, with the approval of Robert Murphy, our first postwar Ambassador to Japan, I did so. Ambassador Murphy, one of our ablest career officers, had had a distinguished career in Europe, having been Ambassador to Belgium before he came to Tokyo. During World War II, he had been political advisor to General Eisenhower and after the war had served in occupied Germany as political advisor to General Clay, the military governor of the American zone of occupation. Bob had never served in Asia and, while he got along well with the Japanese, was inclined, as are most Americans coming to Tokyo for the first time, to judge them by American or European standards and assume they would react to the same pressures.

America was anxious at that time to have Japan take a larger share of the burden of its own defense, and a large part of my speech dealt with this problem and the reasons why Japan should do so. I showed the text of my speech to Bob, and he thought it was not half strong enough, and at his urging I put a little more punch in it. However, both Bill Turner, Bob's number two man, an old prewar Japan hand, and I thought the Japanese would think the speech too tough. Bob still believed it was not strong enough, although he reluctantly approved it in its revised form. The speech was given before a large audience of Japanese leaders and American residents, and the public reception was good. Almost ten years later, after I had retired and was living in Honolulu, a prominent Japanese-American attorney with whom I had become friendly told me he had been present at my speech in Tokyo. He said that all his Japanese friends had been most discouraged by what they considered the harshness of the speech and my seeming misunderstanding of the Japanese viewpoint. They had not dared to say that to me at the time. It was too soon after the end of the Occupation.

By the time I got back to Washington, the Republicans had won the election and it was announced shortly that Foster Dulles would be the next Secretary of State. A month or so before General Eisenhower was to be inaugurated, Mr. Dulles was given an office, not far from mine, on the third floor of what we then called New State, where he was briefed and given access to papers so that he would be prepared to take over the complicated duties of Secretary of State. I had seen him briefly in New York before he came down to Washington, and he had told me he didn't yet know exactly what my future would be but that I shouldn't worry and just carry on with my present duties.

As is customary with all Ambassadors and appointive officers of the rank of Assistant Secretary of State and above, I submitted my resignation to President Eisenhower. It was never accepted, and for some three months after his inauguration I continued to serve as Assistant Secretary in charge of Far Eastern Affairs.

One day shortly before Christmas, 1952, Mr. Dulles had called me into his temporary office and asked me what I knew about a certain businessman in San Francisco. I told him what I knew, which wasn't much, and then asked him why he was interested. "Oh, I'm thinking of giving him your job" was the reply. I said that was interesting and asked what was to happen to me? "Oh, you're going to Japan as Ambassador." I was told that the President knew and approved but that it would not be possible to make any announcement for some time, because there was a prominent Republican politician in Honolulu who wanted the job and who had considerable political backing. Mr. Dulles told me under no circumstances to mention the matter to anyone but my wife and not to get impatient if it took some time to get everything worked out. He also added that he didn't want me to leave Washington until he had a satisfactory replacement for me. I then raised the question of what would happen to Bob Murphy who had been in Tokyo less than a year and was an extremely able, hard-working career officer. Mr. Dulles told me not to worry about Bob, as General Eisenhower wanted him for an important position back in Washington and "Doc" Matthews, the then Deputy Under Secretary of State, would shortly be communicating with Bob about his future.

So I went back to my office hoping that my inner excitement would not be obvious to my staff. But there was work to do, as much as ever, and I didn't have much time to think about the future. A week or two before he finally left office, President Truman gave a dinner at the White House for his Little Cabinet, the Under Secretaries and Assistant Secretaries of all the Executive Departments. After an informal cocktail hour, during which we all had an opportunity to talk briefly with the President, we were led into a specially prepared dining room where the tables were set up in the shape of a large U. In the center and facing toward the base of the U, where the President sat, was a large television set. Just before the dessert course, President Truman rapped on his glass with a spoon and said, "Gentlemen, I hope you will bear with an old father who wants to hear his daughter sing." With that the TV was turned on, and we heard and saw Margaret Truman.

All of us had another opportunity of experiencing the humanity of President Truman when, just a few days before he was to leave office, we received personal letters thanking us for our work in his administration. These were not brief general notes of thanks but were directed to the specific matters with which we had been concerned. After thanking me for my contributions "to the conduct of our foreign affairs, particularly during the period that you have served as Assistant Secretary of State for Far Eastern Affairs," the letter went on to say:

> The particular area which is your concern has been the Nation's very acute concern in this period. It has confronted us with some of our greatest challenges, and I feel fortunate for myself and the country that your abilities and experience were available in this spot.
>
> I feel that United States foreign policy has made particularly significant progress in the Far East, especially in the successful United Nations resistance to aggression in Korea, the restoration of Japan to a place of equality and opportunity in the free world, and the completion of the initial steps in a system of collective security among the free nations of the Far East. To all these you have made important contributions.
>
> You have my best wishes for the future.

Is it any wonder that all of us who worked for him were sorry to see him go?

Before President Truman's administration finally came to an end, there was last minute work to do for those of us in the Bureau of Far Eastern Affairs. In early December 1952, Secretary Acheson was going to Europe, and before he left I sent him a memorandum on Japan and our policies regarding it which I suggested he might wish to discuss with Mr. Eden while in Europe. In view of the continued Chinese Communist charges today (February 1972) that Japan, under American pressure, is becoming a militaristic threat, it may be interesting to look at some of the things said in this twenty-year-old memorandum. I pointed out that the then authorized strength of the Japanese National Safety Force was 110,000 and that we believed this force should eventually be increased to ten divisions or 325,000 men. We said that we originally had believed this figure could be reached by the end of March 1954, but due "to the political difficulties which rearmament faces in Japan" we thought the program would be delayed a year. In February of 1972, twenty years later, the strength of what is now called the Self Defense Force is still under 200,000, and the defense budget approximates only one percent of Japan's gross national product as compared with around four percent in most other nations, many of them smaller than Japan. And, in contrast to Communist China, Japan has no nuclear capability. Does this look like militarism or overpowering American pressure to make Japan militaristic?

On December 4, 1952, the day after I sent the above memorandum to Mr. Acheson, Mr. Dulles told me of a conversation he had had with Jiru Shirasu, who was in the United States on a personal mission for Prime Minister Yoshida. Mr. Dulles reported that Shirasu had said that Mr. Yoshida was greatly concerned over the pressures to rearm to which the Japanese Government was being subjected. Yoshida believed that it would not be possible to develop any large-scale rearmament in Japan without first re-educating the people, because they had been taught during the Occupation that it was wrong to have a military establishment and that this was stated in the new Japanese Constitution. Yoshida urged that time be given to avoid a political upheaval that would put the Socialists into power on a "neutrality" platform. Mr. Dulles told Shirasu that he believed the Japanese people must realize they would not be a fully sovereign nation as long as they were wholly dependent upon another nation for their protection and that they must realize, as a matter of their own self-respect, that they would have to bear some responsibility and a fair share of the common burden of defense of the free world.

Mr. Dulles said that military security information which might come to him later might lead him to feel there was great urgency but that, "if the information made him feel that way the same information would probably lead the Japanese Government and people to feel the same way." The fact that this just isn't so and that the Japanese Government and people seldom feel and react the same way we do was one of the facts I found most difficult to impress on Washington during the four years I was Ambassador in Tokyo.

As the weeks dragged by I began to wonder whether or not I really was going to Tokyo. Finally, at the end of February or in the first week in March, Mr. Dulles told me the problem of the politician in Hawaii had been solved and that the White House would shortly announce my appointment. Almost ten years later, after I had retired from the Foreign Service and had come to live in Honolulu, I was a guest at a local discussion club one evening and during the cocktail hour a prominent local business-man, who had been Chairman of the State Republican Com-mittee, came up to me and said, "You know, John, when I first heard you were coming to Honolulu to live I made up my mind to hate you. You beat me out of one of the few jobs I have ever really wanted, American Ambassador to Japan. Now that I've met you, I guess you're not so bad and I'm glad you have come to live among us." Randolph Crossley was a real gentleman.

Two or three days after Mr. Dulles had told me my designa-tion as Ambassador to Japan would shortly be announced, I attended a meeting in the Cabinet Room of the White House with Harold Stassen, Director of the Mutual Security Program, and the late Joseph Dodge, Director of the Bureau of the Budget, to discuss economic aid problems related to Korea. The meeting adjourned just as members of the Cabinet began to file into the room for the regular Friday morning meeting. Presi-dent Eisenhower also strolled in. I had never met him, and I asked Joe Dodge, an old friend whom I had worked with in connection with Occupation financial problems in Japan, to introduce me. He took me up to the President and after the introduction, President Eisenhower, with his infectious grin, said as he grasped my hand, "You're the young man we're send-ing to Japan, aren't you?" At last, I had the news from the highest source.

On Saturday morning March 7, 1953, the first page of the *Washington Post* carried three banks of eight-column headlines announcing the appointment of Malenkov as Stalin's successor as Premier of the Soviet Union. Also on the first page were pictures of four men: Malenkov, Molotov, the new Soviet Foreign Minister, Beria, the new Soviet Interior Minister, and John M. Allison, who, the paper said, had "been nominated yesterday as Ambassador to Japan." The weeks of waiting were over, but I still had to appear before the Foreign Relations Committee of the Senate to be confirmed.

While waiting to be called before the committee, I was kept busy winding up my duties in the Bureau of Far Eastern Affairs and taking part in the briefing of my successor as Assistant Secretary of State for the Far East. Walter Robertson, a Richmond, Virginia, investment banker who had served with General Marshall on his diplomatic mission to China at the end of World War II, had been chosen by Mr. Dulles after he investigated many possibilities. I am sure that Walter's intense hatred of communism was one of the reasons Mr. Dulles picked him. From Mr. Dulles's point of view the appointment was a good one, and the two men worked well together. From the point of view of American policy in Asia, the appointment was not so good. Walter was an honorable Virginia gentleman who was completely inflexible in his approach to postwar Asian problems and saw everything in terms of an imminent, rather than a possible, Communist threat to vital American interests. However, in spite of his rigid anti-Communist stand, Walter Robertson did not kowtow to Senator Joe McCarthy and stood up bravely for some career members of his staff who were the victims of McCarthy's unscrupulous and irresponsible charges.

In a memorandum to Mr. Dulles shortly after he took office, I discussed the problems arising from British concern that ANZUS was seeking to extend its scope throughout the Pacific, including Southeast Asia, and Churchill's statement to President Eisenhower that it was unreasonable for ANZUS to proceed with their planning without direct United Kingdom assistance, as their interests were closely involved. The old story in a new form.

When President Eisenhower took office he appointed Admiral Radford, who had been Commander-in-Chief, Pacific, as Chairman of the Joint Chiefs of Staff. On February 4, 1953, I had a long talk with the Admiral on Far Eastern problems. He was critical of the lack of aggressiveness of the French in Indochina and to a lesser degree of the failure of the United States to provide spare parts for planes and other military equipment in our aid program. He agreed with the State Department that it would not be wise at that time to bring the United Kingdom into ANZUS, and he thought he had sufficient authority to cope with any Chinese Communist reaction to the change in the orders of the Seventh Fleet. However, he cautioned that any decision to blockade the Chinese coast should only be taken after a thorough study of the possible consequences, with special reference to its effects on Hong Kong. While on some things, such as possible reversion to Japan of the Bonin Islands, "Raddy" was completely inflexible, on most matters he was easy to work with and showed an appreciation of the political aspects of strategic decisions.

It was not until the end of March 1953, that I was called before the Foreign Relations Committee of the Senate to be questioned about my qualifications for the position of Ambassador to Japan. When I was working with Mr. Dulles on the Japanese Peace Treaty, we had several meetings with the committee and particularly with its Far Eastern Subcommittee, so when I was called into the committee's large meeting room in the Capitol, I was greeted by old friends on both the Republican and Democratic side of the great oval table. Senator Griswold, of my home state of Nebraska, was also there to introduce me officially to the committee. The forty-five minutes I spent before the committee proved a pleasant interlude in an otherwise exhausting schedule. When, on April 2, my nomination was reported to the floor of the Senate, Senator Sparkman of Alabama, former Democratic nominee for Vice President, and Republican Senator Smith of New Jersey both made complimentary statements on my behalf and Senator John Wiley of Wisconsin, Chairman of the Foreign Relations Committee had placed in the Congressional Record a most flattering statement about my qualifications and my appearance before the committee. The nomination was approved unanimously.

On the same day my nomination was confirmed, that of William Howard Taft III as Ambassador to Ireland was also confirmed unanimously. Bill Taft was the son of Senator Robert Taft, and many people thought he had received his position through his father's influence. I had met Senator Taft several times at dinners given by Bill Bullitt, former Ambassador to the Soviet Union and to France, and while I seldom agreed with his policies, I liked him as a person. At the spring, 1953, Gridiron Club dinner given shortly before I left for Tokyo, I was seated near one end of an extremely long head table, and Senator Taft was seated at the same table but close to the center. During one of the frequent intermissions between skits the Senator got up and came around to my seat and said he just wanted to let me know that he had had nothing to do with his son being nominated as Ambassador to Ireland. The Senator said he believed in the Foreign Service career system and he hoped I would understand. I had never doubted the Senator's honesty, and I was glad to learn quite by accident a few days later that the Senator had indeed had no hand in his son's appointment. I have always considered his action in coming over to speak to me showed his great thoughtfulness and human understanding.

On April 8, 1953, I was finally sworn in as United States Ambassador to Japan, and immediately afterward Walter Robertson was sworn in as Assistant Secretary of State for Far Eastern Affairs. We were to leave for Tokyo toward the end of

April, and, as is usual in Washington, far too many people thought they had to give us a farewell party of some sort. The day before we took off by train for San Francisco, I was to be received by President Eisenhower for a brief farewell visit. As I remember, my appointment was for eleven o'clock on a Saturday morning. On Friday I completely lost my voice as a result, probably, of too many parties. Fortunately at one more party that evening, the wife of a good friend from the British Embassy gave me some pills which she had used to cure the same affliction, and on Saturday morning I was able to talk.

During my talk with President Eisenhower I mentioned the matter of a brilliant young Japanese economist, Shigeto Tsuru, who had been an advisor to the Japanese Socialist party and wanted to return to the United States to visit his alma mater, Harvard. There was considerable opposition among the McCarthy type of American to his being given an American visa, as he was a far left wing Socialist and many even accused him of being a Communist.

I told the President I was inclined to give Tsuru a visa. I said it had always seemed to me that the people who wanted to keep all Communists out of the United States were exhibiting but little faith in our system of government. I asked why we shouldn't be able to change the Communist's ideas as well as he was said to be able to change ours? The President said, "I believe you're absolutely right. Do what you believe to be best." Later the pressures of the extreme conservatives in his own party were to cause him to be more cautious in his approach to these problems, but I was never criticized when later I approved the Consular section of our Embassy giving Tsuru a visa.

The President signed and gave me the usual Presidential photograph, wished me Godspeed, and then, after twenty-three years of struggling through the ranks of the Foreign Service, I was off to take up my assignment as an American Ambassador, the personal representative of the President in a foreign country.

# X

# The Garden of Live Flowers

## 1953–1957

IN HIS STIMULATING BOOK *The Twilight of the Presidency,* George Reedy, former Special Assistant to President Lyndon Johnson, maintains that the life of the White House is the life of a court and that the perquisites and privileges which go with the office of President inevitably cause the occupant of the office to lose contact with reality and to act more and more as if he were in fact royalty and not just being treated as royalty. To some extent the same criticism could be applied to an Ambassador who goes abroad as the personal representative of the President and receives in many cases much the same perquisites and privileges, to a somewhat lesser degree, as does the man in the White House.

While all of us who have been Ambassadors, even for a short time, have succumbed to some extent to the reflected glory of being the President's personal representative, I believe it has been easier for those of us from the career service to resist the temptation to believe we are a special breed. We have worked for Ambassadors as junior officers and have seen their faults and foibles as well as their virtues. Members of our own staff have often known us when we were holding the most humble posts and, while polite, do not hesitate to tell us when we are being silly.

And so it was when I arrived in Tokyo. My wife and I sailed to Japan on the *President Cleveland,* the ship on which we had first met a little over five years before. We were met by a group from the Embassy headed by my friend Bill Turner, who would be my number two man until he departed in a few months to become Consul General in Bombay. Bill had given me my first Japanese language examinations back in 1932, and we had worked and played together for many years. It would be useless for me to try and pretend I was a special breed of cat with Bill around to guffaw at any incipient pomposity. He knew Japan well and was a great help during my first months of getting broken in to my new job. When Bill left he was succeeded by J. Graham (Jeff) Parsons who had been private secretary to Ambassador Grew back in 1932 and 1933, when I was a language student at the Embassy. It would be impossible for me to try and fool Jeff any more than Bill Turner, so I started out under good auspices.

We arrived in Japan on May 23, 1953, and just five days later I presented my credentials to the Emperor. As I recall, I was to be at the Palace at eleven o'clock in the morning. At shortly after ten o'clock, Mr. Goto of the Imperial Household arrived to conduct me and my senior staff to the Palace. Today I believe he arrives only about fifteen minutes ahead of time as the journey to the Palace is made by motorcar and takes no more than ten minutes or so. But in 1953 we were taken in Imperial carriages drawn by beautiful black horses preceded by Imperial guards also mounted on horses. The Emperor's coach, in which I rode alone with Mr. Goto, was lined with gold. The coachman's and footman's hat bands were gold with the Imperial Crest. The bridles and harnesses of the horses also had the Imperial gold crest as did the hubcaps and the doors of the coach. The coachman and the footman were in special uniforms with knee trousers and long white stockings. The drab morning coat, striped trousers, and high silk hat which all of us wore, hardly seemed elegant enough to go with the nineteenth-century splendor of the coach and horses. At the slow majestic pace of the horses it took us almost a full forty-five minutes to reach the Palace. Tokyo traffic today will not permit such a ceremonial procession.

Upon arrival at the Palace, we were led to a reception room where my staff waited while I was shown into the Emperor's presence to present my credentials. I had been coached about the three bows I should make and how I should hand my letter of credence to the Emperor's aide. I managed this without stumbling and after my last bow found myself immediately in front of the Emperor. He smiled and put out his hand for me to shake. I bowed again and gave my short speech (which had been approved in advance by the Foreign Office and the Imperial Household Department), the Emperor replied briefly and then the members of my staff were brought into the room, and I presented them to the Emperor. There was more bowing and the ceremony was over. We backed out of the room and together with Mr. Goto returned to the Embassy, where our wives were waiting. Mr. Goto joined us in a glass of champagne.

Now that I had presented my credentials to the Emperor, I immediately had to start on one of the most wearisome tasks that is required of every new Ambassador. I had to make calls on all the other Ambassadors in Tokyo, beginning with the Dean of the Diplomatic Corps, the British Ambassador. This, at least, would not be a chore, because I had known Sir Esler (Bill) Dening for several years. We had worked together in London during the war, and before and during the negotiation of the Japanese Peace Treaty we had seen each other several times in Washington, London, and Canberra. Bill had been born in Japan of missionary parents, spoke the language and had lived there many years before the war. He was a good friend and counselor during my years in Tokyo. He was also an avid collector of Chinese ceramics, as was my wife, so he was always welcome in our home. Because Bill was Dean of the Diplomatic Corps, he had to be the first to leave a dinner party so that junior members of the Corps could go. Often, when at our residence for an official dinner, Bill would leave the party at the accepted time of around ten-thirty, but as soon as he was out of sight of the other guests, he would go to our upstairs study, where we would join him, after the remaining guests had left, for a final nightcap and usually a chat about Chinese porcelain.

Not only did an Ambassador have to make calls on all his colleagues who had arrived before him, he had to receive all of them as they returned his call. With most of them I had but little in common, and I had work to do as many of them did not. Once in a while one of my colleagues would actually have some information about local conditions which could have been obtained in no other way, but this was rare. However, if you skipped anyone he would claim to have been insulted and that his country had also been insulted. After all, diplomats are supposed to make friends not enemies, so you put on your short black coat, your striped trousers, took your black Homburg, and went out to have coffee or sherry and fifteen or twenty minutes of desultory conversation about how you liked or didn't like Tokyo and whether or not you played bridge, golf, or tennis. I had to explain that my bridge was terrible and that as for golf and tennis, I agreed with Dr. Johnson that any man who had walked upstairs at night and downstairs in the morning had had enough exercise for any normal human being.

While the calls went on, I had to find time to pay attention to other pressing matters. When we arrived in Tokyo I found present a team of Inspectors from the State Department, headed by the Chief Inspector, Raymond Miller, who was anxious to see how a comparatively new postwar Embassy was operating in a former enemy country. We both agreed that the American staff was far too large. There were 185 Americans as well as several hundred Japanese. What would Ambassador Grew have thought of such a mob? When war came in 1941 he had only some thirty people on his staff.

The Inspectors had made a thorough study of the operation of the Embassy, and Ray told me they wanted to put in a report recommending a cut of fifty positions. After studying their report I agreed, and we did succeed in cutting the American staff down to 135. Our triumph was not to last. Before I left Tokyo four years later, the American contingent was up to 169 as the result of pressure from various Washington agencies. I remember my amazement when I received a cable informing me that the FBI wanted to send an agent to the Embassy to be called a legal attaché. I pointed out to the Department that the army had both Intelligence and Counter-Intelligence units in Japan, that we had a swarm of CIA agents, and that the Embassy already had a legal attaché who was doing valuable work. The Department insisted, I continued to protest, and finally J. Edgar Hoover sent out his personal assistant on a special mission to convince me of the necessity of such an appointment. I got no support from Washington, so I reluctantly consented, and a nice young man showed up who seemed to be inoffensive and usually kept out of sight. I never did see any results of his work, but I heard that he got along well with the Japanese police. Eventually, of course, he had to have an assistant, presumably to play cribbage with him during the long hours when he had nothing to do.

My experience with the FBI should have taught me my lesson, but when some time later Harold Stassen, then Director of the Mutual Security Agency, wanted to assign a staff of his men to Tokyo to assist the Japanese improve their industrial productivity, I again protested. I was back in Washington on consultation, and I took the matter up personally with Secretary Dulles, but he only said, "Go over and see Harold and see what you can work out." It was obvious I was to get no support at the top. I did go and talk with Stassen who was determined to send his men to Tokyo. His voice almost choked as he asked, "How will we be able to live with ourselves five years from now if Japan's economy has gone to pieces and we have done nothing to help it?" We had a perfectly good economic section already in the Embassy which worked well with the Japanese, but Stassen's men came to Tokyo nevertheless. He did agree his Mission would be kept to fewer than twenty-five and that our Economic Counselor, Frank Waring, who had a Ph.D. in economics from the University of California, could be Deputy Head of the MSA Mission. To my pleasure he assigned as head of the Mission Clarence (Chief) Meyer, who as I have told, was head of Standard Oil in Japan before the war and had come home with me on the *Gripsholm*. Chief had headed an aid mission to Korea and most recently had been head of the MSA Mission in Vienna. Of course, Japan's economy did not go to pieces, and its productivity has long exceeded ours.

One of the other problems we had to deal with resulted from the large American military establishment of which the headquarters of the Commander-in-Chief, Far East, was located in Tokyo with a four-star general at its head. It was only little more than a year since the peace treaty had gone into effect and our military had lost their Occupation status and become troops based in Japan at the consent of the Japanese, who were no longer subject to an American military command. Many of the same men who had been in Japan under the Occupation were still there, and it was hard for them to become reconciled to their change in status. It was also difficult for some of them to understand that the American Embassy was no longer a subsection of the Military Headquarters and was not subject to military command. It was just as difficult for some of their dependents to understand the new situation. The wife of one of our Air Force Generals, at an Embassy reception, talked about the possibility of putting on a "debutantes' ball" and said, in a patronizing manner, "We'll invite some foreigners, too, and I'm sure they will love it." When I broke in to say that, after all, we were the foreigners in Japan, the good lady was visibly shocked. The ball was not held.

When we first arrived, General Mark Clark was CINCFE, and, while in some ways he was a bit of a prima donna, he did show an understanding of our problems and on several occasions was most helpful to the Embassy and the State Department in our disputes with the Pentagon over the best methods of persuading the Japanese to take more responsibility for their own 'defense. After General Clark departed, I was fortunate in having General John E. Hull, who turned out to be a most agreeable man to work with. He was followed by General Maxwell Taylor, who left shortly to become Army Chief of Staff. My last CINCFE colleague was General Lyman Lemnitzer. We had our differences and arguments, but in the end we got along without having to refer any matters to Washington for final settlement, and we are still friends today.

Another thing we had to remember in Embassy relations with our military was that the Japanese were watching our every move. They were asking themselves whether or not the Americans really meant it when they claimed that the military was subject to civilian control. The Japanese had had no experience with such a military, and their doubts that such a military could exist was one of the factors causing them to hold back on the development of their own defense forces. As one small contribution to their education in this regard, I insisted that new military commanders arriving in Japan should call first upon me at the Embassy, as the civilian personal representative of the President. In my day-to-day dealings with CINCFE, we worked out a system that whenever the General wished to see me about something he came to the Embassy. If I wished to see him, I went to his headquarters. After a few months, the Embassy set up with the Far East Command a Joint Consultative Group, headed on the military side by the Chief of Staff and on the

Embassy side by my Deputy. This group would meet alternately at Pershing Heights, the headquarters of the Far East Command, and at the Embassy. It would consider, and usually settle, all problems which arose. In the few cases where a stalemate resulted, the matter would be referred to the Commander-in-Chief and the Ambassador. As I have said, we never found it necessary to refer any problem to our superiors in Washington, a record of which I am proud.

One of the first things an American Ambassador in Japan had to do twenty years ago was to address the America-Japan Society. This speech was expected to give an indication of what the new Ambassador hoped to accomplish and also to set forth overall American policy toward Japan. At noon on June 12, 1953, I appeared at the Tokyo Kaikan to be greeted by 378 members and their guests. Among those at the head table was Admiral Kichisaburo Nomura, the Ambassador who had had the unpleasant duty of telling Secretary of State Hull that Japanese-American negotiations were broken off, on December 7, 1941, after the bombs had already begun to rain down on Pearl Harbor. I am sure Admiral Nomura had no detailed advance information about when war would come, although I am sure he knew it would come if negotiations failed. We came to be good friends, and he was always available for consultation whenever we desired. Unfortunately, Admiral Nomura and many of the other Japanese of his generation, who were the staunchest members of the America-Japan Society just after the war, were not in tune with the younger postwar Japanese, and their advice about local conditions, while freely given and with sincere good will, was not always relevant.

I spoke for some thirty minutes and dealt with the rise in American interest in Japan, the hopes of the United States for a peaceful and stable postwar world which had been frustrated by the actions of Soviet Russia, and how the Russians had miscalculated American reactions. Toward the end of my talk, I devoted about three or four minutes to a brief description of the American Mutual Security Program and how Japan might be included if she so desired. The local press had been full of reports about the program, and I said in my speech:

> In fact I sometimes think there has been discussion of nothing else. I have been somewhat disturbed by misconceptions which exist . . . It has not been especially devised for the sole purpose of making Japan a slave of U.S. policy. It is not a subtle scheme for getting Japanese soldiers to fight for us in Korea or elsewhere. . . . It is our belief that Japan's first duty for many years to come will be to ensure the integrity and security of Japan.

I went on to explain that planning for the Mutual Security Program had to be done long in advance, and until the treaty of peace with Japan had gone into effect, it had not been possible to include Japan in this program. Now it was, but then I emphasized that:

> Aid under the Mutual Security Program is not something which the U.S. either would or could force upon Japan. It constitutes an offer only and it is for the Japanese government and people to decide whether they wish to participate in this program. If they do so decide, the aid will apply to Japan in the same way that it applies to all the other nations . . . who have joined in this cooperative enterprise for peace. None of these nations has been compelled to accept arms — none of them has been asked to contribute more than her economic circumstances would permit. In all cases decisions as to what to do under the program are made voluntarily after mutual discussion. So much for MSA — it is Japan's if she wants it — if she does not, that is for Japan to say.

My discussion of MSA took less than five minutes, but in the press reports of my speech, which were in all the Tokyo afternoon papers, mostly in the leading position on the front page, the emphasis was given to those few minutes. According to a message the Embassy sent that night to the State Department, the headlines generally proclaimed that the United States did not intend to make unreasonable demands nor attempt to involve Japanese troops in fighting abroad. The head of the

American Bureau of the Foreign Office was reported to have been enthusiastic over the extent and nature of the press coverage and expressed great satisfaction that so much attention had been given to the MSA program. My own feeling of satisfaction at what seemed to be a good press was destined to be short-lived.

Shortly after the America-Japan Society address, I was called upon to speak to a combined meeting of the American Chamber of Commerce and the Japanese Chamber. In view of the audience I laid particular stress on the fact that the American Government and its leaders were keenly aware of the economic problems confronting Japan, and I stressed the fact that President Eisenhower realized the concern felt by the people of Japan over the problem of how to create means to defend themselves, so that they would not be dependent upon others and at the same time not weaken the economic fabric of the nation. I pointed out that the President believed that if a country does not have a sound economic base, the mere possession of arms will be of no avail.

It is difficult for those who look at the economic giant Japan is today to realize how real were the concerns of the people in 1953 about their economic future. Based on Japanese Government statistics, and the reports of my own economic staff, I predicted in my talk that the trade deficit in 1953 might well reach the figure of $1.15 billion, which would certainly be in excess of the special dollar receipts from United States expenditures in Japan, amounting to a little more than $800 million, and would result in a reduction in foreign exchange reserves of approximately $350 million. Not quite twenty years later the Japanese Government is concerned about too large reserves. In February of 1972, the Minister of International Trade and Industry predicted that before March 1973, Japanese currency reserves would top the $20 billion level and might force another yen revaluation unless checked.

I knew that one of the principal tasks during my first year in

Tokyo would be to persuade the Japanese Government to begin to take part in the provision of their own defense. Only as their own strength was developed would it be possible for American troops to be withdrawn. It was not necessary to be long in Japan to realize that while the government and business circles were happy about the number of dollars being spent annually in Japan by the United States, at the same time the presence in the country of foreign troops and dependents, often living on a higher standard than the local population, was a constant source of friction and did little to advance Japanese-American friendship. It was hoped that the MSA Program would be the means by which Japan could gradually increase its defense posture and thus permit our troops to begin to leave.

On the day before my talk to the America-Japan Society, Foreign Minister Okazaki had invited me to lunch at his home, where he plied me with questions about MSA and what it would mean for Japan. He told me of the great concern of the Japanese people over the possible creation of another military caste and their fear that any participation in an American security program would mean Japanese forces would be sent abroad to fight America's battles. Even if this was not so, the people feared that the dire economic straits in which Japan then found itself would not permit the building up of a defense force. The people were also concerned that Japan, as a defeated former enemy, would be placed in an inferior position to other countries with which the United States had security agreements. Without over-stressing MSA, so that it would appear to be the only thing with which the United States was concerned in its relations with Japan, I had tried in my two talks to set at rest some of the concerns expressed by Mr. Okazaki. Before our negotiations were over, it would be necessary to repeat and expand these points many times.

Mr. Okazaki was a pleasant and easy man to deal with. Not easy because he agreed with everything I said, but because he was completely frank in explaining the Japanese point of view while at the same time understanding, as many Japanese did not, the underlying reasons for the position of the United States. Mr. Okazaki and I had first met in Nanking, China, back in January of 1938, when he had come to present the official Japanese Government apology for the incident in which I had been slapped by a Japanese soldier. We never mentioned this meeting, but I suppose it was often in the back of both our minds. As time went on we became the best of friends. I learned that he had been a student and graduate of the Atsugi Middle School, where I had taught English conversation when I first came to Japan in 1927. We once made a joint pilgrimage back to the old school, and some of the same teachers who had been there when I was, were still there. Although Mr. Okazaki had graduated before I arrived, he often referred to me as his teacher, just as Prime Minister Yoshida often spoke of me as a fellow "jail-bird."

Before we could get started on real negotiations, it was necessary for me to have several conversations with Okazaki to answer questions about MSA which had been posed by the Prime Minister and other Cabinet members. Finally, I suggested that the Japanese Government write the Embassy a letter setting forth the matters on which it required elucidation and which I could send to Washington for an official reply. The reply could then, if satisfactory to the Japanese Government, be made public. This was agreed to. The Government presented its questionnaire, the American answer was considered satisfactory, and it was made public on the afternoon of June 27, 1953.

At the same time as the American note was published, Prime Minister Yoshida issued a public statement making clear that he was in favor of Japan's accepting Mutual Security aid. Mr. Yoshida's statement said, "In the light of the American reply to the Japanese Government's inquiry I think there should be no objection to accepting MSA assistance." But then, with his usual caution, the Prime Minister added that the government had not made any official decision on whether or not to receive the aid.

Before this happened, however, we were to have the first of many flaps caused by indiscreet and impatient American officials in Washington who still seemed to think Japan would automatically agree to anything the United States suggested. General George Olmstead, then Director of Military Assistance, in testimony before the House Foreign Affairs Committee, was quoted in press reports reaching Tokyo as saying that discussions and negotiations "leading up to the bilateral agreement which is required for eligibility under the Military Defense Aid Program are progressing." This was directly contrary to statements Prime Minister Yoshida had made in the Diet, that no negotiations had yet taken place. I reported this to the Department on June 18 and said the Japanese press was again accusing Yoshida of bad faith and of carrying out "secret diplomacy." Even more disturbing was the statement attributed to the Assistant Defense Secretary, the late Frank Nash, that Japan could proceed with the development of safety forces despite constitutional limitations and that the constitutional provision is "an excuse for not doing something rather than the real obstacle that prevents our going and doing it." I pointed out that I realized the State Department had only limited power in preventing the publication of such statements but it would be most helpful if the Department could issue some clarifying statement to rectify the false impression given. I stressed that while General Clark and former Ambassador Murphy had talked with Yoshida, and I with Okazaki, these were strictly of an exploratory nature and "cannot legitimately be classed as negotiations." Fortunately the Department agreed and did issue a statement which said that an effort had been made to keep the Japanese Government informed about the general nature of the Mutual Security Program but that there had been no formal exchanges and nothing that could be described as "negotiations." This statement was released on June 23, and the Japanese Government agreed to the publication of the American note mentioned above.

The American note was published in full in the morning *Nippon Times* of June 27, 1953. Three specific points were made. First, any assistance for which Japan would become eligible under the MSA Program "would be designed to further the main objectives of the Program by enabling Japan to safeguard its internal security" and also to exercise its inherent right of individual or collective self-defense. Secondly, the economic stability of Japan would be "an essential element for consideration in the development of Japan's self-defense capacities." It was also stated, and was stressed in press accounts, that United States procurement in Japan of materials required for the Program would be increased if Japan decided to take part in the Program. Thirdly, the military obligations that Japan would assume under Section 511(a) of the Mutual Security Act would be met in the case of Japan by the fulfillment of those obligations that Japan had already assumed under the Security Treaty between the United States and Japan. The note stated specifically that "there is nothing in the Mutual Security Program or any existing treaty obligation between the United States and Japan which requires Japan to use its security forces except in self-defense."

The *Nippon Times* stressed the last point made and entitled its leading editorial favoring acceptance of MSA aid, "Nothing To Fear." Other papers were not so kind. The *Asahi*, in its editorial comment, maintained there was a possibility Japan would be called upon to despatch its forces abroad if it accepted MSA aid. It also expressed the fear that Article IX of the Japanese Constitution, renouncing warfare, might be turned into a dead letter if Japan concluded an MSA agreement. The *Mainichi* and other papers still concentrated on whether or not there had been secret negotiations and accused the government of "deceit" and "secrecy." The Left Socialist leader, Suzuki, said that preliminary talks had obviously been held and that the MSA Program was just another step toward setting up Japanese armed forces as auxiliary to the United States.

It was obvious that those opposed to the acceptance by Japan of MSA aid had already made up their minds and were not going to be influenced by anything either the Japanese or American Governments said. The only thing to do was go ahead. On June 30, therefore, the Japanese Government made public a note sent to the Embassy proposing talks between the two governments on a possible MSA agreement. The Embassy proposed, and the State Department approved, a reply agreeing to begin *talks*, not negotiations, on a mutually agreeable date.

When the talks began on July 15, 1953, I was somewhat surprised to discover that by then the Japanese Government was prepared to speak of "negotiations" and from then on everyone knew that such "negotiations" were taking place. I soon learned that while our problems with getting agreement from the Japanese to various points were not negligible, our problems with Washington and particularly the Pentagon were no less, and in some cases even more, difficult of solution. The generals and admirals, and some of their civilian colleagues, seemed to think it would be possible to make Japan into a forward bastion of American strategic strength with the Americans calling the tune and the Japanese meekly accepting their secondary role. The Embassy believed this was not only wrong but that any attempt to bring it about would only store up trouble for the future. In our disputes with Washington we were often given help by the top American military officers in Japan. Some of the colonels and lieutenant colonels were a bit troublesome, but we usually got cooperation from the generals and admirals.

It may be of some interest to tell briefly about three of the principal disputes which the Embassy had with Washington during the eight months of talks. These concerned: first, the status and size of the Military Assistance Advisory Group (MAAG), secondly, the control of military procurement in Japan, and thirdly, the American desire for a speedy buildup of Japanese defense forces. The first two of these disputes were principally with the Pentagon, but the third involved Secretary of State Dulles as much as the admirals and generals.

One of the matters that especially concerned the Japanese was that the MSA agreement with them should be on all fours with similar agreements signed by other nations with the United States. In all other previous agreements, the MAAG had been placed under the control of the Embassy and had usually been small in size. The Pentagon began by insisting that the MAAG in Japan should be under the exclusive control of the Commander-in-Chief, Far East. The Japanese made it clear early in the negotiations that they would not accept any MAAG that was not under the Embassy. I personally couldn't have cared less whether the MAAG was under the Embassy or CINCFE. However, I was convinced from my talks with the Japanese that the Pentagon would have to back down on this point or there would be no MSA agreement. General Clark was most helpful and informed the Pentagon that he saw no reason why the MAAG should not be under the Embassy. Eventually, reluctant agreement was received from Washington. Before this happened, however, we had a long drawn out fight over the size of MAAG. The first Pentagon estimate of the proper size for the MAAG was 1489, which would mean that it would be the largest MAAG in the world. I urgently cabled the State Department that I was shocked at this estimate. I pointed out that on Formosa there was a MAAG of 772 to deal with defense forces totalling 300,000 to 500,000, while on the most optimistic estimate the Japanese defense forces would not exceed 200,000 over the next two years. (Japanese ground forces are still less than 200,000 almost twenty years later.) Again General Clark agreed with the Embassy that the Pentagon estimate was too large. I told the State Department that I did not believe the Japanese would agree to more than 500. The Pentagon maintained that the size of MAAG could be reduced after there had been an opportunity to train Japanese to take over certain of their functions. We eventually reached a compromise, and the Embassy agreed to an original MAAG of 944 men which would be reduced to 500 by the end of 1954. Even this was much larger than the Japanese desired, but they finally agreed.

While the negotiations were still going on, the Defense Department proposed that it should appoint a civilian Defense Procurement Coordinator in Japan who would serve under, and be responsible to, CINCFE. In protesting such an appointment, I pointed out to the State Department that it ignored MAAG and its relationship to the buildup of Japanese defense forces and that Japanese agencies concerned with defense production were all civilian and accustomed to dealing on most issues with the Embassy and not the military. I went on to say that the Japanese would interpret the Defense Department proposal as indicating that the primary interest of the United States in Japan was in getting it to act in the military interests of the United States. The creation of a defense industry in Japan was of great political and economic significance for Japan as well as for all United States policy in Asia, and I said that apparently the Defense Department considered only its immediate effect on Japan and not its overall importance to Japan's future in Asia and how that would affect United States relations with other Asian nations. I added that the recent press and Diet questioning of possible United States interference in Japanese internal political and economic affairs had been intense and that the Defense Department proposal would only increase this criticism. The proposal would place in the hands of one man responsible only to CINCFE the power and funds with which to influence the whole gamut of Japanese economic policy. I concluded by pointing out that there was already a considerable amount of coordination between CINCFE and the Embassy on procurement and that the Defense Department proposal not only failed to attack the basic problem of improving coordination in Washington, as the Embassy had previously pointed out, but in fact endangered the then good coordination in Tokyo. The proposal eventually died, and, although the military in Washington made further attempts to take charge of Japanese affairs, the Embassy was able to maintain its right to be concerned in these affairs over which for seven years the military had had sole domination.

While these problems with the Pentagon were keeping us from relaxing and enjoying the alleged special privileges of diplomatic life, we were also worried by some of the actions of our own chief in Foggy Bottom. On July 10, 1953, I reported urgently to the State Department that a bulletin put out by the United Press in Washington stated that the Secretary had said that an immediate goal of ten divisions was envisioned for the Japanese defense forces in the new Japanese budget and indicated that United States funds would be needed to help Japan reach that goal. Such statements would be used by opposition elements to castigate the Japanese Government which had publicly maintained it had no intention of increasing the strength of the Japanese forces at that time. I further stated that the Embassy failed to understand the Secretary's statement, because, in fact, no such increase was provided for in the new Japanese budget. The Foreign Office had indicated that Prime Minister Yoshida was considering a small increase from the current strength of 110,000 to perhaps as much as 150,000 but that this would be impossible if it appeared that the United States was forcing the Japanese to do so. The State Department was requested to make a clarifying statement stressing that the press statement had been based upon a misunderstanding and that ten divisions was an ultimate, rather than an immediate, goal. I also urged that American officials in publicly discussing MSA matters refrain from mentioning the Japanese Constitution.

All was quiet for a time, and the MSA talks opened shortly.

However, the worst was yet to come. On July 29, I read in the morning papers that Secretary Dulles was going to visit Korea, and there was no mention of a stop in Japan. I immediately cabled the Department that it was most important that the Secretary stop in Tokyo for a day or two on his return from Korea. General Clark had telephoned me and said he, too, believed it important for the Secretary to stop in Tokyo upon his return. A visit from the Secretary would help at a time when constant criticism was being heard that Japan was only a United States puppet. It would give Yoshida an opportunity to say that the Secretary had come to Tokyo to ensure that Japan was kept informed on matters of deep interest to it, such as the situation in Korea. The prevalent feeling was that the United States had been unduly subservient to Syngman Rhee, and I said that a visit from Dulles might help to some extent to dissipate this feeling. I privately expressed surprise at the United States attitude toward Rhee and said that some Japanese had expressed malicious pleasure at the trouble the United States was having with him.

The Secretary decided to stop in Tokyo and for a time all seemed well. But on August 4, before he had arrived, another United Press story from Washington caused raised eyebrows in Tokyo. In his press conference on August 4, the Secretary was reported to have said: "The United States is considering the possibility of a mutual security pact covering Japan, Korea and Nationalist China . . . but no decision has been made." We again urgently cabled the State Department referring to previous Embassy reports that "at present" there was practically no chance that Japan would consider joining such a pact and any possibility that Japan might consider doing so was greatly prejudiced by such stories as carried by the United Press. These seemed to imply that the decision about such a pact was one solely for the United States to make and that Japan as well as other Asian countries would then have to agree. Nothing was heard from Washington, but again for a time there was quiet along the Potomac.

Secretary Dulles finally arrived and had long talks with Yoshida and other Japanese leaders. He was also able to give Yoshida a present by informing him that the United States was preparing to hand back to Japan the Amami Oshima group of islands in the northernmost part of the Ryukyu chain. This was done at lunch on a Sunday and created an immediate good impression. Unfortunately, it did not last long. Also in Tokyo was James Reston of the *New York Times* who insisted upon having an interview with the Secretary. None of us approved, but the Secretary finally consented on the condition that it would not be an exclusive interview and that it would be "off the record." The only other American press man available that afternoon was Robert Sherrod of the *Saturday Evening Post*. Both of them came to the Embassy and for about an hour Mr. Dulles talked to them frankly and in detail about his discussions with the Japanese and his disappointment with their slowness in building up their defense forces. In addition to Reston and Sherrod, Assistant Secretary Robertson and Assistant Secretary McCardle, in charge of press relations, and I were present at the interview. Reston and Sherrod finally left, and shortly afterward Mr. Dulles and his party took off for Washington. Reston left for Washington the same evening.

The next morning I was amazed and shocked to see a full column in the Japanese *Asahi* newspaper, which subscribed to the *New York Times* news service, reporting in detail what Dulles had told the reporters. The afternoon English language *Asahi News* also carried the story, with Reston's by-line. I cabled the Secretary at once pointing out that this breach of confidence and lack of responsibility on Reston's part was inexcusable as all present at the interview, including Reston, had expressed their understanding that it was "off the record." In his story Reston reported as fact that Dulles "expressed extreme dissatisfaction with the passive attitude of the Japanese Government toward the defense of Asia." He went on to report that Dulles "had found it difficult to understand why Japan could not have more than four divisions when Korea with only one-fourth the population had plans to build a 20-division army." The rest of the story was just as bad. I expressed the fear that much of the good impression created by Dulles's announcement about the return of the Amami Oshima group would be wiped out by this story, which all Japanese newspapers had repeated and played up in their afternoon editions. I said it would have been hard for Reston to have published anything that could have done more harm to American-Japanese relations, and I urged a strong protest be made to the *Times*. Nothing was done, and Reston continued to be welcome at Dulles press conferences.

During my more than thirty years in the Foreign Service, I have only experienced two cases in which confidences have been betrayed by the press. In addition to the case of Mr. Reston, a correspondent for the *Christian Science Monitor* who attended an "off the record" interview I gave at the request of Phil Potter of the Baltimore *Sun*, published substantial portions of the interview without my permission. My experience with such correspondents as Potter, Keyes Beech of the Chicago *Daily News*, Bob Eunson of the Associated Press, Stewart Hensley of the United Press, Bob Trumbull and the late Foster Hailey of the *New York Times* have been most pleasant, and I think we learned to like and trust one another as friends. Bob Sherrod was always most correct, and I never knew him to betray a confidence. Not only were my relations with these representatives of the press pleasant, they were most useful. I am sure I learned as much, if not more, from them than they did from me.

In spite of the temporary furor caused by Reston's article, the State Department, under Mr. Dulles's guidance, persisted in talking publicly about the need for increased Japanese rearmament. Mr. Dulles had hardly had time to get back to Washington and get settled in his office, when we were faced with another press flap. The Japanese *Asahi* had submitted a questionnaire to Dulles and on August 14 his answers were published. I cabled my concern to the State Department and reported that the Japanese press had published the answers under the headlines: "Dulles Reiterates Hopes Japan Will Boost Defense." I expressed my regret that the answers, which I presumed had been drafted in the Bureau of Far Eastern Affairs, had not been referred to the Embassy for clearance, and I stressed that continued public statements about the United States' desire for Japanese rearmament would have a bad effect in Japan. I stated that Embassy officers would continue to press privately for speedier Japanese action but that public statements by United States officials were considered only as interference and used by the opposition and the Japanese Communists as a stick with which to beat the government. I concluded by pointing out that the present United States Government had not yet taken the Japanese Government into its confidence regarding United States policies in Asia and that until we were willing to talk as frankly to the Japanese as we had to the Filipinos and to the Koreans, the Japanese Government would be slow to respond to United States demands.

All the Embassy protests about public statements seemed to fall on fallow ground. Mr. Dulles was an activist, and he was sincerely convinced that Soviet Russia posed an immediate threat that could only be counteracted if the United States and all its friends maintained a strong military position. Mr. Dulles also seemed unable to visualize what his answers to questions from the press would look like when they appeared in print. He had little real understanding of how the Japanese or any other Oriental people thought and assumed they would automatically respond to ideas in the same way as Westerners.

Once again in early September, in a Washington press conference, Dulles returned to the fray. He was quoted in the Japanese press as again urging Japanese rearmament, and nearly all stories contained such statements as "Dulles urges Japan to hike own defense" and "Dulles urges Japan to rearm." I reported to the State Department that the manner in which the Japanese press had reported the press conference might indicate a definite attempt by the Japanese to blame the United States for unpopular actions that they knew were necessary instead of having the blame attached to the Japanese Government. The austere economic measures required by increased rearmament activity were most unpopular, and we reported that many Japanese leaders were talking to the press with the same attitude as was prevalent during the Occupation, when unpopular measures were taken by the government but explained as being the result of United States demands. In addition, I feared Japanese officials might take increasing advantage of such statements as the Secretary's to justify their actions that publicly they would not advocate. If Japanese leaders acted only on our insistence and made no real effort to educate their public as to the soundness of such action, we might find we had obtained a defense establishment without the one thing necessary, the belief of the Japanese people in their own cause with consequent strengthening of their will to defend their way of life.

While our troubles with Washington concerned us, we were equally concerned at the prodigal attitude of the Japanese Government, which seemed confident that the United States would bail it out of any economic troubles. We reported to the State Department that past Japanese policies such as tax reduction, deficit financing, easy credit facilities, and nonessential investment had created problems which the Japanese Government had not been willing to face up to. We expressed the fear that the increase in special dollar earnings by Japan, which were estimated to reach more than $1 billion in fiscal 1954, as compared with $816 million in fiscal 1953, would only add to the difficulties and make possible continued Japanese refusal to face up to hard facts.

In late August 1953, Mr. Dulles had written Prime Minister Yoshida inviting him to Washington, but Yoshida hesitated to go before he had achieved a stronger position politically so that he could give definite replies to the questions he expected to be asked by the Americans. We reported to Washington that prospects for a merger of the conservative parties were not good and that we had received reports from good Japanese sources that the Reston article had delayed efforts of the government party to bring about the merger, because the opposition parties interpreted it as meaning that Yoshida had lost the confidence of the United States. In early September Yoshida decided to send one of his most able and trusted advisors, the late Hayato Ikeda, to the United States as an advance emissary. Ikeda was later to become Finance Minister under Yoshida, and eventually he served as Prime Minister of a united Conservative government.

In reporting the forthcoming visit of Ikeda, the Embassy urged the State Department to use the visit as an opportunity to develop new policies toward Japan aimed at remedying, at least in part, the bad Japanese fiscal policies mentioned above. We suggested that the United States should stop demanding publicly that Japan reform its fiscal policies but only permit a higher flow of special dollars if Japan began to correct the defects noted. We also said that while maintaining pressure for the expansion of Japanese defense forces, we should give much more attention to getting Japan to adopt corrective economic and financial measures. In short, we recommended that Japan be given a second dose of the medicine prescribed by Joseph Dodge, then Director of the Bureau of the Budget, when he acted as a financial advisor to General MacArthur during the Occupation. However, we again warned the Department to remember that Japan was no longer an occupied country and that it would not take this medicine merely on demand. We urged that Ikeda be talked to frankly and be given a detailed explanation of American thinking about Japan's position in Asia and the reasons for our concern over the lack of what we thought adequate Japanese action in both the economic and defense fields. We informed the Department that we understood Ikeda did not have detailed negotiating authority in the defense field but was prepared to discuss all matters in a general way. The talks with Ikeda might pave the way for commitments by Yoshida if he later went to Washington or, if not, in Tokyo.

While Ikeda was in the United States, we were shocked to learn that the Defense Department was planning to build up United States troop strength in Japan to four divisions and keep them there without reduction until Japanese ground forces reached at least 200,000. (If this policy had been carried out, there would still have been four United States divisions in Japan in 1972.) We pointed out to the Department that this buildup was being considered at a time when the Japanese were assuming that as they increased their forces, United States forces would be withdrawn. In my opening statement at the inauguration of the MSA negotiations only about two months previously, in referring to the development of Japanese strength to protect itself, I had said: "As Japan develops this strength it is the expectation of my government that United States forces in Japan can be progressively reduced." Revelation of the plan to increase United States forces could destroy a major incentive for the buildup of Japanese forces.

In a second message to the Department on the same subject, on October 5, I said that if the State Department was convinced of the necessity for this United States buildup, I could not emphasize too strongly the need for making clear to Ikeda the reasons for this. On the previous evening, the former Ambassador to Russia and France, Bill Bullitt, en route to Korea, had told me there was a strong feeling among Washington leaders that time was running out and that great speed was needed in developing a worldwide defense system. If this was so, I had been given no information which would enable me to argue the point successfully with Japanese leaders, and I suggested that if Yoshida went to Washington, the leaders there should be frank with him, and that I should go along to get the benefit of their thinking.

The amazing thing to me was the way in which Washington leaders apparently took no notice of what Japan was doing in the defense field under serious handicaps, some of them of American origin. The Japanese people had become thoroughly disillusioned with their former military caste and did not want to build a new one. General MacArthur's statement that Japan should become the "Switzerland of Asia" still had a powerful grip on them. Their antiwar Constitution, again largely due to General MacArthur, was considered by the people as a safeguard which should not be tampered with. In spite of all this, Japanese leaders had gone far ahead of their people in realizing that in the real world of the 1950s Japan should begin building an adequate defense establishment. On September 27, 1953, Prime Minister Yoshida and Mr. M. Shigemitsu, leader of the opposition Conservative party, had a conference on defense matters and in a public communiqué had linked Japan's defense buildup to withdrawal of United States forces and had also agreed that the National Safety Agency law should be immediately amended to convert the National *Safety* Force to a National *Defense* Force. This was a big step forward as seen from Tokyo although not perhaps from Washington. But Washington still wanted everything to be done at once and couldn't understand why the Japanese leaders seemed to be continually dragging their feet. However, the four divisions did not come, whether due to the Embassy's protests or because the Far East Command was also skeptical, I don't know.

During all these exchanges between Tokyo and Washington,

our talks with the Japanese about the MSA agreement continued. For a time the talks went well and at one point it looked as if they could be concluded before the end of 1953, but early in December of that year I reported to the State Department that the Japanese were insisting on an advance understanding with the United States on force goals for Japan before signing the agreement. We were told by Mr. Shimoda, head of the Japanese drafting group, later Ambassador to Washington, and now, in 1972, a member of the Japanese Supreme Court, that the Japanese insistence was due to their hopes of being first able to complete their defense plans and budget in order that the government would not be embarrassed in the Diet by its inability to explain satisfactorily the scope and extent of the assistance contemplated under the agreement.

The Japanese later altered their position and wished the United States to sign the agreement without a firm Japanese commitment of how much they would increase their defense forces. At the end of December, Foreign Minister Okazaki, in a meeting with General Hull and me, urged that the United States take it on faith that the Japanese Government would decide early in 1954 on defense levels, which would be the maximum politically possible. He said he did not wish to bargain in this sensitive area. General Hull and I agreed that while the effort decided upon was far from impressive by United States standards, it would put Japan on the road toward assuming responsibility for its own defense. I urged Washington to accept the views of General Hull and myself and again emphasized the fact that the present Japanese Government was far ahead of Japanese public opinion.

The talks jockeyed back and forth for several more weeks, and it was not until March of 1954 that the agreement was finally signed. In an effort to get speedy agreement in Washington, we had pointed out that the Embassy believed there was little prospect of improvement in the Japanese position. We reported that the effort to unify the conservative parties was gaining strength and that prolonged wrangling over the defense issue between Japan and the United States, which could not be kept secret, might well scotch the efforts to create a strong conservative party.

At last in early March of 1954, all the minor technical points had been cleared up and on March 8, the agreement was signed by Foreign Minister Okazaki and me at a public ceremony at the Foreign Office. In addition to the Mutual Defense Agreement, we signed three allied agreements: an Investment Guaranty Agreement, an agreement for the purchase by Japan in yen of needed agricultural products, and a companion Economic Arrangements Agreement.

In emphasizing two points that were of constant concern, I said in a public statement: "This agreement takes us one step nearer the time when the Japanese people will not need to rely on American forces for protection. It takes us one step nearer the time when the United States can withdraw its forces from Japan." I added: "It is also important . . . to point out that this agreement is not unique but that in signing it the Japanese Government is following a pattern already set by many countries in all parts of the world."

In June 1953, Mrs. Eleanor Roosevelt visited Tokyo. Her visit was at the invitation of the Japanese Committee of Intellectual Interchange. Her obvious friendliness, sincerity, and real interest in the Japanese people, of all walks of life, and their problems made her visit a great success. She met with women's groups, farmers near Sendai in northern Japan, and finally with the Emperor and Empress. The audience at the Palace lasted almost an hour, an unusually long time, but both the Emperor and Empress were interested in everything Mrs. Roosevelt had been doing and questioned her at length. She was tremendously impressed by the Imperial couple, and after she returned home she wrote an article about her audience which she hoped to publish. Fortunately she sent me a copy and asked whether or not I thought she should publish it. From an American viewpoint it was a good story and placed the Emperor and Empress in a favorable light, but the officials in the Imperial Household were still hesitant about allowing any direct quotation of the Emperor and made it clear to me that they would much prefer that Mrs. Roosevelt not publish the article. When she was informed of the Japanese reaction she graciously withheld her article. While one could often disagree with Mrs. Roosevelt's ideas and question some of her actions, it was not possible to spend time with her and not realize that here was a great lady.

In the fall of 1953, the return of the Crown Prince from an extended tour to the United States, the United Kingdom, and Western Europe was hailed by the whole country. The British Ambassador and I decided we would each give him a dinner if the Imperial Household would grant permission, which in due course it did. Prior to World War II members of the Imperial family seldom were entertained by the foreign embassies, and when they were, it was an extremely stiff and formal occasion with both guests and hosts being glad when it was over. Since the war the younger brothers of the Emperor and their wives, Prince and Princess Takamatsu and Prince and Princess Mikasa as well as Princess Chichibu, the widow of the Emperor's oldest brother, often attended Embassy receptions and dinners and were most informal, but the Crown Prince was in a slightly different category. The British Ambassador decided that he would follow a modified Japanese style at his dinner party, and when the Crown Prince arrived the Japanese guests were lined up in one group and the foreigners in another. The Prince first shook hands with the foreigners and then went down the Japanese line, bowing in Japanese style to each.

When it came our turn to have the Prince, we made inquiries at the Imperial Household to find out whether or not it would be all right if we followed American custom. We were told that the normal polite way of receiving distinguished guests at an American dinner party would be acceptable. When the Prince arrived at our residence, all the guests, both Japanese and foreign, were lined up together side by side completely intermixed. To the astonishment of our Japanese guests, the Prince went down the line and shook hands with them as well as with the foreigners. A precedent had been broken. It was not the first time this had happened at the American Embassy. The late Joseph Grew, Ambassador in Tokyo before World War II, tells in his *Ten Years in Japan* how, at the reception given at the American Embassy when his youngest daughter was married, he introduced Prince Chichibu to the Canadian Minister, the Dutch Minister, and several other Ministers. Prior to that time the Imperial Princes had only been introduced to Ambassadors. The problem would not arise today, of course, when inflation has hit diplomatic titles as well as the dollar, and those who were once Ministers are now almost all Ambassadors, whether they come from large or small countries.

Vice President and Mrs. Nixon had been sent by President Eisenhower on a worldwide "Good Will" tour, and in November they were scheduled to visit Japan. The Japanese Government invited them as the first State Guests since the end of World War II, and elaborate plans were made for their reception. The Nixons accepted the Japanese Government's invitation to be State Guests, but indicated they would prefer to stay at the American Embassy residence while in Tokyo. Our Japanese housekeeper, a charming, efficient lady, who had lost her husband during the war, was all aflutter at the prospect, but she assured my wife that she and our fine staff of servants would be able to cope with the situation.

Several weeks before the arrival of the Nixons, an advance party of Secret Service and White House officials showed up and gave us our first inkling of what to expect. We were told that in addition to the Nixons, a Secret Service man and the military aide to the Vice President would stay at the Embassy residence. We were told that in addition to the usual greeters at the airport, high Japanese Government officials and the whole Diplomatic Corps, the Vice President wanted assembled where he could greet them, a group of the "common people," the ordinary Japanese men and women who usually watched from afar. We were told that the highway from the airport to the Embassy, some fifteen miles, should be lined with Japanese school children carrying American and Japanese flags. Finally we were told that the police should keep the highway clear of other traffic, because the Vice President would wish to alight from his car from time to time to greet and shake hands with people on the sidewalks and have his picture taken by press photographers, who would be in a car immediately behind that of the Vice President. I incautiously remarked that I didn't know that Mr. Nixon was running for office in Japan and was glared at by members of the advance party.

After having been told all that we were expected to arrange, we were finally asked a question. One of the Secret Service men wanted to know what kind of presents the members of the Vice President's party, including the Secret Service members, might expect to receive from the Japanese. I stated that I was sure the Vice President and Mrs. Nixon would receive a large number of valuable and interesting presents, as befitted their position, but that I did not anticipate that other members of the party would receive anything, and I certainly did not intend to suggest to the Japanese that they should. My popularity with the advance party received another blow.

We informed the Foreign Ministry of everything the advance party had told us and were assured that the Vice President's wishes would be carried out to the best of their ability. The great day finally arrived, and at one-thirty on the afternoon of November 15 the Nixons arrived at the old Haneda Airport. The Japanese Cabinet and the members of the Diplomatic

Corps were lined up on the airfield at the foot of the plane's gangway. Behind a temporary fence about one hundred feet away, were the "common people" waiting to be greeted by Mr. Nixon. It was obvious that the Vice President was displeased, but he went down the line and shook hands with the members of the Cabinet and the diplomats and then strode over and reached across the barrier to shake hands with twenty or thirty of the people nearest him. We then got in our motorcars and began the long journey back to the Embassy.

The school children were just where they should have been and as they grinned and waved their Japanese and American flags, the Vice President's mood seemed to brighten. We were preceded by motorcycle policemen and a car full of Secret Service men. Just behind was the press car full of photographers, and then came the car with Mrs. Nixon and other members of the party. After we had gone a mile or two and had reached the more built-up outskirts of the city, the Vice President asked me to tell the driver to stop the car, and we all got out. Foreign Minister Okazaki was riding with us, and he looked on with a rather sardonic smile as Mr. Nixon went from one side of the street to the other shaking hands with astonished Japanese, most of whom seemed embarrassed rather than pleased. After about five or six minutes of this we got back in the car, but every mile or two the performance was repeated, and the press was kept busy taking pictures.

We finally arrived at the Embassy residence, and our whole staff of servants were lined up in a semicircle before the door, dressed in their finest ceremonial kimonos, waiting to greet the Nixons. The press photographers surged around and bulbs flashed, while the Vice President shook hands with all the servants and patted the shoulders of dignified, old Funayama-san, our Chief Butler, who turned as red as if he had just finished a quart of sake. The Nixons were conducted to the guest suite, a Secret Service man was installed in an adjoining bedroom, and Brigadier General Paul Caraway, the military aide, had the next bedroom and shared a bath with "Bill," the Secret Service man, whose last name we never learned. Nobu-san, our housekeeper, went up with Mrs. Nixon and asked her if there was any laundry or pressing needed, but Mrs. Nixon apparently preferred to do everything herself, as all she asked for was an iron and ironing board, which was reluctantly provided, because Nobu-san thought it was a reflection on the staff that Mrs. Nixon would not let it take care of these matters.

It was a busy day for the Vice President. He had left Seoul, Korea, that morning and on the plane had been briefed about Japan by Jeff Parsons, our Minister Counselor of Embassy, who had flown to Korea to meet him. At three o'clock that afternoon Mr. Nixon was given a more detailed briefing at the Embassy by General Hull and myself and our senior staffs. It was the first time many of us had met the Vice President, and it was his first visit to Asia. We were all impressed by the intelligent questions he asked and the obvious diligence with which he had done his homework. The briefing lasted until approximately five o'clock, and then at seven-thirty the Nixons had to appear at a black-tie dinner we gave for thirty-five leading Japanese officials, senior American officers of the Far East Command and their wives, the President of the American Chamber of Commerce and his wife, the Parsons, and ourselves. After dinner we were joined by some sixty more representatives of the American civil and military communities and senior members of the Embassy staff and their wives. There were also present the three members of the House of Representatives Appropriations Committee who were visiting Tokyo at the time. The Nixons retired shortly after ten, and by eleven o'clock, when the last guest had departed, we fell into bed exhausted, both physically and emotionally.

The following four days were among the most hectic I have ever experienced. The Vice President had two interviews with

Prime Minister Yoshida. He and Mrs. Nixon had an audience and luncheon with the Emperor and Empress after which Mr. Nixon attended a program arranged by the Far East Command, and Mrs. Nixon was given a reception by a group of women's organizations at the Prime Minister's official residence. The Prime Minister gave them a dinner, the Speaker of the House of Representatives and the President of the House of Councillors gave them a reception, and they spent part of an afternoon at the Kabuki-za, the old traditional Japanese theatre. Mr. Nixon had meetings with Japanese and American businessmen, and the whole Nixon party spent a day visiting Kyoto, Nara, and Osaka. A free day was scheduled but unexpected appointments broke it up. The whole visit was climaxed by a luncheon, given jointly by the America-Japan Society and the American Chamber of Commerce in Japan, where some seven hundred Japanese and Americans heard the Vice President admit that the United States had made a mistake in 1946 when it urged the Japanese to forgo the maintenance of a military force and encouraged the military and economic disarmament of Japan. To read Mr. Nixon's speech of November 1953, with its talk of the necessity of free world rearmament because of the threat of international communism, and then read President Nixon's February 1972 Report to the Congress on U.S. Foreign Policy for the 1970s, with its acknowledgment of the end of a monolithic communism and the need for establishing a peaceful dialogue with Soviet Russia and the People's Republic of China, gives one a graphic picture of how the world has changed in twenty years and how Mr. Nixon has changed with it.

On the morning of November 20, the visit of the first State Guests of postwar Japan came to an end, and the Nixons departed for Okinawa and Manila. Their plane was full of presents of all kinds, including a suit of Samurai armor. As far as I know, the members of his party, including the Secret Service men, received no gifts, and I suppose they still blame me for this, although I was never consulted by the Japanese regarding the matter and never volunteered any comments. The Vice President was again slightly annoyed during his departure, because the school children with their flags were all on the wrong side of the road. The Vice President took the seat of honor on the right in our car going back to the airport, and the school children were all lined up on the left side of the road, just as they had been when the Nixons arrived. After again shaking hands with members of the Cabinet and the Diplomatic Corps, saying a few words to the press, and submitting to myriads of photographs, the Nixons took off promptly at seven-thirty in the morning. The Embassy gradually settled down, and I finally caught up with what had been happening in the world during the four days our guests had been with us.

However, of guests we never lacked. During our first year in Tokyo we had a total of more than fifty house guests, mostly Senators or Congressmen, government officials, or people with letters of introduction from Senators or Congressmen. This continued all during our stay in Japan, and while most of our guests came to be good friends, there were those who didn't.

Shortly before Christmas, during the last three years we were in Tokyo, we held an open house at the residence, and the Embassy Wives' Club sold tickets at a dollar apiece to raise money to support a nursery for a group of poor children whose fathers had vanished and whose mothers worked. There was still a substantial American military establishment in Japan, and the wives of the soldiers, sailors, and air force men seemed to have an inexhaustible desire to see the Embassy residence and have pointed out to them where General MacArthur slept when he lived there. On the day of the annual reception a thousand women and a few stray men marched through the residence. Embassy wives were stationed in each room to explain the different kinds of furniture, the paintings, and various art objects. In the guest suite, my wife, with tongue in cheek, had placed a card with a long list of names and the heading, "The following people have slept here." She then listed our guests, Republicans and Democrats alternated, beginning with Mrs. Eleanor Roosevelt, Senator William Knowland, Adlai Stevenson, Senator and Mrs. Smith of New Jersey, and Senator Estes Kefauver. At the bottom of the card was the additional statement: "But be it distinctly understood, not all at the same time!" But they still wanted to know where General MacArthur slept. I was a bit flattered when I was told that one lady even asked "Where does the Ambassador sleep?" but I was somewhat appalled when I discovered that the Embassy wife's reply was, "I really don't know. You see I've only been here two weeks."

The Japanese were gradually regaining their self-confidence and toward the end of July, the Japanese Supreme Court held unconstitutional by an 11–4 decision a Japanese law which incorporated an Occupation directive banning the circulation of Communist literature. The Court's decision established the principle that all post-treaty Japanese legislation based upon Occupation directives must meet the test of validity under the Japanese Constitution. This was one of the first indications that Japan would no longer automatically acquiesce in American desires about Japanese policy. During the next three years we often wondered whether the State Department or the Pentagon had ever heard of this decision.

At the end of September Foreign Minister Okazaki and I signed an agreement removing the extraterritorial status of United States forces stationed in Japan and made them amenable to Japanese jurisdiction in the same manner as American troops in NATO countries were amenable to local jurisdiction under the Atlantic Treaty Status of Forces Agreement. This was a big step toward removing one of the chief causes of friction between our two governments. According to the *Nippon Times* of September 30, 1953, even the right and left wing Socialists "hailed the signing of the protocol. They said 'it proves another forward step' made toward Japan's real independence." Although during the remainder of my time in Tokyo, the Japanese waived jurisdiction over the vast majority of cases in which they could have prosecuted American military men and gave lenient sentences in those cases in which they did assume jurisdiction, many Americans, including visiting American Congressmen, continued to denounce the agreement as placing "American boys under alien laws." Of course, many of the Japanese laws had been revised during the Occupation to bring them into line with international standards, but this was seemingly forgotten.

In the autumn of 1953, it looked as if the friction between Japan and Korea might become truly dangerous. President Rhee of Korea had established a line some fifty miles off the Korean coast and declared that any Japanese fishing vessels found between that line and Korea would be confiscated and its crew imprisoned. Already some five hundred Japanese fishermen were in jail in Korea, and the Japanese public was becoming increasingly agitated. For a time it looked as if Washington wanted to wash its hands of the whole matter, but Foreign Minister Okazaki pointed out the absurdity of this when he raised the question with me of what would happen if an armed Japanese frigate, loaned by the United States to Japan, should, in protecting Japanese fishing boats, engage in hostilities with an armed Korean frigate, loaned to Korea by the United States.

This problem of Korean-Japanese friction was to be with us for some time and took up much of the time of our staff and that of the American Embassy in Seoul. By the end of the year, Washington had agreed to the provision that American observers sit in on negotiations between the two countries which were designed to settle all outstanding problems. The Koreans, under the instigation of Rhee, adopted a most intransigent line, and, in the opinion of most of us in Tokyo, were being completely unreasonable. The Japanese had offered many concessions on the fishing problem, and we believed that if Korea showed any good will, the Japanese could be persuaded to offer more in the general financial and economic talks being conducted at the same time as those on the fisheries problem. At the end of the year Rhee was due to head a high-level Korean Mission to Washington, and I recommended to the State Department that we make clear to him that we endorsed what General Hull had told his superiors in Washington, namely; we must face up to the fact that Korea is a small nation surrounded by three powerful neighbors, only one of which, Japan, was friendly to the free world, and it is therefore essential that Korea realize that its safety and future progress, as well as that of the West, depends upon the renewal of friendly relations with Japan, and this can only come about through compromise and cooperation on both sides. It was several years before a Japanese-Korean settlement was agreed upon, but at least, in the meantime, we did manage to keep the incipient fire from bursting into flames.

On the last day of 1953, the Embassy was able to report to Washington that the government and many conservative leaders finally seemed to be concerned about Japan's economic plight and that there was increasing support for the firm stand Prime Minister Yoshida was taking in pushing through an austerity budget as well as politically unpopular economic measures and domestic reforms. We told the State Department it was just possible that the Japanese people were at last beginning to find themselves and were starting on the difficult road back to a viable economy and a stable society under a conservative leadership.

With the coming of the New Year and the New Year's Reception for the Diplomatic Corps by the Imperial family, the Americans again broke tradition. Traditional Court protocol had decreed that when diplomats entered the room where sat the Emperor and Empress, flanked by the other members of the Imperial family, they would bow three times as they approached the Throne and then back out of the room by another door, making three more bows en route. Their wives, who followed them, would make three curtsies as they entered, and as they left, the Imperial presence. My wife would have nothing of it. She claimed the curtsy was a European, and not an American, way of showing respect and that it was not a traditional Japanese custom either, because the Japanese bowed when showing respect. To the undisguised horror of the wife of my Deputy Chief of Mission — who, although an American citizen, had been born and brought up in Canada and had been visiting her uncle, the Canadian Minister to Japan, when she and her husband met — Toots announced to the Embassy wives that she intended to make three traditional Japanese bows rather than curtsy. She said the wives could do as they wished, but she just wanted them to know what she was going to do. I confess that I, too, was somewhat disturbed when I first heard what she intended to do. However, I knew there would be no turning back once my wife had made up her mind, and so I merely looked up the shipping schedules to see about passage back to America when the Japanese asked for my recall.

New Year's Day dawned bright and clear, and just before noon we all drove up to the Palace and were herded into a large reception room with other members of the Diplomatic Corps. The Europeans were all in their splendid uniforms complete with medals, swords, and plumed hats, while we were decked out in sombre white tie and tails. Peggy Parsons, the Deputy's wife, was obviously nervous, but she was a good sport and a loyal friend. If the Ambassador's wife was going to bow, she would bow too, although I'm sure it seared her soul. I had to precede my wife, so I could not see what happened, but she told me later that although the Emperor and Empress kept straight faces, she noticed that Princess Chichibu and Prince and Princess Takamatsu gave what seemed to be an approving smile and nod. A few days later at a reception at one of the Embassies, Prince and Princess Takamatsu both came over to my wife and told her how much the whole Imperial Family had appreciated her making a traditional Japanese bow that they knew had taken her some time to perfect. As soon as we reached home she called in Nobu-san, our wonderful housekeeper, who had been the instructor in Japanese bowing, and gave her the good news. I threw away the steamship time tables.

The New Year was not destined to be a quiet one for the American Embassy. Shortly after the beginning of the year, my wife had to go to the United States because of illness in her family and I was left alone. There was an unusually heavy snowfall that January. One bleak Sunday evening, after at least six inches of snow had fallen during the day, I was sitting reading a spy thriller in my upstairs study when the telephone rang. It was Sam Berger, head of the political section of the Embassy, who asked if he could come and see me at once in company with an officer of what we sometimes spoke of as "another Agency of the Government," meaning the CIA. I told Sam this was no night to be out (snow was still falling) and asked if the next morning wouldn't be better. He insisted the visit was necessary, so I told them to come ahead and rang for the houseboy to bring up some drinks.

When Sam and his friend arrived and told me what was on their minds, I threw away the story I had been reading, for I realized I was about to be thrown into the middle of a real-life tale of international intrigue. Apparently officers of the CIA as well as intelligence officers of the British Embassy had been cultivating one of the officers of the Soviet Mission in Tokyo named Yuri Rastvorov. The young Russian was a keen tennis player and most contacts with him had been made at the Tokyo Tennis Club. He now wished to defect and had chosen to go to the Americans rather than the British, because he thought the Americans would be able to get him safely to Okinawa, then under American jurisdiction, more easily than the British could get him to a safe spot away from his Soviet colleagues. That

Sunday afternoon he had gone off with one of his American friends and was now hidden in his home. The problem was what to do with him. I first asked what evidence the CIA could give that Rastvorov was defecting voluntarily and not being kidnapped. I was shown his Soviet passport, which he had handed over, and a statement in Russian and English signed by him saying it was his wish to get to America, where he hoped his wife and child would be able to join him later. I was told that all arrangements had been made to fly him to Okinawa that night and that it only needed my permission to set the wheels in motion. I was on the spot. To take him out of the country without informing, and getting the permission of, the Japanese Government would be a technical violation of Japanese sovereignty, which I was reluctant to agree to. Yet not to let him be taken out of the country secretly might well endanger his life and that of his family who, I understood, were just on the point of leaving Russia for a neutral country. Sam and I discussed the matter, and I finally said I would agree to the CIA's taking Rastvorov out of the country on condition that they would get approval from their Washington headquarters for me to inform the Japanese what had been done at the earliest possible date.

The local papers the next few days were full of stories about the disappearance of the Russian diplomat and speculation as to what had happened to him. I was bombarded with questions by the American press, and for the only time in my thirty years in the Foreign Service I told a deliberate lie when I told them I did not know anything about Rastvorov. I received permission to tell the Japanese authorities what had happened, and one morning after breakfast Deputy Prime Minister Ogata and Foreign Minister Okazaki came to the Embassy residence, where a representative of the CIA and I told them the whole story and the reasons we had thought it necessary to act so quickly and secretly. They were rather shocked at first but agreed we had done the right thing. If we had waited to consult them first, they would not have been able to give us the permission we needed without the danger of publicity. The papers continued to scream, but our Japanese friends did not waver in the slightest degree in their determination to keep the secret. Eventually, after Rastvorov arrived in the United States, Japanese officers were given the opportunity to question him. Except for the extreme left wing of the Japanese press, the Soviet charge that Rastvorov had been kidnapped by the United States was not seriously entertained. However, when in August the Russians were officially notified of Rastvorov's defection, and he gave a public press conference in Washington, the Japanese press was full of stories that the incident vividly demonstrated Japan's lack of real independence.

By about the middle of February the initial press interest in the Rastvorov case had begun to slacken, and we began to hope we would have a quiet time for a while. Our hopes were not destined to be fulfilled. On the morning of March 16 the Yomiuri newspaper reported that a Japanese fishing boat, the *Fukuryu Maru*, which on March 14 had pulled into its home port of Yaizu, had been sprinkled with radioactive ash from the American nuclear bomb tests at Bikini in the South Pacific, and that both crew and fish had been contaminated. This was the beginning of one of the worst periods we had to endure during our four years in Japan.

The Embassy's negotiations with the Japanese Government over this incident did not end until January 4, 1955. On that day I signed an agreement with Mamoru Shigemitsu, who had become Foreign Minister, in which the United States agreed to pay Japan $2 million as compensation for losses in Japanese life and property, as a solatium apart from the question of "legal liability." According to the *Nippon Times* of January 5, 1955, Prime Minister Hatoyama said that "the settlement of the Bikini compensation problem was an indication of U.S. goodwill toward the Hatoyama Cabinet."

Before this comparatively happy ending we had many headaches and suffered through a long period of anti-American agitation. In the July 17, 1954, issue of the *Saturday Evening Post* my friend Robert Sherrod, the *Post's* Tokyo correspondent, had a long article about the incident which gives a good account of some of the problems we faced in dealing with the case of *Lucky Dragon*, the ironic English translation of the ill-fated fishing boat's name. He wrote:

In Tokyo, American Ambassador John M. Allison radioed the State Department immediately after he heard about *Lucky Dragon*. On March seventeenth, the day after the story broke, he called at the Foreign Office to propose a joint Japanese-American investigation and to offer his Government's services in treating the twenty-three *Lucky Dragon* fishermen. He announced that six doctors — three Japanese, three American — were coming up from the Atomic Bomb Casualty Commission at Hiroshima, following "an invitation from Tokyo University Hospital," where Yamamoto and Masuda lay. Mr. Allison expressed "the concern felt by the United States with regard to the unfortunate incident."

For you and me, this seems quite reasonable. For some Japanese it was considered inadequate. "Ambassador Allison did not express his apologies," the newspaper *Asahi* observed coldly. Time after time Japanese have told me that Allison failed to say "sorry" or to use the word "regret."

John Allison's original expression of "concern" which was as much as the rules of diplomacy allowed before he actually knew what happened, might have proved satisfactory if several American Congressmen hadn't felt a compulsion to get into the act. Chet Holifield of California said the March first explosion at Bikini had got "out of control" — a statement which Admiral Strauss later denied, but one which convinced the Japanese their danger was infinite. W. Sterling Cole, Chairman of Congress's Joint Atomic Energy Committee, presumably mindful of the record of pre–World War II Japanese fishing vessels, was quoted in the Tokyo press as saying that *Lucky Dragon* might have been spying. Senator Pastore, of Rhode Island, who chanced to pass through Japan in mid-March, opined upon returning to the United States that the Japanese press was exaggerating the illness of the irradiated fishermen.

The Japanese newspapers, without realizing that Congressmen must always appear to their constituents to be both omniscient and clairvoyant, leaped on the statements. The net result was to convince the sensitive Japanese people that Americans were crassly indifferent to the fate of the twenty-three, and, for that matter, to a Japan which might one day be done to death for lack of fish or by a single radioactive shower. On April ninth Ambassador Allison adjusted his apology to the Japanese conception of English semantics and said, "I wish to express again, in the name of the United States Government, our deep regret for the unfortunate accident."

As I look back on this tragic incident, I am inclined to believe that I should have made an apology at the very beginning. I had lived in Japan long enough to know how much store the Japanese people set in apologies and what they call "sincerity." Much of the bitterness and emotionalism which characterized the Japanese reaction might have been mitigated had I at once said, "I'm terribly sorry. It is most regrettable and we will do everything possible to make amends." Of course, Washington would have been horrified, for they would have interpreted my statement as acknowledging America's complete responsibility and a commitment to pay damages no matter what investigation proved to be the truth. However, it is not at all certain anything could have helped for, as we reported to the State Department, the incident coincided with the worst possible combination of factors. First, there was the World War II atomic legacy. Then, the high seas fishing area open to Japan had already been made smaller by the action of Communist China, the Republic of Korea, and the U.S.S.R. To all this was added the danger to fish, a main item of Japanese diet. Finally, the incident took place at the height of the tuna season, thus affecting both food supply and dollar exports. Then, in September, one of the crew died. Fortunately Washington reacted promptly, when I reported this sad event, and the very next day authorized the immediate payment of one million yen to the widow. A note of condolence and a check were presented to the widow through the Foreign Office, and it was reported on all Japanese radio stations throughout the afternoon. This helped somewhat to moderate public opinion, but it would still be several months before the matter was finally settled. In the meantime, I had to fly to Washington to discuss the settlement with all the American agencies concerned, and Prime Minister Yoshida made a good will trip to Europe and the United States. Shortly after his return to Tokyo, he was forced out of office to be succeeded by Ichiro Hatoyama of the opposition conservative party, whose Cabinet agreed to the final settlement of the *Lucky Dragon* case.

In the middle of May, we negotiated an agreement for the lease of four United States naval vessels to Japan, and it was to these vessels that the Foreign Minister referred, when in October he raised the question of what would happen if one of them engaged in hostilities with a similar vessel loaned to the Koreans by the United States.

By the middle of the year, the optimistic prediction we had made on the last day of 1953, that Japan seemed at last to be starting on the difficult road back to economic viability, had proved to be premature. The economic experts in the Embassy pointed out that Japan was further from a self-supporting economy than it had been three years earlier, and we warned the State Department that unless Japan was willing to undertake and implement a rigorous austerity program, such as had been done by West Germany, the Netherlands, and the United Kingdom, further United States aid would merely perpetuate the unstable situation and postpone the inevitable adjustment, which would be much more severe. We outlined some of the steps Japan should take and stressed that despite rising national income Japan had reduced taxation and had apparently been depending upon special U.S. dollar spending in Japan to maintain a higher standard of living than it could otherwise afford.

It is interesting to note, in view of what has happened since, that in reporting to the State Department our views on policy toward Japan for the coming months, we emphasized the importance of associating Japan with our overall policy toward Asia and particularly Southeast Asia. The Embassy's political and economic officers worked together on this problem, and we telegraphed the Department our approval of the idea of economic provisions in the projected Southeast Asia Treaty Organization. We said that if the United States wanted the cooperation of neutral Asian states, we must make clear that military force was not the only solution we favored, and we urged that, to the greatest extent possible, Japan should be included in such an economic program. We urged integrating Japan and Southeast Asia both politically and economically and pointed out that in the long run, and short of war, the greatest source of weakness in Japan was the fear that it would not be included in the future of the Far East. Japan had made a defense commitment in the recently concluded MSA agreement and any greater commitment would not be looked on with favor by most of the countries of Southeast Asia.

Mainland China again came into the picture, and we reported that while responsible Japanese opinion was still reserved on whether or not the Chinese Communists had found the solution for the problems facing underdeveloped countries, the recent Geneva Conference dealing with Indochinese and Korean problems, where Chou En-lai and the Chinese Communist delegation played an important part, had caused the Japanese increasingly to believe that the Communist revolution in China would not only last but that, for the first time in centuries, China was again a major power whose economic and military strength would increase in the future, and these changes were due to the Communist regime. There was little to show that Washington read our messages very carefully or was seriously considering what Japan's future position in Asia should be other than as a safe base for American military activity. During the Dulles period economic and purely political activity took second place to the building up of a strong military base, which it was believed would deter further Communist expansion in Asia.

Shortly after we had sent these messages to the Department, Ikeda, the Secretary General of the Government party, was reported in the press to have made a statement to a meeting of Liberal party leaders which had overtones of an anti-American character. He allegedly interpreted the Indochina truce arranged at Geneva as a defeat for American policy, and he stated that this was not the time for Japan to choose between East and West, but rather a time to decide its own policies in light of what action either East or West would take economically and politically and that Japanese foreign policy should become more flexible and not be tied just to the United States.

Two or three days later I had lunch with Ikeda along with two senior members of my staff. Mr. Ikeda was accompanied by two of his experts. During the course of our frank, but still friendly set-to, I pointed out that Japan had not made the same progress as West Germany in recovering from the effects of the war. In reply, Ikeda made a statement which greatly impressed me and did give an insight into Japan's psychological state as a result of the war. He said, as nearly as I remember it, "What you forget, and what Washington forgets, is that in the lifetime of the leaders of today's Germany they have gone through two defeats. This is the first time in 2500 years of Japanese history that we have ever suffered a similar defeat." In 1954, the Japanese were only beginning to recover from the great trauma caused by their defeat. In this at least, Ikeda was right. It would be another fifteen years or more before its effects were overcome, and even today, every now and then, we can still see the evidence of its effects.

One encouraging event that year was the inauguration on July 1, 1954, of Japan's new defense establishment. On that day the National Safety Agency became the National Defense Agency, and the new law gave as its mission the defense of Japan against

direct aggression. The changeover was commemorated by ceremonies in Tokyo and at camps and bases throughout the country. I attended the one in Tokyo and afterward reported to
Washington that while some of the newspapers worried over the
possibility of militarist intervention in politics and other prewar
abuses, "on the whole, the press, which only a year ago would
have shuddered at the military trappings of the ceremonies,
seemed to take the whole affair in stride." The new legislation
had been agreed to by both of the conservative parties, and for a
time we thought this might signal an early merger of the two.
However, this was not to come for almost six months.

During this summer I had a salutary lesson on how important
it is for an Ambassador to show no signs of favoritism, or even
seem to, toward an opposition party. American diplomats have
often been criticized for knowing the present government of a
country but knowing nothing about the next. To some extent
this is true, but there are reasons for this, particularly in Asia.
The American Ambassador in London is not criticized if he has
meetings and talks with members of the opposition party, nor is
the British Ambassador in Washington if he does the same. But
in Asia they have not had as long experience with representative
government, and they are much more sensitive.

It was well known in Japan that my wife was a student and
collector of early Chinese porcelain, which, from the thirteenth
to the middle of the nineteenth century, had been exported by
the Chinese, particularly to Japan and the countries of Southeast
Asia. One Saturday afternoon we were invited by Mr. Y. Suma,
a former Japanese diplomat who was then a member of the
opposition conservative party, to have tea at his home and see
the extensive collection of Chinese ceramics that he had collected during his diplomatic service in China. The only other
guests present were the Vice Minister of Foreign Affairs, an old
friend, and his wife, who spoke no English. We spent an hour
or so looking at Mr. Suma's collection, which my wife told me

later would be more noted for its quantity than its quality. We then had tea and left for home. Not a word was spoken about either international or domestic politics.

The next Tuesday morning I was reading telegrams in my office, when the phone rang and Mrs. Kazuko Aso, the daughter and official hostess of Prime Minister Yoshida, and an extremely close friend of ours, almost shouted at me in her excellent, colloquial English, "John, what's this I hear about you having a meeting with the opposition party to plot against Father?" She said that a story was circulating in the Diet corridors that I had been plotting with Suma against the Prime Minister. I told Kazuko the whole story of what had happened and suggested that she could confirm my account by talking to Vice Minister Okumura. I then said I would see what could be done to stop the story which had absolutely no basis in fact.

I immediately telephoned Suma and asked him to come to see me as soon as possible at the Embassy, and he agreed to do so. Although I was certain that Suma had deliberately spread the story to make trouble for Yoshida, I did not accuse him of doing so. Instead, I told him I had heard about the story going around the Diet, that it was most embarrassing to me, and that, as he knew the true facts of the case, I would greatly appreciate it if he would do everything in his power to correct the false account. He promised to do so, and I was later told that he did modify the story, at least enough to get me back into the good graces of Mr. Yoshida and his charming daughter.

Although I did not suspect it then, it would only be a few months before Mr. Yoshida would be forced out of office. The old gentleman, who was far from being a fool, probably realized the precariousness of his position and was thus especially sensitive to any indication that he might be losing the confidence of the United States.

In October Sam Berger came to me one day and said that Nobuske Kishi, the Secretary General of the opposition conservative party, had, through an intermediary, requested a meeting to discuss the political situation. Mr. Kishi knew it would not be possible for him to see the American Ambassador, but he did want to establish a contact with the Embassy. I agreed that Sam should meet Kishi but that the meeting should be kept as secret as possible. It was finally arranged and one evening Sam, along with Bill Leonhart and Dick Lamb, one of our officers who was fluent in Japanese, met Kishi and one or two of his associates at a Japanese restaurant.

As Sam later told me the story, Kishi started out by saying that although Sam had been long enough in Japan to understand that the Japanese never talked business on a first meeting, nevertheless both he and Kishi were busy men, and therefore he wondered if Berger was prepared to talk business at once. On being assured that he was, Kishi then came right out and asked, "Why is the United States supporting Yoshida?" Sam replied that Kishi must misunderstand our practices. Yoshida was the Prime Minister and naturally we dealt with him. Sam went on to say that the conservative party was the only one in Japan at that time capable of running the country, and it was a shame it was split into factions; it should be united.

Kishi, a most sophisticated politician, was apparently still somewhat under the spell of the Occupation, as were many Japanese at that time, and after Sam's statement he inquired, "But what about Yoshida, would he be the head of a united party?" Sam replied, "That is not a matter for the United States to decide, it is a matter for the Japanese to decide." Kishi appeared satisfied and made arrangements to keep in touch through Bill Leonhart, who was senior enough to know what was going on and yet junior enough not to cause comment if he happened to be seen with Kishi.

From that time on, activity designed to oust Yoshida apparently picked up speed. I knew nothing about it, however, for I had to go to Washington to be there with the Prime Minister, who was visiting the United States as the last stop after his goodwill trip to the United Kingdom and Europe. He was given a luncheon at the White House by President Eisenhower and had talks at the State Department as well as being given an official dinner by Secretary Dulles. The *Mainichi* newspaper published a picture on November 15 of a smiling Yoshida being seen off in Washington on November 13 by Assistant Secretary of State Robertson, former Ambassador Joseph Grew, and me. Less than a month later this grand old man, who had done so much to guide Japan back into the family of nations after the war, would be out of office and settled back in his country villa in Oiso, about two hours southwest of Tokyo.

I returned to Tokyo shortly before Thanksgiving, and the day before that holiday Bill Leonhart came to me and reported that Kishi had asked to see him Thanksgiving evening and that he supposed he would have to pass up his turkey dinner and see him. I was sympathetic but agreed that Bill's duty came before turkey. On the following Friday morning, Bill came in and reported a most interesting two hours with Kishi in which the latter had outlined the course that would be followed in bringing about a merger of the conservative parties over the ensuing year or two and the names of the men who would be involved. Kishi then went on to discuss Japan's foreign policy and told Bill that for the next twenty-five years it would be in Japan's best interests to cooperate closely with the United States. He went on to warn that this did not mean that Japan would automatically agree to everything the United States desired. He believed the basic need for United States-Japan partnership took priority over all other issues and that both nations would have to make adjustments in their policies and programs but that these were unimportant details in comparison with the overriding need for close cooperation. He said that the aims of the two nations in the Far East were identical, and although Japanese-American relations could never be as intimate as American-British relations, he hoped that Japan could be America's second closest associate.

Kishi's prediction of how the conservative merger would evolve was, in the main, borne out as time went by. During the first week in December it was announced one noon over the radio that Mr. Yoshida had resigned. Within one hour of this announcement I had received a telephone call, from a mutual friend of mine and Mr. Kishi's, inquiring whether or not I could see the latter in the near future. It was now proper for Kishi to see me openly, as he was no longer in the opposition but would be part of the governing party. When Kishi and I met, he said he wanted to confirm everything he had said to Bill Leonhart on Thanksgiving night. He particularly wanted me to know and report to Washington his ideas about the importance of American-Japanese cooperation and to say that this would be the fundamental policy of the new government, although from time to time it might diverge in detail from American policy. After all, Japan had to stand on its own feet and have a policy of its own and not just be a puppet. During the last two years of my tour in Japan, as Kishi became increasingly influential in the Japanese government, he proved a good and strong friend of the United States.

On December 10, 1954, the new Hatoyama Cabinet was sworn into office and Mamoru Shigemitsu, who was to become a close friend, was named Deputy Prime Minister and concurrently Foreign Minister. It is interesting to note that not only Prime Minister Hatoyama, but three of the Ministers appointed by him, had been purged by the Occupation and prevented from engaging in politics for at least two or three years. The Deputy Prime Minister, Mamoru Shigemitsu, and the Secretary General of the Party, Nobuske Kishi, had both been tried as Class A War Criminals, and Mr. Shigemitsu had been given a sentence of seven years, of which he served four before being paroled in 1950. Mr. Shigemitsu had signed the Instrument of Surrender of Japan on board the U.S.S. *Missouri*.

In spite of their treatment by the Occupation, all of these

men proved good friends of the United States, and I was able to work closely with them. In fact, almost once a month Mr. Shigemitsu and I had private informal meetings in his hotel apartment, where we could meet without the publicity that always followed a meeting at the Foreign Office. When Mr. Shigemitsu had been Consul General in Shanghai in the early thirties, he had lost a leg when a Korean terrorist threw a bomb at a group of Japanese dignitaries during an official celebration. Admiral Nomura, who was Japanese Ambassador in Washington at the time of Pearl Harbor, lost an eye in this same incident.

After two or three of these meetings the Foreign Minister apparently felt we were on sufficiently friendly terms so that as I was ushered into his study one day, I saw him sitting in an arm chair and his artificial leg standing in a corner across the room. He was really relaxed. At this meeting he first brought up informally the question of China. He said that the Japanese Government agreed with the United States that the government and people on Formosa should not be allowed to be taken over by the government in Peking by force. But, he went on, "from that point the Japanese people are not sure what should be done." He stressed the cultural, historical, religious, and even economic ties to the mainland of China which were felt by the Japanese, and he told me that eventually these ties would have to be recognized in some manner. He raised the question of what would happen if Chiang Kai-shek, not a young man, should die, and he said he would like to have talks with the United States Government about what mutually acceptable policy could be developed to meet this situation. In almost every monthly meeting Mr. Shigemitsu would raise the same question in one way or another, and once a month I would report it to the State Department, but I would get no reply. Later, after I had left Japan, I understood that talks on China policy did take place, but obviously they didn't go very deep or the shock when President Nixon announced his plan to visit Peking would not have been felt so greatly in Japan.

Article XXV of the Administrative Agreement on the means of implementing the Security Treaty between Japan and the United States provided that Japan should furnish annually $155 million for the support of United States forces in Japan "until the effective date of any new arrangement reached as a result of periodic re-examination." This meant that every year, as the Japanese prepared their new budget, they opened negotiations with the United States to see if this sum could not be reduced. In effect this meant that the United States was intimately involved in the preparation of the Japanese budget. After the 1954 negotiations had been completed at the end of four months of haggling, I cabled the State Department my concern that these long, drawn out talks, although successful, had resulted in an immediate strain in our relations with Japan and a strong undercurrent of criticism at what was claimed to be United States interference in Japan's sovereign right to formulate its own budget.

During the course of these discussions, in July, I stated in a cable to the Department: "I think we must face up to the fact that in general the trend is definitely in the direction of restricting, rather than broadening, U.S. rights and bases in Japan . . . any effort we make to fight this trend head-on by insisting on our 'rights' is not likely to be successful and can only result in further aggravating our current relations with Japan to the detriment of our long-term base position here."

In the Embassy we began to think it might be helpful for the United States to propose, before the Japanese did, the revision of our Security Treaty to bring it more into line with the existing situation. We believed that all our really important interests could be preserved if we took the initiative but that it might be difficult to do so if we waited until the Japanese had become completely fed up with the present Treaty and Administrative

Agreement and demanded a change. Secretary Dulles did not agree. He apparently did not relish the idea of submitting a new treaty or agreement to the perils of legislative discussion in either Washington or Tokyo. In September, when Mr. Shigemitsu did plead for revision, Mr. Dulles was still adamant in his opposition.

Toward the end of August, 1955, the Foreign Minister made a pilgrimage to Washington, and I was called back by the State Department to be there during his visit. In addition to the normal Foreign Office contingent, Mr. Shigemitsu was joined by Nobuske Kishi and Ichiro Kono, the Minister of Agriculture and Fisheries. The latter two were leaders of an important faction in the Government party, and while genuinely interested in furthering Japanese-American cooperation, they were also interested in seeing to it that Shigemitsu did not get all the credit and thus gain more influence in the party and become a potential rival to Prime Minister Hatoyama, to whom they were both loyal. While this intraparty rivalry created some slight difficulties, the three-day conference that took place in Washington was, on the whole, successful.

It is interesting to note that Mr. Dulles stated at one point that a favorable U.S. balance of trade with Japan was normal and could be expected to continue. He said Japan should make up for it by invisible earnings from three-cornered transactions with other nations as was the case with the United Kingdom. How smoky are the glasses through which even the most far-seeing leaders look! Some twenty years later the United States now has more than one billion dollar adverse trade balance with Japan.

One of the positive results of the conference was the setting up of an advisory committee to consider joint U.S.-Japan defense problems, including the possibility of devising a formula which would enable the annual budget meetings to be conducted less acrimoniously. Mr. Shigemitsu's desire for revision of the Security Treaty was not met, although Mr. Dulles did agree to discuss the matter later when Japan had taken further steps to strengthen its defense establishment.

After the talks in Washington Mr. Shigemitsu went to New York for a few days, and I was asked to accompany him in his visits to the United Nations and to a rather extraordinary stag dinner given for him by the late Bernard Baruch at his Long Island home. In addition to the Japanese Observer at the United Nations, Toshikazu Kase, who had accompanied Mr. Shigemitsu when he signed the Japanese surrender on the U.S.S. *Missouri*, the other guests were mostly leaders of the New York press, including Roy Howard of the United Press International, Arthur Sulzberger of the *New York Times*, Ogden Reid, then of the *Herald Tribune*, and several others. Former Ambassador Joseph Grew and former Governor of New York Thomas Dewey and I were the only nonpressmen included. Mr. Baruch's great friend Herbert Bayard Swope, former editor of the old *New York World*, was also present. At dinner we were seated at two tables on the verandah. As we were eating our dessert Mr. Baruch left his seat at the table with the Foreign Minister and came around and traded seats with the man on my left. He then turned to me and Swope, who was sitting on my right, and asked, "What should I do about a toast, should it be to the Emperor?" I said that as this was not an official party I thought it would be sufficient if he just proposed a toast to our guest of honor, Foreign Minister Shigemitsu. Swope leaned across and said he heartily agreed with me. Mr. Baruch thereupon stood up and asked his guests to rise and join him in a toast to Mr. Shigemitsu. As we were about to resume our seats Mr. Dewey said, "Gentlemen, before you sit down let us drink to the Emperor of Japan." The rather startled guests did so and as we sat down, Swope again leaned across me and growled, "That'll teach you fellows — the God-damned S.O.B." A few minutes later Governor Averell Harriman, who had been campaigning for re-election, arrived and came over and sat next to me and Swope, and we told him the story. He laughed and said it was that sort of action by Mr. Dewey which was helping his re-election campaign. I made up my mind I would never like Dewey.

Both Governor Harriman and I were wrong. Harriman did not get re-elected and several weeks later when Dewey came to Japan, and I was instructed by the State Department to entertain him, I found him a most delightful guest, an extremely intelligent and well-informed man, and a real help to me in some of my talks with Japanese conservative leaders whom we were still trying to persuade to agree to a unification of the conservative factions.

Just before I had gone to Washington to be with Foreign Minister Shigemitsu, my wife and I were involved in a fantastic enterprise. Tide Water Oil Company had commissioned the Mitsubishi Shipbuilding Company to produce for them what was at that time the largest tanker yet built. The M.S. *Veedol*, 45,000 tons, was to be launched at the Mitsubishi shipyards in Nagasaki on August 7, 1955, and Mrs. Allison had been invited to christen the ship. When a huge Japanese company and a vigorous American enterprise get together almost anything can happen. And it did. A private train, complete with first-class sleeping accommodations and a never-closed bar, which provided both Japanese and Western drinks, soft and hard, was chartered by Mitsubishi. In addition to large contingents from both Tide Water and Mitsubishi, some fifty or more representatives of the American business community and their wives were invited as were half a dozen members of the Embassy staff to watch over my wife and me.

When we reached Nagasaki, the day before the launching, Mrs. Allison and I, along with the President of Tide Water Oil and Mrs. David Staples, were driven to a famous old geisha house, set in a beautiful stylized Japanese garden, which had been taken over for our exclusive use by Mitsubishi. Air conditioners had been installed in the rooms where we were to sleep Japanese style on the floor, and all our wants were attended to by attractive young kimono-clad waitresses who might have just come from playing the part of the "three little maids from school" in *The Mikado.* The other guests were put up in hotels, but we all met for a gala banquet that evening.

During the late afternoon my wife spent some time being instructed in the art of ship launching in Japan. It is like nothing else anywhere. The launching party would be stationed on a huge platform high above the ground and just in front of the bow of the tanker as it rested in its ways, waiting to slip into the harbor. In front of us would be a long wooden table with seven electrically connected buttons and across which was draped a thick red and white silken cord. At a special signal, my wife was to cut this cord with one sharp blow. She told me later that she did it on the first practice try.

The banquet that evening was also memorable. After a super-abundance of cocktails we were led into a huge Japanese-style room, where we were seated at low tables and served a delicious Japanese meal. Toward the end of the dinner a geisha troupe appeared and put on a splendid traditional geisha dance performance. Then the Japanese officials from Mitsubishi removed their Western-style coats and put on short Japanese *hapi* coats emblazoned with the three diamonds trademark of Mitsubishi and the company's name in Japanese ideographs. They then performed the famous "Dragon dance" in which they wound in and out among the guests alternately bowing and threatening with wooden swords. When they finished there was no resisting the pressure for the Americans to do the same. So six of us, including President Staples of Tide Water and me, donned the *hapi* coats and pranced around the room looking incredibly silly. Thanks to the lavish libations with which everyone had been supplied it didn't seem as silly then as it does now, when one looks at photographs taken at the time.

The next morning, Sunday, August 7, we all journeyed to the shipyards and marched up the winding ramp to the platform. There were the usual speeches by the head of Mitsubishi and Tide Water and others, but for once not including the American Ambassador. Then the moment came, Toots was given the signal, and down came the silver hatchet in a mighty chop. The cord broke apart, a bottle of champagne on a flying cord struck the bow of the *Veedol*, smashed into a hundred pieces, and the big ship began slowly to slide down the ways. At the same time hundreds of balloons and streamers were released, confetti rained over the tanker, and a flock of beautiful white doves swarmed from their cages over the ship as it sped down into Nagasaki harbor, while more than 10,000 Japanese cheered. And then — then — the *Veedol* didn't stop as it reached the water, but in spite of being held back by 100 tons of drag chains it kept right on going across the 2000-foot-wide waterway and climbed up into the Yamamoto shipyard on the opposite shore. As *Life* reported with pictures in its August 29, 1955 issue, little damage was done, but it took seven tugs seven hours to pull the tanker back into the harbor.

The party was still not over. We were all driven up to the cool mountain resort, Unzen, for an overnight stay and then back to the special train, which returned us to Tokyo in the same luxury in which it had brought us to Nagasaki. When we got back to Tokyo Station and it was all over, I understood how Cinderella must have felt when the clock struck twelve.

When we weren't arguing with the Japanese about economic debts or the beefing up of their defense program, and even while we were, there were other aspects of our life in Tokyo which made it very pleasant to be Ambassador there. One of these was the annual Imperial Duck Netting Party, which took place during the winter or early spring at the Imperial hunting lodge about an hour's drive from Tokyo. In the 1920s the participants in these annual events were required to wear morning coats and high silk hats, but by the 1950s informality had infiltrated the Imperial Household, and the men wore slacks and sport coats and the ladies usually tweed suits.

Representatives of three or four diplomatic missions would be invited to each party, and one of the Imperial Princes with his consort would act as host. We would arrive at the Lodge about ten o'clock in the morning and be divided up into groups of ten, and each of us would be given a number from one to five. The wild ducks, of which there were thousands on the nearby lake, would be attracted by tame decoys into narrow canals which were built up to mounds on each side. The participants would be given large nets, like giant-size butterfly nets but with a broad mouth, and at a signal from a Japanese steward, would dash out to a marked position on each side of the mound corresponding to the number each had been given. The sound of the guests dashing to their positions would frighten the wild ducks, and they would fly up out of the canal only to be caught in the nets being waved about by the stouthearted diplomats. It was almost impossible not to get at least one duck, and some of the more hardy campaigners managed to snare two or three. Of course, sometimes all that was caught was the hat of a colleague on the opposite side of the canal. The ducks that had been caught were turned over to the Japanese stewards, and the more sensitive of the guests refrained from asking what happened to them. But when we went to our cars to return to Tokyo, each guest was given one duck to take with him, so, if your wife was with you, you had two ducks to turn over to the cook when you got back to the Embassy.

After the netting all the guests assembled before the lodge, where for about half an hour or so drinks were served, and people could, if they wished, engage in minor sports such as slinging horseshoes or quoits or playing Ping-Pong, which was not at that time involved in international diplomacy except strictly as a game. We were then all taken into the lodge and seated at little tables for six. Each guest had before him an individual hibachi on which he cooked his own slices of duck to eat with the rice and the many Japanese delicacies spread out on the table.

Most diplomats would agree that ninety percent or more of the official occasions requiring their presence could be missed with no regret whatsoever, but I don't know of any diplomat in Tokyo or his wife who did not look forward eagerly to the annual invitation to the Imperial Duck Netting Party.

There was still another annual event sponsored by the Imperial Household which was equally enjoyable. This was the Cormorant Fishing Party at the Imperial fishing grounds on the Nagara River near Gifu, a relatively small, but famous, city located almost halfway between Nagoya and Kyoto. Along with twenty other diplomats representing eight countries, Mrs. Allison and I were invited to the first of these parties in July of 1954. We arrived on the afternoon of July 19 and were put up in rooms at the Nagaragawa Hotel just above the river. We were joined at six o'clock by Governor Muto of the Prefecture, Mayor Higashi of Gifu, and about forty other notables for a reception at the hotel. About seven o'clock we were taken aboard large sampan-style boats, decorated with bunting and huge Japanese lanterns, where we were served a sumptuous European-style dinner complete with wines, as we slowly moved upstream to the point where we would meet the fishing boats coming downstream.

Waiting on the dark river, we suddenly heard the paddles of the fishing boats approaching, and as they came around a bend in the river with bright bonfires in large receptacles strung above the bow of each fishing boat, we all burst into spontaneous applause at the spectacle. There were six fishing boats, and one after the other they came near our boats, and we were able to observe closely the skill with which the fishermen handled their birds.

After the fishing boats had passed us, the head Fishing Master, Yamashita, came aboard with one of his trained cormorants and explained in detail how the fishing was done. The trained fishermen, all of whom had served a long apprenticeship, could control as many as twelve birds at a time, while the younger men controlled six. Each bird had a band around its neck which prevented it from swallowing the larger fish, and as they came back to the fishing boats they would drop the fish in baskets. If the bird happened to catch a fish by the tail, it would toss it up in the air and catch it by its head so that the scales of the tail would not scratch its throat.

As we turned and went back toward the hotel, we were caught in the midst of hundreds of other boats filled with tourists from nearby hotels who had come to enjoy the sight. Most of the boats were filled with prosperous-looking Japanese men decked out in the distinctive *Yukata*, or night kimono, provided by the various hotels, singing lustily with gaily clad geisha. As we returned to the hotel, we were treated to a munificent display of fireworks and an abundance of drinks.

We learned later that the Fishing Master Yamashita was a "Living National Treasure" and that he was a friend of another Living National Treasure who lived and worked near Gifu, and whom we had come to know because of the interest he shared with my wife in early blue and white Chinese ceramics. The Japanese have a wonderful policy of designating as Living National Treasures any person over sixty who is judged to have contributed something unique to the arts or crafts of Japan. Those so designated are given special privileges, among which is the right to ride without cost on any of the Japanese national railways. Our friend, Mr. Toyozo Arakawa, was a famous potter, who since we first met him has become even more famous and whose works are eagerly sought by collectors and bring fantastic prices. Many of them were specially designed utensils for Japanese tea masters.

The last full year we were in Tokyo, 1956, was a busy one. In addition to the normal Embassy activities, the continuing negotiations to settle GARIOA debt (the same $2 billion spent by the United States during the early days of the Occupation to feed, clothe, and house the Japanese people), numerous meetings and discussions with the Far East Command and the Japanese authorities about problems arising from the presence of American forces in Japan and the land and buildings they occupied which the Japanese wanted to recover, and similar official concerns, there were a number of unofficial events and visitors which required our attention. Among these was a visit by the one and only Samuel Goldwyn and his wife, and we had the pleasure of having them to dinner. After meeting and visiting with them we were glad that we had not, as he might have said, "included him out" of our guest list. There was also the great Walter O'Malley and his Dodgers, then still based in Brooklyn, and we saw them in action against a Japanese team and entertained them at the Embassy. The hard-bitten warrior O'Malley looked as if he might have been an old-style sea captain or a Tammany ward politician, but he turned out to be a charming gentleman who had a tremendous knowledge of, and love for, flowers and gardens of all kinds.

O'Malley and the Dodgers were not the only American baseball heroes to visit us. During our four years, there were also Leo Durocher and the Giants, Casey Stengel and the Yankees, and Ed Lopat and his All Stars. The Giants and the All Stars were in Tokyo at the same time, and both teams came to the Embassy for a reception the same afternoon along with leading Japanese players, managers, and plain enthusiasts. Nobu-san came to me in despair and wanted to know what "She, she Ginger ale" was. It was being demanded by most of the players and turned out to be Canadian Club and ginger ale which fortunately we were able to provide. Leo Durocher, then married to Laraine Day, had instructed his team to wear their best blue blazers and dark blue ties, and we were told there were signs up all over the Imperial Hotel, where the team was staying, signed by Durocher and warning his men of dire punishment if any of them were late for the bus that would take them out to the Embassy. In a nation of baseball fans, who in the 1930s had gone wild over Babe Ruth, these baseball teams did much to increase friendship and regard for the United States. We were proud of them.

One of the more serious talks I had to make during the spring of that year was before the America-Japan Society of Osaka, where I was attending the opening of the third annual Japanese Trade Fair. Although my talk to the society covered eight pages, the press the next day emphasized only one paragraph. The *Nippon Times* headed its story, "Japan's Trade Desires Questioned by Allison." The paper began its account by saying that I had "questioned Japan's sincerity in its 'oft-expressed desires for real economic cooperation with the United States.'" The concluding paragraph of the *Nippon Times* story is worth quoting in full. It says:

> Although it is recognized in the U.S. that Japan must export to live, Allison urged Japanese leaders to recognize that trade is a two-way street, that all right is not on one side. In this connection he pointed out that exports of sewing machines from Osaka during February were double those of January and that, of these exports, those to the U.S. were nearly four times as great as in January. "And this at a time," he said, "when an American sewing machine company is being denied the right to compete on equal terms in the Japanese market."

Sixteen years later American Ambassadors in Tokyo were still making the same complaint, and it was not until President Nixon shocked the Japanese economic community by his monetary and trade restrictions of August 1971, that the Japanese really began to take the matter seriously, although for years they had been giving lip service to the necessity for true trade cooperation. Whether it had anything to do with my Osaka speech and the representations I had been making to the Foreign Office, or for some other reason, the Singer Sewing Machine Company was allowed to come into Japan not too long after I had left Tokyo.

One of the most arduous duties we had during our time in Tokyo was providing the annual Fourth of July celebration. The custom had grown up around the world that all diplomatic missions would celebrate their national day by giving receptions for local government officials and the Diplomatic Corps. In Tokyo we also had to include members of the American unofficial community as well as senior officers of the Far East Command and their wives. We soon discovered they could not all be accommodated at one function. Therefore we had two receptions. The first was from 11 to 12:30 in the morning for Japanese Government officials, members of the Diplomatic Corps, and senior officers of the Far East Command. This numbered more than 500 persons. In the afternoon there was another reception for members of the American community and unofficial Japanese, numbering approximately 1000. In addition to standing in line for these two receptions, I had to steal away from the morning reception about 11:45 to dash over to the reception being given by the American members of the Tokyo Club and then on to the noon reception being given at the American Club. At each place I had to make a speech and propose a toast to the President. At the end of the afternoon reception I had to go to the Philippine Embassy which then celebrated Philippine Independence, also on July 4. Fortunately my wife could skip the outside receptions, but she bore the brunt of the ones at our Embassy.

When President Kennedy took office he decreed, with great wisdom, that these large receptions were a waste of money and served no really vital purpose. Today American Ambassadors give small receptions, when deemed absolutely necessary, for local officials and diplomats and then join with members of the American community in informal hot dog and beer parties, where the expense is shared. Not only does this save money, but it also saves many headaches for American Embassy protocol officers. The American community in Tokyo had grown to fantastic size after the war, and it was impossible to ask everyone, so only the one or two most senior members of each organization were asked. There were always some who felt discriminated against, and the "snobbish, cookie-pushing Ambassador" was always to blame.

One of the more pleasant chores of an Ambassador in Tokyo is accompanying prominent citizens of his country to an audience with the Emperor and Empress at the Imperial Palace. Before a private citizen is received by the Emperor he has to be recommended by his Embassy, and if the audience is approved, he must be accompanied by the Ambassador. Before the war it was necessary for both the guest and the Ambassador to be attired in morning coats and wear high silk hats. After the war, as was true with the Imperial Duck Netting parties, things became more informal and guests were permitted to wear dark business suits, although, for a time, Ambassadors were still required to wear the more formal dress. Later even this requirement was lifted, and we all could appear in business suits.

During my four years in Tokyo I had the pleasure of taking some distinguished Americans to the Palace. I have already mentioned Mrs. Roosevelt. Among the others there were Dr. Grayson Kirk, then President of Columbia University, Howard Shepherd, Chairman of the Board of the First National City Bank of New York, and Helen Keller. The Emperor seemed to be quite interested in the fact that Dr. Kirk, a University President, was also a member of the Board of Directors of a huge industrial concern. In Japan this never happened. The Emperor was also intrigued by his talk with Mr. Shepherd, who was one of the few men in the international financial community he had ever talked with. Helen Keller was, of course, unique. I had had some qualms about this visit, but it went off splendidly. Miss Keller was obviously pleased and charmed by the attention of the Emperor and Empress, and they, in turn, were tremendously impressed by what this gallant lady had accomplished under such great handicaps.

We had not known just what we should do for Miss Keller during her visit to Tokyo, but in response to the request of some of the Japanese organizations working with the blind and deaf we gave a tea at the Embassy residence, inviting members of the Japanese organizations, a few American educators and missionaries also interested in work with handicapped persons, and some of the staff from the Embassy. As the afternoon wore on, Miss Keller and her companion, Miss Thompson, began to look a bit weary, and when they had refused a second cup of tea I had one of my staff ask them if, by any chance, they would like a drink of something stronger. When Miss Thompson relayed this message to Miss Keller with her fingers, Miss Keller's face lit up, her fingers worked furiously, and, according to Miss Thompson, Miss Keller's reply was, "The marines have landed!"

There were two Americans who wanted to meet the Emperor whom I declined to recommend to the Imperial Household. One was Margaret Sanger, the great birth control advocate. She had been kept out of Japan by General MacArthur, during the Occupation, as a controversial character. In the eyes of the Japanese officials and leaders in the 1950s she was still controversial, and although I received her at the Embassy and was glad to introduce her privately to Japanese leaders, I did not believe it appropriate at that time to take such a controversial figure to the Imperial Palace. She never forgave me. If it had been ten years later, I'm sure there would have been no problem.

The other American whom I refused to recommend to the Imperial Household was Frank Buchman, leader of the Oxford Group and the founder of the Moral Rearmament Movement.

One of the pageants put on by his followers in Tokyo had caused antagonism by the way in which it seemed to equate the Communist and non-Communist worlds, and the arbitrary demands made by members of his group upon the Japanese for free accommodation and financial support had aroused considerable ill-feeling. Not only did Mr. Buchman never forgive me, but I received a personal letter from my predecessor in Tokyo, Bob Murphy, then Deputy Under Secretary of State, saying that my action had been brought to the Department's attention by Senator Alexander Smith of New Jersey with a request for an explanation of the reasons for my action. Senator Smith was a good friend and a man of considerable common sense, but I knew that his son-in-law was a high official of the Moral Rearmament Movement. I wrote Bob a letter outlining my reasons and giving in some detail an account of the performance put on by the MRA people in Tokyo. I asked him to pass the information on to Senator Smith. That was the last I heard of the matter, and Mr. Buchman did not meet the Emperor.

On the night of September 28, 1956, I made one of my last public speeches in Japan. It was at a banquet given by the America-Japan Society in commemoration of the 100th anniversary of the arrival in Japan of Townsend Harris, the first American consul. Prince and Princess Takamatsu were present as was Foreign Minister Shigemitsu and former Premier Yoshida. Some four hundred guests sat through seven talks and seemed to enjoy them. The honeymoon period in American-Japanese relations was not yet over, although, for those who were willing to look, there were signs of troubles ahead. The *Japan Times*, the next morning, while giving considerable space on its front page to the banquet and the optimistic talks about continuing good Japanese-American relations, also reported on its front page that "a high level Japanese spokesman warned yesterday that his nation may drop its voluntary export textile quota unless the U.S. takes positive steps before the end of the year to stop dis-

crimination against these goods." In following years this problem continued to mar the relations between the two nations,
until in 1970 and 1971 it was one of the causes of the Nixon
economic shock given to Japan.

At the banquet, however, we were not thinking of these
future troubles but were recalling the history of past relations. I
pointed out that Townsend Harris came to Japan at a time when
China was being opened by guns but that "Harris came without
guns and his only weapons were his powers of persuasion and an
inexhaustible store of patience and good will." I referred to the
entry Harris had made in his diary for September 4, 1856, the
day on which the American flag was first raised at Shimoda.
After reflecting on the significance of this act, he wrote:
"Query, if for real good of Japan?"

Mr. Yoshida seemed to think the answer to this query was in
the affirmative, for in his short talk that doughty warrior, at a
time when the then Japanese Government was beginning to
make friendly gestures toward Moscow, stood up and said: "I
feel keenly at this moment the need of a clear restatement of
Japanese-American relations . . . Let me say boldly and in all
sincerity that, with the cold war still on, this is no time for us to
flirt with Moscow while making pious protestations of friendship
for America; no time for us to debate this or that Article of the
San Francisco Treaty.

"It is high time Japan and America got together and worked
freely and heartily together without reservation."

Today, while most Japanese leaders would agree that Japan and
America should work together, I believe that most of them
would probably eliminate the words "without reservation." The
Vietnam war, a growing spirit of neutralism and pacificism in
Japan, the Nixon Doctrine, growing fears of U.S. withdrawal
from Asia, and the Nixon shocks over China and trade have all
contributed to creating a Japan vastly different from the one we
lived and worked in between 1953 and 1957.

Not long after the Townsend Harris banquet my wife and I

returned to Washington on home leave. I had been warned in a letter from Walter Robertson that as I had been in Tokyo almost four years I should be expecting a transfer in the not too distant future, but he gave no indication of where I might be sent. Sure enough, while we were home the press announced that I was to be succeeded in Tokyo by Douglas MacArthur II, then Counselor of the State Department. He was a nephew of the General and his wife was a daughter of former Vice President Barkley.

I had at least been warned and actually had been told as soon as I reached Washington, and before the public announcement, of the change. In the past I have known of Ambassadors who first learned of their recall by reading it in the morning papers, so I guess I was lucky. There is no good reason why the State Department must act in this manner, and it does nothing to enhance the prestige of the Department's representatives abroad.

I was told that the two most important posts open to which I might aspire were Indonesia and Pakistan. After consulting with my wife, I informed the Department that Indonesia was the more appealing to us. Before our return to Tokyo in early December, I was told we would go to Djakarta but that I could say nothing about this until the agreement of the Indonesian Government had been obtained. When we arrived back in Tokyo, therefore, everyone knew we were shortly to be succeeded by the MacArthurs, but there was no indication of where we were going next or even that we were getting another post. It could have been an embarrassing two months, but fortunately my staff at the Embassy was most understanding, and my Japanese friends assumed all would work out for the best. It was not until January 8, 1957, that the *Japan Times* published a story from Washington saying that "responsible informants disclosed yesterday that John M. Allison, U.S. Ambassador to Japan, is to be assigned as Ambassador to Indonesia."

The last few weeks were hectic. Kishi had just become Foreign Minister in a new government, and I had to have many conferences with him about the problems he would be taking up with MacArthur. On January 10, 1957, the *Times* reported that he had had an hour and a half conference with Far East Commander General Lemnitzer and me the day before, which Kishi told the press was largely confined to defense matters and provided the basis for future talks. The new Prime Minister was Tanzan Ishibashi, who had been purged by General MacArthur.

Whether or not my four years in Tokyo could be considered a success is difficult to say. In the April 1957 issue of *Fortune*, John Osborne had a long article entitled "The Importance of Ambassadors." He spent several weeks in Japan, and he used me as an example of what an Ambassador does. He described many of our problems and at one point said:

> Allison's basic diplomatic task was to deter — nobody could reasonably have expected him to prevent — the drift of the Japanese Government toward some degree of political and economic accommodation with the Soviet Union and Communist China. His means of determent were of course such powers of persuasion as he possessed, plus a stream of admonitions and reassurances from Secretary Dulles in Washington . . . In Tokyo, as in every other capital of a committed ally in Asia, a tangible and specific fear existed from early 1954 through 1956 that the U.S. . . . might leave its friends out on a limb. Whether or not this fear was ever justified is beside the point. It existed and it created a major problem for Allison and other Ambassadors similarly situated. The U.S. may thank Allison in part for the fact that Japan has moved no further toward the Communist camp and away from the U.S. side than it has.

# XI

# Advice from a Caterpillar

## 1957–1958

MY ELEVEN MONTHS in Indonesia might — like Sir Nevile Henderson's memoirs of a generation earlier — be called *Failure of a Mission*. The failure was in not being able to persuade my own government to give me the means with which to persuade the Indonesians, who wanted to be persuaded, that their best interests lay in cooperation with the United States and the Western world rather than with the then still monolithic Communist world. It was at the same time the most fascinating and frustrating period in my thirty years in the Foreign Service.

The people in Washington were on an entirely different wavelength from President Sukarno, that vain, mercurial, sometimes arrogant, and often charming leader of the Indonesian people. While in Washington after leaving Tokyo I had been shown the documentary film made by the U.S. Information Agency of President Sukarno's 1956 visit to the United States. It was in color, showed Sukarno to good advantage, and only lasted about thirty minutes. From the American viewpoint, it was a splendid production. In the second or third talk I had with Sukarno after my arrival in Djakarta, he complained to me about this film. He agreed that it was a good technical production and that he could find no fault with its accuracy. What then was wrong? After his return from Washington, Sukarno had gone to Peking, and the Communist Chinese had also made a documentary film recording his visit. The Chinese film lasted two hours which was the usual time for any Oriental film that was supposed to be first class. Didn't the Americans appreciate Sukarno or understand his importance? If so, why a film of only thirty minutes? Here again was an object lesson that the Asian and Western minds did not work in the same way.

In 1957, the term "culture shock," now so common, was unknown to me, but its effects became vividly evident during my first few weeks in Indonesia. Coming directly from Japan, where everything worked, even if not always in the way one liked, to a country where nothing seemed to work, and no one really seemed to care, was a traumatic experience. I remember telling one of my colleagues after my first two weeks in Djakarta that the Indonesians weren't worth shooting. I was wrong. Eleven months later when we left the country both my wife and I had a high regard and a real affection for the gentle, soft-spoken Indonesians. We had learned that the reason things often went wrong, or didn't go at all, was that in this country of, at that time, almost eighty million people, the number of trained administrators, entrepreneurs, or government leaders was negligible.

When Indonesia gained its independence from the Dutch in 1949, after some three hundred years of Dutch occupation and rule, the national literacy rate was less than ten percent. Only a few of what the Dutch considered the more amenable Indonesians had been given a university education and brought into the government. These men had been kept in minor positions, and their frustrations caused many of them to join the independence movement and become the leaders of the nationalist revolution. Some of them had received further administrative training during the Japanese occupation. With this scant training and but little experience they were now trying to run a modern nation.

It was not only the Indonesians who caused us headaches during our first weeks. The physical plant provided by the United States Government for its employees in Indonesia was shocking. In a city only three degrees south of the Equator, where the climate is always hot and sometimes hotter, there was but little air conditioning. The offices occupied by many of our staff were little better than pigsties, often with no cross ventilation. Plumbing and sanitary facilities were primitive at best and sometimes nonexistent. Plans had been approved for a new Embassy Chancery, but it was not completed during our stay in Djakarta. I was horrified when I saw the plans that had been approved by the State Department for an apartment to house our lady secretaries. They not only lacked air conditioning facilities or cross ventilation, but there was no provision for servants' quarters. Of course, in Washington, the young ladies would not have had servants, but this was Asia where everybody has servants, even the servants.

The kitchen of our residence was completely outside the residence itself and had no running water. The cook had to go to a tap outside the kitchen. There was only one small air-conditioned bedroom in the residence, because my predecessor didn't approve of air conditioning. The downstairs toilet facilities available to guests were outrageously primitive. I was told that my predecessor had said that people who were invited to diplomatic receptions and dinners should have attended to all their natural functions ahead of time.

Before our eleven months in Indonesia were up Toots had succeeded in getting a renovated powder room for our lady guests and having air conditioning installed in the two large bedrooms. She had persuaded the State Department to do over completely the kitchen and serving areas, although only the plans for this had been completed before our departure. We also received approval for a slight raise in pay for the Embassy servants and provided them with a regular ration of orange juice, for repeated sicknesses had been diagnosed as being probably due to a deficiency in Vitamin C. These efforts on behalf of our servants made us unpopular with a few of our diplomatic colleagues who claimed we were being sentimental and were making it impossible to get good servants cheaply.

One of the most pleasant features of life in Indonesia was the weekend resort in the hills a little more than an hour's drive south of Djakarta, just beyond Bogor where President Sukarno had his fine country estate with the beautiful mansion where Sir Stamford Raffles had lived and done most of his work, when the British, for five years, ruled Java. There were three houses on an old tea plantation, not much more than two thousand feet above sea level. There we could enjoy roaring wood fires and had to have blankets on our beds at night. This retreat was a life saver for those of us who worked all week in the steaming oven which was Djakarta. It also gave us an opportunity to meet, under the most informal conditions, many of our diplomatic colleagues and many official and non-official Indonesians who also came up to the hills over the weekend.

The three houses on the tea plantation were all under the control of William Palmer, a bachelor, who was at that time the representative in Indonesia of the American Motion Picture Producer's Association. Bill had been brought up in Thailand by American missionary parents and had lived most of his life in Southeast Asia. Between a large house, occupied by Bill and his numerous weekend guests, and a middle-sized one, occupied by the Allisons, was a smaller cottage used on alternate weekends by Greg Hackler, head of the Embassy political division and his family and by Lieutenant Colonel Smith, the Air Attaché, and Mrs. Smith.

One of the by-products of weekends in the Puntjak, as the area was known, was an introduction to Indonesian magic. There was a swimming pool located on the slope of the hill in front of Bill's house. About a year before we arrived, according to Bill, the pool began to leak and none of the efforts to repair it proved successful. Bill finally consulted one of the wise old Indonesian women who lived on the plantation, and she told him that the reason it leaked was that the pool had been built over the grave of an old Indonesian gentleman and that he was unhappy about it. Bill asked what could be done and was told that he should give a *selamatan* to appease the old gentleman. This is a semireligious feast to which all the local villagers are invited, and the local priest comes and blesses the event. The selamatan was given, and after an hour or so Bill asked the old lady if she thought the old gentleman was satisfied; she replied "Not yet." This happened two or three more times, until finally, after the feast had been going on for some time, the old lady said she believed the old gentleman was now happy. The proceedings were brought to a close, and from that day on the pool never leaked.

We were told that we should have a selamatan to bless our moving into our home in the hills, and not wanting to offend the local villagers we put one on. There must have been fifty or more people who attended along with the village priest. In order to ensure good weather and keep the rains away, we were told we should put the underpants of a virgin boy on the roof of our house. So three-year-old Jeffrey Hackler contributed a pair of his best pants, and one of the Indonesian servants climbed to the roof and secured them to a beam. The sun was brilliant, and there was not a cloud in the sky. After about three hours we were getting a bit tired, but it looked as if the feasting would never cease. We had one of the boys climb up and remove the pants. Within fifteen minutes the sky had clouded over, and the rain came in torrents.

There were more urgent matters than Indonesian magic to occupy my mind. In my first talk with President Sukarno it was obvious that he was still tremendously concerned with the problem of West New Guinea, or Irian Barat, as the Indonesians called it. He repeated, in almost the exact words, what he had said to me when I visited him in 1952, as Assistant Secretary of State for the Far East. If only the United States would support, in principle, the Indonesian demand that the Dutch open negotiations concerning the inclusion of this territory in the Republic of Indonesia, Sukarno could, he said, relegate the Communists to a position of no importance and no influence in the country. As long as the Soviet Union and the People's Republic of China were the only big nations to give public support to Indonesian desires, what grounds did Sukarno have, he asked, to condemn Communists in Indonesia?

There were other early indications that everything was not going to be sweetness and light. During the first few days I was in Indonesia I was invited to a large cocktail-buffet reception at the home of the manager of Standard Vacuum Oil, just across the circle from the Embassy residence. During the evening I had an interesting talk with a Dr. Sumitro, who, I was told, had been a former Finance Minister and was then Dean of the Economics faculty of the University of Indonesia. The few minutes I had with him made me wish for a longer talk and the next morning I asked Frank Galbraith — then head of the Political Division in Djakarta, and now our Ambassador to Indonesia — if he could arrange for me to see more of Sumitro. In a day or two he reported that Sumitro had vanished. We learned later that he had gone first to Sumatra and then to Singapore. He was one of the first Indonesian leaders who decided he could no longer work with Sukarno.

The Indonesian Prime Minister, when I arrived, was Ali Sastroamidjojo, whom I had known well when he had been Ambassador in Washington during the time I was Assistant Secretary of State. During my first visit he was polite but evidently under a strain. Although he was one of the leaders of the PNI, a powerful political party thought to be the special favorite of Sukarno, I got the impression he was not completely

sure of himself or his position. He was also a fanatically loyal
follower of Sukarno and was in some ways even more extreme.
Five months earlier Sukarno, who was developing his conception of what he was to call "Guided Democracy," had proposed
the abolishment of all political parties. Now Ali was afraid that,
as an active political party leader, his days as Prime Minister
were numbered. His fears were well founded. In February of
1957, Sukarno proposed the construction of a *gotong-rojong*
Cabinet on the basis of the representation of all the parties in
Parliament.

Frank Galbraith taught me the meaning of gotong-rojong: the
cooperative manner in which, from ancient times, the Indonesians had worked together to accomplish whatever they desired. It had been of real value in times past, but one wondered
whether or not it was an adequate tool for twentieth century
Indonesia. A literal application of the principle in 1957 would
have meant that the Communist party (PKI) would have had
to be included in the Cabinet. The army wouldn't agree to this,
and so for a time Ali stayed on as Prime Minister. However, by
the beginning of April, Sukarno decided a change must be made.
After the head of the PNI, Suwirjo, had been unsuccessful in
forming a new Cabinet, President Sukarno, as the *Times of
Indonesia* stated, "consulted the Supreme Commander of the
Armed Forces, another man named Sukarno, and then called
upon a private citizen, also named Sukarno . . . to form a
cabinet."

Although the editor of the *Times* denounced the unconstitutional manner in which Sukarno had formed the Cabinet, he
had good words to say about the men who were actually chosen.
Of the Prime Minister he said: "Prime Minister Djuanda Karta
Widjaja takes on his thirteenth ministerial job. He can never
stand up to President Sukarno but he is an honest, capable man
who commands respect." I found this to be an essentially correct description of Djuanda, who became a close friend during

the coming months. Of the Foreign Minister, the editor said: "Dr. Subandrio, who had the prescience to join the PNI a couple of months ago, is undoubtedly a sound selection for the Foreign Affairs portfolio although, probably not to be out of step with President Sukarno, he pretends to believe that the West is out to balkanize Indonesia: Indonesia's foreign policy as carried out by him under the President's control, will probably see a shift to the left." Once again I found this to be a good description of the rather brilliant, extremely articulate, and opportunistic Foreign Minister whom I grew to like but never to trust.

The editor of the *Times*, who had made these judgments, was a most interesting person. He was a Tamil from Ceylon who had become an Indonesian citizen. He was an Oxford graduate, had a Filipino wife, and was coal black. This last quality seemed to set him apart, and he apparently had a grudge not only against the white foreigners in Indonesia but also against many of the lighter-skinned Indonesians. Charles Tambu was his name, and he was a brilliant man. Fortunately the head of the United States Information Service (USIS) in Indonesia, Lionel Landry (now Executive Vice President of the Asia Society in New York), was a man of great sensitivity and considerable experience in Southeast Asia. He has a charming Burmese wife, and it was at their house that my wife and I got to know the Tambus during the course of an informal evening. I learned a lot about Indonesian politics that night and also a lot about what I suppose today would be called the "hang-ups" this fiercely independent, intelligent black man had, as a result of living in an almost exclusively brown and white society.

Several days after the evening at the Landrys' my wife and I met Charlie Tambu again at some diplomatic reception, and he asked whether the two of us would be willing to come to an informal dinner with just him and his wife at their "very small and humble house," as he described it. We, of course, said we would be delighted, and a week or so later we did go to what was, indeed, a "very small and humble house." The sparkling conversation and wit of our hosts soon made us forget our surroundings and far too soon it came time to go home. After this dinner Charlie decided it was possible for an American Ambassador and his wife to be human, and, while he did not refrain from criticizing America in his paper whenever he thought it wrong, he also made sure that unfair and inaccurate criticisms of America were denounced for what they were. He was a rare person, and we were both grieved when several years ago we heard that he had been forced out of Indonesia by the Sukarno Government and had died abroad.

The flight of Sumitro, and the increasingly arbitrary actions of Sukarno, made me think hard about what American policy should be toward Indonesia at this stage in its development. The only instructions I had been given before leaving Washington had been almost entirely negative. "Don't let Sukarno get tied up with the Communists. Don't let him use force against the Dutch. Don't encourage his extremism." The only positive note was when Secretary Dulles said, "Above all, do what you can to make sure that Sumatra [the oil producing island] doesn't fall to the Communists."

There were at least three Indonesian elements which we would have to take into account. There was, first, the increasing disaffection among many of the leading intelligentsia as well as political leaders with the actions of Sukarno, who, they feared, was leading the nation into a dictatorship and possibly into the hands of the Communists. Secondly, there was the dissatisfaction of the regional leaders over the domination of the Central Government by the Javanese and the fact that while the regions, particularly Sumatra and Sulawesi, produced the vast majority of the foreign exchange the nation received, only slightly more than ten percent of it was spent in the regions. Then, last but by no means least, was Sukarno's determination to see West Irian incorporated into the Republic of Indonesia. It was not long before I began to see there was a fourth element to be considered. That was the growing conviction in Washington that communism was at the bottom of all the trouble in Indonesia and that Sukarno was motivated solely by a desire to bring Indonesia into the Communist camp.

The complaint of the regions had considerable merit, and their attempt to solve their problem through large-scale smuggling and increasing challenges to Central Government authority were looked on with some sympathy by the political leaders who distrusted Sukarno. The Embassy was concerned because of the Standard Vacuum and Caltex installations in Sumatra and the large number of American men, women, and children living there. Fortunately their safety was not seriously threatened while we were in Indonesia, but my successor, Howard Jones, was faced with a real problem, for by that time the rebellion of the regions was in full bloom.

The intellectual and political leaders as well as the army commanders, who, in effect, controlled the regions, did not in the beginning have any desire to see Indonesia fragmented. They merely wanted to persuade Sukarno to pay more attention to the needs and wishes of the regions, to govern in a less dictatorial manner and more in accord with the Constitution, and, above all, to stop courting the PKI and listening to the slanted advice of its leaders. The army leaders in Djakarta, who were probably the strongest anti-Communist force in the country were, at first, sympathetic with the problems of their military colleagues in the regions. It was not until the latter, having completely lost hope of getting any relief from Sukarno, openly defied the military commands of their Djakarta superiors, that the army reluctantly agreed on the necessity of taking action against them. General Nasution, the Chief of Staff of the army, was far from being a Communist and he did not approve of Sukarno's flirting with the PKI, but he believed firmly in the maintenance of military discipline, and, although a Sumatran himself, he sincerely believed in the necessity of supporting a unified Indonesian State. Unfortunately, neither Nasution nor his principal officers had a good knowledge of economics, and they often ignored or swept aside the legitimate economic demands of the regions. Sukarno was almost an economic illiterate and was vastly more interested in leading a revolution than in the humdrum, prosaic tasks required to make the new revolutionary government work, after the revolution itself had succeeded.

Sukarno's insistent demand for the inclusion of West Irian in the Indonesian Republic was an example of his tendency to ignore economic factors and stress only political achievements. West Irian would mean many economic headaches for Indonesia, but it had been a part of the Netherlands East Indies, and therefore Sukarno believed it should be a part of the Republic of Indonesia. When Indonesian independence had been granted in 1949 it had been impossible to agree as to the status of West Irian, and the problem was finally postponed for one year.

The Dutch and the Indonesians never agreed on the true interpretation of this West Irian agreement. The Indonesians took the position that the only thing to be discussed at the end of the year was when and how the area would be incorporated into Indonesia, while the Dutch claimed that the whole question of whether or not it should even be included in Indonesia should be discussed. It would take a Philadelphia lawyer to settle the legalities of this issue. Among other things, the Dutch claimed the Indonesians were not justified in taking over West Irian, because its Papuan population was not of the Indonesian race. But neither was it Dutch.

I gradually came to two conclusions. The first was that the West Irian question was not one of interest only to Sukarno. The great mass of the Indonesian people, including most of the regional leaders and the dissident political and intellectual leaders, agreed with Sukarno on this point. My second conclusion was that whatever the legal rights might be, the political realities were that if Indonesian desires were not, in some manner, recognized, Sukarno could, and probably would, lead his close to 100 million people into the Communist camp. At the same time I was sure that if the Indonesian demands were granted, the slightly more than 10 million Dutch would protest vigorously, threaten to leave NATO, castigate the United States — if we had helped Indonesia — and then accept the situation. There was nothing else for them to do. They certainly did not wish to become Communists. In view of the strategic location of the Indonesian islands, lying as they did across the lines of communication between America's Philippine and ANZUS allies, and because of the all important Indonesian oil production, it seemed to me our interest lay more in keeping the Indonesians out of the Communist camp than in worrying about ruffling the feelings of the Dutch.

During the summer months of 1957, we had a vivid example of how easy it would be for the Indonesians to move into the Communist camp without the majority of the people either wanting to be Communists or really understanding what communism was. During the months of June, July, and August local elections were held which resulted in the PKI winning almost thirty percent of the votes cast. This was partly due to the fact that during this time Indonesia was visited by the head of the Soviet Government, Kliment Voroshilov. He was taken on a whirlwind tour around the country by Sukarno, and the Red and White Indonesian flag and the Hammer and Sickle of Russia were entwined together wherever one looked. There were almost fifty political parties competing for votes, and due to the still large percentage of illiteracy, the ballots not only carried the names of each party but also a symbol to represent it. Naturally the PKI symbol was the Hammer and Sickle. The people had just seen their President traveling throughout the country with the head of the world's greatest Communist power and the

Hammer and Sickle flag crossed with the Indonesian flag on all public buildings and flag poles. Why shouldn't they put their cross opposite the Hammer and Sickle on the ballot?

Another thing we learned from this election was how the old Indonesian philosophy of gotong-rojong, or mutual cooperation, influenced the voting. Professor Guy Pauker, then of the University of California at Berkeley and later of the Rand Corporation, was in Indonesia observing the elections. He told us of one family of four he had interviewed. By family agreement the father, a good Mohammedan, had voted for the Masjumi party, the Muslim party. His wife had voted for the PNI, the Nationalist Party; the older son had voted for the PSI, the Socialist Party; and the younger son had voted for the PKI. They told Pauker they believed all the principal parties should be represented as everyone should work together. It was a nice thought but not very practical in the real world of the twentieth century.

The closeness in the timing of the visit of Voroshilov and the setting up of the National Council by Sukarno apparently reinforced Washington's belief that Guided Democracy was, at least in part, Communist inspired. When Sukarno had visited the United States in 1956, he had expressed great admiration for the American system of government, and Washington assumed that the American example would be followed in Indonesia. When this did not happen, it could only be because Sukarno was falling into the hands of the Communists. I was not at all sure that the Indonesian people, who had never known representative government as understood in America, were ready for American-style democracy. Perhaps, at this stage of their development, some form of Guided Democracy was what they needed. In the same conversation in which he had criticized the USIS documentary film of his visit to America, Sukarno had explained that while he had been greatly impressed by what he saw in the United States, it did not seem to have much relevance to the problems he was facing in Indonesia. What he saw in Communist China did, and although he would never be a slave to communism, he did believe it had certain lessons for any underdeveloped country.

While it was possible, and in fact, easy, to disagree violently with Sukarno, it was difficult not to like him. Often arrogant and imperious, he could also at times be completely informal and go out of his way to be thoughtful and considerate. When it was impossible for him to attend our Fourth of July reception at the Embassy he did not merely have an aide inform us, but he sat down and wrote me a personal letter of regret in his own hand. He said: "I feel very sorry about it; the more sorry, because, as you know, I am an ardent admirer of your revolution for independence." In signing his letter, this leader of the revolution against the Dutch used the Dutch spelling of his name, Soekarno. This was typical of many of the leaders of Indonesia and still is. They hated Dutch policy but liked the Dutch as people, and in private they often spoke Dutch among themselves.

The economic situation continued to deteriorate. The Chief of the Embassy economic section, Walter Smith, warned me of the problems which the government was facing. He pointed out that the continued deficit financing of the government was reaching grave proportions and that the central bank's advances to the government to make up the deficits had already exceeded the legal limit. The deficit in 1956 had been almost three billion rupiahs, and the estimated 1957 deficit was about the same. He told me that the number of civil servants was three times what it had been under the Dutch and that efforts to cut down the public payroll had been unsuccessful. While over forty percent of the government's foreign exchange earnings came from export of rubber, the government had made no serious effort to increase replanting of improved stock and had given no encouragement to the estates. Other commodities such as tin, coffee, sugar, tea, and copra likewise showed no prospects of increasing substantially. Oil was the only bright spot, but even here much more could be done if the government were to grant new concessions freely.

Sukarno appeared to take but little interest in what was happening to the economy of his country. His public speeches became increasingly hostile to Western-style democracy, and he intensified his campaign for the return of West Irian and increased his praise of the Communists both at home and abroad for backing him in this campaign. Washington became alarmed and sent out the head of the Far Eastern Section of the CIA to look into the situation on the spot. I spent a long and fruitless afternoon with him and the local CIA Station Chief on the verandah of the Embassy residence. I do not know what his qualifications were for assessing Asian affairs, but he had served in Paris before assuming the position he then held and apparently had been brainwashed by the French as to the imminent Communist danger in Asia. When he returned to Washington I heard, at second hand, that he reported that Sukarno was beyond redemption and that the American Ambassador seemed confused and was inclined to be soft on communism.

Unfortunately, the head of the CIA at that time was the younger brother of the Secretary of State. The latter had great confidence in his brother and normally would accept his reports and advice without question. This was perfectly natural, but it had unfortunate results for American policy in Asia. I had great regard and considerable affection for both Foster and Allan Dulles, and there was no question in my mind about their intelligence, patriotism, or good intentions. But they did not know Asians well and were always inclined to judge them by Western standards. In addition they sincerely believed in the imminence of the Communist threat. On top of all that they were both activists and insisted on doing something at once to remedy the situation.

We began to get worried cables from Washington. The setting up of the National Council, the fiery speeches of Sukarno, his continued neglect of the economic problems of the country, and the CIA reports seemingly convinced the State Department that something must be done soon or all Indonesia would fall to the Communists. It was also apparent that no one in the top echelons of the Department had read the history of the Indonesian revolution, for their telegrams implied that Sukarno was adopting an entirely new line in favor of the Communists and against Western democracy.

In a response to a message from Walter Robertson, I pointed out to him that recent actions of Sukarno were not, "except perhaps in degree, different from, or out of line with, his previous statements or deeds." Referring to Professor George Kahin's fundamental book, *Nationalism and Revolution in Indonesia,* I pointed out that in a speech on June 1, 1945, Sukarno said: "[our] need is not for the democracy of the West but for . . . politico-economic democracy able to bring social prosperity." Again in December 1946, when Sukarno increased the size of the National Committee (the forerunner of the Cabinet) he jumped the PKI representation from 2 to 35 while keeping the Nationalist Party (the PNI) to its original 45. Finally, I pointed out that he also appointed at that time, as new members, representatives of the peasantry, labor, and the regions outside of Java, thus to some extent forecasting the composition of the recently appointed National Council. I was not surprised that Washington did not seem to know these facts. My predecessor, I had been told, had forbidden any of his staff to read Kahin's book as it was apparently too anti-Dutch for his taste. He was now head of the Research and Intelligence Office of the State Department, and his staff was probably still forbidden to read this "subversive" book!

In this same telegram to Walter Robertson I stated that I could think of nothing which would more certainly ensure Indonesia falling to the Communists than to terminate or slow up American aid. It was important to look at the historical record from the Indonesian point of view in order to understand why it was so easy for the Communists and their Russian friends to gain popularity in Indonesia and so difficult for the United States. I reported a recent conversation with Roeslan Abdulgani, former Foreign Minister and at that time Secretary General of the new National Council. He had pointed out, during a friendly discussion about the reasons for American difficulties in Indonesia, that the people had been greatly disillusioned by lack of anticipated American support after the war, and they had not forgotten that it was American tanks and arms which the Dutch used in their effort to regain control of Indonesia. I concluded that Indonesians might be unfair in their attitude, but we could not ignore it if we hoped to stem the Communist tide.

The day after sending the above message I journeyed to Surabaya with Sukarno, the Prime Minister and the Foreign Minister, other members of the Cabinet, and ten members of the Diplomatic Corps, including the Russian and Yugoslav Ambassadors, to participate in the ceremonies opening a great new cement plant, largely financed with American money. Sukarno made a speech, I made a speech, the engineers in charge of the plant made speeches, and a luncheon was given for several hundred people. Sukarno appeared with me for numerous press photographs, and anyone observing his actions would believe that America was the greatest country on earth. The next day, of course, he would make similar gestures toward the Russians.

From the Masjumi party leaders I was learning that, in their opinion, Sukarno could only be influenced to change his ways by use of superior strength, and it was therefore important, if the United States wished to reverse the trend, to take some action which would gain the support of the masses. Only with some mass support would it be possible for the anti-Communist forces to sway Sukarno. And it was clear that the masses, as well as all these leaders, agreed with Sukarno about West Irian.

It therefore seemed to me essential that the United States take some action with regard to the West Irian problem which would commend itself to the Indonesian masses and to Sukarno. Sukarno was still telling me at every opportunity that he could cut the Communists down to size if only the United States could support him in his demand for West Irian. Before I had made up my mind as to the best means of getting Sukarno to make good on his statement I had a further message from Walter Robertson informing me that an Ad Hoc Inter-Agency Committee was being set up in Washington to consider the whole Indonesian problem and come up with suggestions as to what the United States might do.

In a reply to Walter I pointed out that the whole tenor of his message seemed to imply that the United States could, by giving some sort of aid and comfort to the anti- and non-Communist forces, "reverse the present prospective growth of Communist forces." While agreeing that we should be prepared to give such aid if we could do it in a manner which wouldn't be counterproductive, I said the matter was much more complicated than merely doing what we could to step up anti-Communist strength and activity and that in any case our capabilities are limited in an independent country. Witness, for example, the recent election of a pro-Communist Mayor in Naha, the capital of Okinawa, where the United States then had complete control and readily available forces. As long as the overall policies of the United States did not appeal to Naha voters as being in their interest, our controls amounted to nothing. This would be even more true in independent Indonesia, and unless we could take action which would convince the masses that we were on their side, no amount of aid to anti-Communist forces would be of help, for they would not be able to carry the masses with them. I referred to the contention of the Masjumi leaders that Sukarno was only susceptible to superior strength and added that at that time Sukarno was the only available leader capable of keeping Indonesia out of the Communist orbit.

Between 1954 and 1957, the West Irian issue had been submitted four times to the United Nations, and it was due to be voted upon again in the forthcoming UN session. I therefore recommended to Washington that the United States support the Indonesian Resolution. This resolution did not call for West Irian to be turned over to Indonesia but merely called for discussions to be held.

With reference to the studies being made by the Ad Hoc Committee, I urged that it consult with Jim Baird, head of the ICA (Aid) Mission in Indonesia, who was then in Washington on consultation, and also Val Goodell, CIA Station Chief in Djakarta, who was shortly due to go to Washington for consultation. I reported that both Baird and Goodell agreed with me that I, too, should be brought to Washington for consultation. As far as any visible results were concerned, Washington never read this message. I remained in Djakarta, the Ad Hoc Committee continued its deliberations, and in due course produced an amazing document. But before I learned of the committee's recommendations, President Sukarno had invited me to the Palace for a long talk.

He began by again stating that if only the United States would support the Indonesian resolution in the United Nations he could bring the local Communists under control. He implied it would also then be easier for him to take the advice of men like former Vice President Hatta and Sjafruddin, President of the Bank of Indonesia, who disapproved of taking drastic action against the Dutch and who advocated that more attention be given to the economic problems facing the country. But Sukarno wasn't really interested in economic problems; his flair was for the dramatic, and the real reason for this talk with me soon became evident. He wanted to invite President Eisenhower to visit Indonesia. Sukarno claimed that if only President Eisenhower would come to Indonesia, it would be possible to make the people forget all about the visit of Marshal Voroshilov, the Soviet head of state, whose visit had proved so helpful to the PKI. Since Eisenhower was still recovering from a heart attack, Sukarno said he would not put on too strenuous a program, and the American President would be the first guest at a new weekend home Sukarno was building in Bali. He urged me to cable the President immediately and extend his invitation. I promised to do so.

It was about two weeks before a reply came from the White House. An official letter on White House stationery, personally signed by the President, was sent me with instructions to deliver it personally to President Sukarno. A carbon copy was forwarded for my information. As I had anticipated, it was a polite rejection of the invitation. I was invited to have tea with President Sukarno and to bring the letter from President Eisenhower the next afternoon. I didn't look forward to the task, for I feared Sukarno's reaction when he read the letter. When I arrived at the beautiful Bogor residence, with its huge expanse of lawn where more than a hundred small deer roamed at will, Sukarno greeted me as if he had not seen me for months and insisted on showing me through the different rooms before we settled down for tea. He was obviously expecting an acceptance of his invitation — no one could possibly turn down President Sukarno! Finally, he indicated he was ready to receive the letter and I shuddered inwardly as I handed it over. I had always believed the expression "his jaw dropped" was an exaggeration, but I literally saw Sukarno's jaw drop as he read President Eisenhower's letter. He couldn't believe it. There was not much I could say, and I was shortly in my car and on the long, rough road back to Djakarta.

It was not long before Sukarno was to receive another affront. In early September, the Under Secretary of State, the late Christian Herter, was going to a SEATO meeting in Bangkok, and I hoped he would make the short side trip to Djakarta. Instead, I was ordered to go to Bangkok to brief him about the situation in Indonesia. Mr. Herter was an intelligent and kindly man and seemed a bit embarrassed when I asked him why he had not come to Djakarta. He explained that the people in Washington dealing with Indonesian affairs did not want to do anything which would build up Sukarno's prestige among the Indonesians! This at a time when, in the eyes of the mass of Indonesians, Sukarno was "Mr. Indonesia," whose prestige could not be any higher. The refusal of the Under Secretary to come when he was so near only heightened Sukarno's suspicions of Washington and encouraged him to turn more and more to the PKI and their Russian and Chinese friends.

I was convinced that it was not only the fear of building up Sukarno's position that was back of the Washington action. In addition, Sukarno was to the good people of Washington just not a nice man. He was a playboy who must always have the ladies around, and he was a demagogue. Dennis Bloodworth in his perceptive book about Asia, *An Eye for the Dragon*, in talking about Sukarno, says: "In the West he was depicted as a sex-soused megalomaniac, fumbling compulsively with girls and glory. But distance plays tricks with values as with light, so that images may appear upside down, and what marks a man for disgust in the Occident may mark him for distinction in the Orient. Asian peasants, ignorant of nations but loyal to their leaders, expect divine despots to be demanding and the incarnation of Vishnu to be virile beyond the potency of ordinary men." Whether Sukarno was divine or not, the Indonesian masses certainly considered him to be. And, from any viewpoint, he was not an "ordinary man."

Upon my return from Bangkok I found a cabled summary of the three principal recommendations made by the Ad Hoc Committee in Washington. First, we were to employ all feasible means to strengthen and encourage the determination and cohesion of the anti-Communist forces in the outer islands, particularly Sumatra and Sulawesi (the Celebes) so that they would be able to affect favorably the situation in Java and provide a rallying point if the Communists should succeed in taking over Java. Secondly, if the situation in Java continued to deteriorate, we should move faster along the lines of the first recommendation. Thirdly, we should utilize whatever leverage was available, or might be built up by the anti-Communist forces in the outer islands, to stimulate into action the non- and anti-Communist forces in Java.

The report gave no real consideration to the reasons for Communist gains or the increasing reliance of Sukarno on Communist support, and the Embassy replied that no valid recommendations could be made for a cure without considering the causes of the disease. While the report recognized the key position of Sukarno, it apparently presumed he was beyond redemption, as there were no recommendations that attempts be made to influence him to change his ways. I repeated what had been said before, that Sukarno must be made to realize that his long-term interests lay in cooperating with the United States and not the U.S.S.R. or Communist China.

There was but little evidence that Washington had paid much attention to my comments on the Ad Hoc Committee report and this, coming on top of other Washington actions, or lack of actions, during the past month or two, was so discouraging that on September 25 I wrote a long letter to Walter Robertson detailing the causes of my discontent and stating that if the Department no longer had confidence in my judgment, I was prepared to resign as Ambassador and request retirement from the Foreign Service. One of my chief complaints was the tendency in Washington to accept CIA reports in preference to those from the Embassy. My letter to Walter read:

> I have not seen any significant report since my arrival here from CIA sources which did more than corroborate information received from other sources in one form or another. I have seen many contradictory reports and reports that were later proved incorrect.

Yet Washington had insisted that CIA reports from Indonesia were "more productive" than those from other sources. As a specific example of the incorrectness of this judgment, I stated:

> In connection with the recent National Conference I received absolutely no reports of any kind from CIA sources during the course of the Conference. Such reporting as we did . . . was the result of efforts of myself and the Embassy's political staff plus the office of the Army Attaché.

Over two months later I received a reply which attempted to reassure me that the reports and judgments of the Embassy were of value and that my superiors in the Department had to "avail ourselves of all the information available, no matter what the source . . ." and therefore the CIA, the Air Attaché, and my predecessor were all consulted. But I was listened to also, and the Embassy reports "receive wide distribution in the Department and are important in our consideration of the Indonesian problem . . . and we are appreciative of the full reports which we have been receiving." This at a time when press reports from Washington indicated the Department was dissatisfied at the meagre reports from the Embassy. Nothing was said about my offer to resign, and I decided the only thing to do was stick it out a while longer.

About this time the local Communists as well as their friends abroad began to take the position that the American Ambassador, who was suspected in Washington of being naive about Sukarno and the Communists, was, in fact, one of their bitter enemies and must be removed. On September 28, 1957, the *Blitz* newsmagazine of Bombay published a long story, datelined from Hong Kong and headed AMERICAN PLOT TO OVERTHROW SUKARNO, which accused me of being the leader of the plot.

On October 9, Acting Foreign Minister Hardi called me to his office to discuss the *Blitz* story. He obviously did not believe the story, but he needed something to tell Sukarno and the local press when they, as he was sure they would, published the story. I was able to point out to Mr. Hardi that the photographs of the forms on which the alleged telegrams were printed were of ones that had been discarded by the State Department at least two years before the dates given on the messages and that the spelling used was the British form and not the American.

Attacks on me in Indonesian left-wing and Communist papers continued and as time went by increased in fervor. A former Indonesian employee of our USIS office, who had been converted by the PKI, began drawing a series of cartoons for the Communist press which featured the bald-headed American Ambassador as the instigator and supporter of all anti-Sukarno and anti-central-government activity in Indonesia. His zeal was somewhat dimmed when I asked Lionel Landry, his former employer, to tell him how much I enjoyed the cartoons and to pass on my request for copies of some of the originals.

Trouble in the outer regions did not lessen, the economic situation grew no better, and Sukarno kept up his campaign for West Irian and Guided Democracy. With respect to the latter we had several arguments, and it was about this time that he first asked me, "What is it that makes fifty percent plus one right?" It is not an easy question to answer.

In the fall of 1957 Sukarno decided to make an extensive tour of Sulawesi, one of the more vocal disaffected areas. As usual he took with him a large party consisting of Cabinet members, government officials, newspaper correspondents, and foreign diplomats. I was included. It turned out to be one of the most interesting and exhausting six days I ever endured. It was also a fine opportunity to get to know Sukarno better and to see how he dealt with the mobs of people who flocked to see and listen to him. Queen Victoria's first Prime Minister, Lord Melbourne, once said: "For recruiting the spirits there is nothing like lying a good while in bed." He and Sukarno would never have understood each other. Every morning we were up and eating breakfast with the President by seven o'clock, and we seldom got to bed much before midnight. In the meantime, Sukarno had made five or six speeches, the shortest of which was at least thirty minutes long, and most of them lasted at least an hour.

He had also interviewed countless residents of the cities and towns we visited, attended luncheons and dinners, and every evening taken part in local dances in packed public halls where he danced every dance. Sukarno was about five or six years older than I, but he thrived on this program; I almost withered away.

At a time when, and in an area where, there had been great vocal dissatisfaction with the central government in Djakarta, it was most interesting to see how Sukarno was received by the people. School children gathered around him and shouted "Great President!" I was reminded of the way high school girls in America used to surge around Frank Sinatra. Sukarno was a man who liked to have people around him at all times, and he always insisted they come close to him and sit at his feet, close enough to touch him. When he made speeches he would start out quietly so that you had to strain to hear him; gradually he would build up to a crescendo at which point his listeners would often shout with uncontrolled emotion. I never saw him use a note while speaking. All his talks had the same central theme, but each was adapted to the local audience. After listening for two or three days to these speeches I was almost able to understand what he was saying, although my knowledge of Bahasa Indonesian (the postindependence national language) was negligible.

Our first stop was in Macassar, the largest city of Sulawesi, where we took part in the opening ceremonies of the Indonesian Olympic Games. Representatives from all parts of the country were present, and on the evening we arrived, the night before the games opened, each region presented its native dance.

The next day we went to the opening of the Olympic Games and witnessed a parade of the delegations from all parts of Indonesia, including Central and North Sumatra, all dressed in special uniforms representing their regions and yet, when the marching ceased and they all faced the grandstand where stood Sukarno, they all joined in singing the National Anthem, *Indo-*

*nesia Raya.* Many of them came from parts of the country and from ethnic groups that had never used the national Indonesian language until after independence, and from areas where there were incipient rebellions against the central government. Yet all joined in this noteworthy demonstration of unity. The President stood on a special platform during this ceremony, and at the end of the singing the crowd cheered him over and over. Was there really a rebellion about to break out?

In his speeches in Menado, Sukarno received a tremendous ovation when he said, "We have no intention of changing the color of our flag — it will remain red *and white.*" Eighty percent of the people in the Menado area are Christian, the majority Protestant. Sukarno talked at a Protestant church and at a Catholic school. These speeches were somewhat shorter than normal, and in each he stressed the fact that Indonesia was founded on the foundation of a belief in God and that no form of political organization was possible which denied that belief in God. Taken literally, this would of course rule out the Communists who could take no pleasure from any of the speeches the President made on this tour.

At his worst Sukarno was certainly a rabble rouser, but in his more lofty moments he was the creator of a spirit of unity for all Indonesia. Superficially, there were no signs on this trip that Indonesia was breaking up, although there were numerous signs of discontent with the central government, signs which were often painted on cloth and wood and displayed prominently. Whenever Sukarno spoke he always requested that such signs be removed, and they were. There was no evidence of any anti-Sukarno activity or of a desire by the regions to withdraw from Indonesia, only of a desire that the central government take their desires and problems into account and pay more attention to the regions.

Several so-called fellow-traveler members of the Cabinet were on this trip. The one who became most friendly was Chairul

Saleh, the Minister for Veterans Affairs. I had been warned against him by my predecessor who believed him to be a dangerous revolutionary and an enemy of America. On one or two of the long drives from one Sukarno speech to another I shared a car with Saleh, and we talked at length. After a bit, as he seemed to be talking rather frankly, I told him that many Americans considered him a Communist. He looked at me and a friendly grin appeared for a moment; then he said in a rather solemn tone, "I really don't know what I am, but I am not a Communist." He added, "I am not anti-Communist either, but I have no desire to help them." He said that both the United States and Russia made great mistakes with the Indonesians as a result of two attitudes. The first was particularly true of the Americans and to a lesser degree of the Russians, and this was that we did not make sufficient effort to understand the Indonesians; second, that judged them by our own standards and backgrounds. He said the second point was equally true of the Russians, and that both they and the Americans spent entirely too much time criticizing each other.

Education Minister Prijono, who had received the Stalin Peace Prize, was another of the alleged fellow travelers whom I met on this Presidential outing. He was a gentle, rather reserved man, but he appeared to be friendly and willing to talk with the American Ambassador. I discovered he was an avid reader of detective stories and was particularly fond of the books by Agatha Christie. I wondered if any real, dedicated Communist would admit to such tastes.

The *Pantjasila*, which had been enunciated by Sukarno in June of 1945, before the declaration of Indonesian independence, was referred to by him in all of his speeches in Sulawesi. It is a statement of five principles which form the basic ideology of the Indonesian State, and the first of these is a statement of belief in God. The other four refer to internationalism, nationalism, the sovereignty of the people, and social justice. They are rather vague principles, as are most statements of Indonesian philosophy, and they have been variously interpreted at different times by Sukarno as well as by other politicians. Yet the statement of belief in God has been continuously stressed throughout the history of Indonesian independence and had been used by all the non-Communist elements to oppose the PKI.

On all occasions when Sukarno was entertained or was giving an informal speech he would introduce to the crowd the foreign guests he had brought with him. I was always called "the bald-headed American Ambassador" and the crowd would always laugh and cheer. None of the other Ambassadors was given any special attention. In Menado and elsewhere in northern Sulawesi the people were extremely friendly toward America. As I appeared on the platform with the President or sitting near him at an evening reception the crowd would often yell, "Bald-headed American Ambassador," and I would be compelled to join in the local dance. As we drove through the countryside around Menado, school children would cry out "American" in English and point at me. Wherever we stopped in that region I was surrounded by children requesting my autograph. Saleh noted this and remarked on the apparent high regard the people had for America.

Not once during the six days we were away from the capital did the President, the five Cabinet members, or any other Indonesian official make any attempt to get into communication with Djakarta, and I saw no one buy a newspaper to see what was going on in Indonesia or the rest of the world. As Sukarno made such trips three or four times a year it was easy to see why it was often so difficult to get high-level decisions from the Indonesian Government. And yet life went on, and every now and then something was accomplished. With it all the President absorbed a tremendous amount of information and found time to read widely, not only in Indonesian but in English and Dutch as well. At a talk at the Protestant church in Menado

Sukarno mentioned that there was too much criticism of the central government and then, in English, referred to the Bible and said: "Let him who is without sin cast the first stone." He was truly a remarkable man. It is a great shame that Washington decided too soon that he was beyond redemption.

Upon my return to Djakarta, hot, tired, and dirty, with most of my luggage apparently still in Macassar, I discovered that during my absence my wife had not been neglected. One morning there appeared at the Embassy residence three young students from the University of Indonesia with their heads shaved to produce a top knot similar to those seen on some American Indians. They explained they were being initiated into one of the university clubs, similar to American fraternities, and had been assigned the task of cleaning up the floor of the residence, and they asked if Mrs. Allison would permit them to do so. She not only gave them permission but sent for the USIS photographer to come and take pictures of the young men at work. She provided them with Coca-Cola and before they left asked them to sign our guest book, which she showed them contained the names of the Crown Prince of Japan, Eleanor Roosevelt, Vice President and Mrs. Nixon, and numerous other world figures. In her turn my wife had to sign certificates for each young man testifying that he had completed his assigned task in a satisfactory manner. The next day pictures of her and the three students appeared in the local press and did nothing to hurt the reputation of America or Americans.

However, the general situation continued to go from bad to worse. Trouble in the outlying regions increased; anti-Dutch activities were stepped up. Sukarno made a public statement that if the Indonesian resolution at the United Nations was once again defeated, he would take drastic action. He did not say what this would be, but from all the reports pouring into the Embassy from various sources among the Indonesians and the Diplomatic Corps as well as nervous Dutch friends it seemed clear that this "drastic action" would mean the expulsion of the Dutch from Indonesia. This would be a great tragedy, not only for the poor Dutch people involved, most of whom had no ties in Holland and whose lives were bound up with Indonesia, but also for Indonesia and its faltering economy. Walter Smith, my Economic Officer, told me that the Secretary of the Dutch Chamber of Commerce had come to him and, almost with tears in his eyes, cried, "Can't you persuade Washington to do something to make those fools at The Hague understand that in order to be permitted to spend 80 million guilders a year to maintain their position in West Irian and supposedly enhance Dutch prestige, they are about to lose 400 million guilders a year in trade with Indonesia?"

While the situation in India drifted inconclusively, my wife and I were to spend four days in Bali participating in one of the most fantastic and fascinating events of our whole diplomatic career.

An hereditary Prince of the district of Gianjar in northern Bali — a former Foreign Minister and Ambassador to France — Anak Agung Gde Agung, invited us to be his guests at the formal ceremonial cremation of one of his uncles and several lesser relatives which would take place at, and near, his family estate on Bali. The people of Bali had remained faithful to the Hindu religion when it had been succeeded on the other islands by Mohammedanism. We had known the Anak Agung (the term means "son of the king") in Djakarta, where he was still officially attached to the Foreign Office in a consultative capacity. He explained to us that for the people of Bali a cremation was not an occasion for sadness but for joy. According to their belief, the soul remains in the vicinity of the body and cannot go to paradise until after cremation. A body cannot be cremated until certain religious rites have been observed, and these may continue for a year or more after death. When the cremation finally takes place, at a time designated by the local High Priest, there is a great celebration. We discovered that between two and three thousand people from all over Indonesia had been invited, although only a small number, among which we were fortunately included, were invited to participate in all the special ceremonies which took place in addition to the main event.

Lionel Landry, through whom our invitation had been sent, was our chief guide. The invitation had come through him because the Anak Agung, a Prince, could not be affronted directly with a refusal. He told us that we should take as presents a silver box, a little larger than an ordinary cigarette box, and a bolt of white linen cloth. Just why we were to bring the cloth we didn't know but were to find out. Bill Palmer had an invitation too, and so we all flew down together, arriving at Den Pasar in the middle of the afternoon. This was before the day of the modern Western-style hotel, and the small hotel there was already filled to overflowing with Indonesian guests. We were taken a little way out of town along the beach to where Jim Pandy, a dealer in Oriental art, particularly Balinese paintings and carved figures, maintained a small guest establishment. The rooms were not air-conditioned, and the plumbing was extremely primitive, but the scenery was magnificent, and Jim offered great hospitality and friendliness.

The next morning we were taken out to the family *puri* (the palace of a prince) which was completely surrounded by a brick wall with a most impressive entrance. Inside the wall there was a series of pavilions, in the first of which various members of the family in gorgeous ceremonial costumes were gathered. We were welcomed and served soft drinks. We also began to be informed about the various stages of the ceremonies we were to witness and were then taken to a second pavilion in which were kept the bodies or replicas which were to be cremated. A cremation is a tremendously expensive undertaking and lesser members of a family often are compelled to wait until some more wealthy member of the family dies so their deceased can participate, at a reduced cost, in the main cremation.

On this occasion there were eleven bodies to be cremated. Two of them were close relatives of the Prince and would thus be placed in the highest of the towers in which the bodies would be taken to the cemetery. The nine others would occupy towers of lesser magnificence. Behind the pavilion were the two main coffins, each carved from a tree trunk in the shape of a bull and gaily decorated with horns in solid gold leaf. The orchestra in the pavilion played a rather humming type of tune in order not to disturb the spirits of the dead. Outside the pavilion was another orchestra complete with drums which were pounded vigorously accompanying a continuous explosion of firecrackers. This was to drive away evil spirits and also prevent rain. When any clouds appeared in the sky the drums were beaten more vigorously than ever. The rain stayed away.

We were also shown the great serpent or *naga banda*, with its brightly painted head, a long rope body and intricately carved and brightly painted tail, used only at cremations of descendants of the highest aristocracy of the land.

After the morning at the puri we were taken outside the wall where tables and chairs had been set up for a luncheon for over a thousand people. The Prince knew that Mrs. Allison was allergic to certain foods, and he had prepared a special table for her with only foods she could eat. There was enough for a dozen people so some of the rest of our party helped her out. Among the guests at the luncheon were not only representatives of the central government but also representatives of the disaffected regions including Colonel Sumual, whom I had last seen in Menado where he was the leader of the opposition to Djakarta.

When the lunch was over we were led back to the puri and conducted to a spot on one corner of the wall where we would be able to have a good view of the ceremonies connected with placing the bodies in the towers. The younger sister of the Anak

Agung sat next to us and explained what was going on. Right in front of us was the main tower which soared eighty-three feet into the air. According to Miguel Covarrubias in his book *Island of Bali* the tower represents the cosmos, with its various projections symbolizing the underworld, the earth, and heaven. There was a ramp leading from the puri to the tower, and it was up this ramp that the bodies or the effigies were taken to be placed in the tower. The rather carefree and careless manner in which the bodies were handled was at first something of a shock, but we were told this was customary and merely illustrated the Balinese belief that the body was nothing and the soul everything. At various points on, and around, the tower were men with stuffed birds of paradise on thin sticks which would pivot with the wind and were supposed to be showing the souls of the deceased the way to paradise. The tower was based upon intertwined bamboo poles, and it was of such height and weight that one thousand men were required to lift it and carry it on their shoulders to the cemetery. Several hundred yards ahead of the main tower was a smaller pavilion also carried on the shoulders of local farmers and in it were the Prince, his brother, and the ceremonial, carved bulls which would be the coffins in which the bodies would be cremated. The High Priest also rode in this pavilion, but before he entered he shot arrows into the air in all directions to determine how the soul should be guided to heaven.

The head of the great serpent, which we had seen earlier, was in the pavilion, and its rope body extended back to the tower where its tail was draped around the base. Over the body of the serpent was held a curtain of white cloth which had been blessed by the High Priest. We discovered the white cloth we had brought was used either for this purpose or to wrap the bodies of the deceased and the effigies. As the tower was lifted onto the shoulders of the men and moved out toward the cremation grounds it swayed back and forth and reminded one of a ship moving out to sea. The family and their retainers followed the pavilion and the towers as they wound their way to the cemetery over a circuitous route that would deceive any evil spirits who might be about. We were taken by a more direct route and were seated directly in front of where the pavilion would be stationed upon its arrival. A ramp was arranged from the tower to the pavilion, and the bodies were brought down and placed in the bulls. Large quantities of holy water were sprinkled on the bodies by the Prince and the High Priest, and quantities of green turf were placed under the pavilion to catch the ashes so that they could later by gathered and placed in urns before they were taken out to sea. When the fires were finally set the surrounding wood was so dry that the crackle of the flames sounded like an explosion of hundreds of huge firecrackers. As the flames began to die down specially selected young men scaled the towers to their very tip to recover the gold nuggets that had been placed there. If they succeeded in this difficult task, the crowds shouted with glee, and the nuggets were theirs to keep.

In the latter part of the next afternoon we returned to the cemetery to watch the ceremonies connected with taking the ashes out to sea. As we sat at the side of the large field where the cremation had taken place, the Anak Agung (the Prince) came over to tell us more about the traditions that governed these ceremonies. As he was talking to us, a young retainer almost literally slithered across the grass on his stomach, in the old servile manner in which generations of peasants had approached the ruling aristocracy, to bring a message to his Lord. The Anak Agung was obviously embarrassed and tried to get the youngster to rise. He later told us that he thought this would have to be the last cremation because not only did they cost too much but the preparations for them, which lasted more than three months, took too many of the peasants out of the fields with adverse results to agricultural production as well as to the income of the workers.

The Anak Agung was a modern-minded man who was trying

to help his people adjust to the twentieth century. He was deeply concerned about the difficulties of doing this and at the same time maintaining as much as possible of the old traditions. He was sure of one thing however, and that was that communism was not the answer. His opposition to the policies of Sukarno, which he believed were leading to Communist domination, were to result in his imprisonment, after we had left the country, from which he was not released until after Sukarno's downfall in 1966.

When we had seen the ashes collected and taken in small, torch-lit boats down the river to the sea, we were again taken to another family puri for dinner. After dinner we were taken up the side of the mountain, across a swaying bridge spanning a river far below, to a clearing where the local peasants were to put on for us the famous *Ketjak* or Monkey Dance. This tells the story from a Hindu epic of how the King of the Monkeys helped the king to rescue his wife from the evil king of Ceylon. The dance was put on outdoors, the only light coming from torches and a flickering moonbeam. All the participants were local people who during the day worked in the fields or at household chores. Some fifty to sixty half-naked men sat cross legged in circles waving their hands above them and chanting the monkey chorus, while local maidens in fantastic costumes danced in and out among them.

Returning to the puri we found that the ceremonies were not yet over. We were taken to a pavilion at one end of which was a stage. We were seated facing the stage, while the Indonesian guests were at the sides. The men and boys were on our left and the women and girls on our right. They were packed so tightly together that they looked much like a typical Balinese painting. Below the stage was a gamelan orchestra composed of members of the family with elaborate instruments which had been in the family for generations. The leader of the orchestra, the drummer, was an uncle of the Anak Agung. The dancers were teenage youngsters in gorgeous costumes, but the star was really the five-year-old nephew of the Anak Agung who did a dance of his own for which he had been well trained. He wore a gold crown made especially for him, and we were told that when the crown became too small for his head it was put aside and never used again. It was late at night when we fell exhausted into our beds, and even the ubiquitous mosquitoes didn't keep us awake.

Upon our return from Bali it was evident that the political situation as well as the economic had not improved. If anything, it had deteriorated. The local press was full of accounts of efforts that were being made to reform the government and bring former Vice President Hatta back into office. For a while it looked as if this might happen, but Sukarno and Hatta just couldn't get along. It is one of the great tragedies of history that these two exceptional men did not trust each other and could not work together. Hatta had the economic knowledge and temperament which would have enabled him to devise policies to rehabilitate the economy of the country. Sukarno had the ability to sell these policies to the people and convince them of the necessity of carrying out Hatta's recommendations.

Any plan which might have any chance of being considered for stopping the slide into the abyss would have to take into account the interests of all parties involved. The Indonesian desire for West Irian would have to be met in some way. The Dutch economic and financial interests would have to be protected. The Australian concern about possible unrest and violence in a territory bordering on Australian territory would have to be assuaged. The American interest in a peaceful, stable, non-Communist Indonesia stretching across the lines of communication between our Philippine and ANZUS allies would have to be taken into account.

Finally, I came up with a plan that I thought might be worth proposing to Washington. Before I did so, I discussed it with my Indonesian friends. All of them expressed some reservations about parts of my plan, but they did say they would agree to consider it as a basis for discussion if it were proposed officially by Washington. When I discussed my plan with Jim McIntyre, the Australian Ambassador, he said that personally he would be inclined to support it but that he doubted his superiors in Canberra would do so.

With a lump in my throat, I sent off two messages to Washington. The first began by saying that with respect to the West Irian problem I believed it had reached a stage where we could no longer sit by and say we were neutral. The agitation for West Irian had been, in the first instance, artificially stimulated and from the viewpoint of abstract morals, Indonesia had no more right to rule West Irian than the Dutch. However, the problem of long-term interests of the Dutch, the United States, and the free world in Asia required some early solution.

The plan proposed to Washington consisted of six points which would have to be generally agreed to as a result of quiet diplomatic negotiations before any public announcement. This would obviously require considerable initiative and responsibility being taken by the United States Government, but I stated that this was essential if we wanted "to keep this important nation of eighty million out of the hands of the Communists." Upon obtaining agreement of the Dutch, Australians, and the Indonesians the plan would go into operation by stages along the following lines:

1. Indonesians would publicly renounce the use or threat of force with respect to the West Irian problem.

2. The Dutch would announce willingness to negotiate providing negotiations would include consideration of the repudiated Indonesian debt, North Sumatra oil, and the position of Dutch commerce and industry in Indonesia. (I made no attempt to indicate what this settlement might be as I considered it a matter to be settled between the Indonesians and the Dutch.)

3. At the end of the negotiations mentioned under the second point (which would take at least six months), it would be announced that at the end of a stated period, say five years, sovereignty over West Irian would be transferred to Indonesia and that:

(a) during these five years the Dutch would undertake training at an accelerated rate of Indonesian and native administrators and Indonesians would provide, at their expense, such administrators as might be available to work under the Dutch for this period.

(b) upon the transfer of sovereignty the Dutch would agree to allow certain officials to remain for a further stated period under nominal Indonesian control and at Indonesian expense.

4. Indonesia would agree that the ANZUS Pact might be extended to cover any hostile attack on West Irian and might even agree to be associated with the ANZUS powers in the limited area of West Irian. (This provision which was designed to bring Australia into the picture was the only one which my Indonesian friends boggled at, but they admitted that if all other parts of the plan were agreed to there would not be much reason to refuse to go along with this point.)

5. The Indonesian Government would undertake to control strictly all Communist activity within Indonesia and would accept American assistance and guidance in antisubversive activities. (This provision was designed to make Sukarno live up to his oft repeated statement that if America would only agree with his position on West Irian he could cut the Communists down to size.)

6. The United States would undertake an expanded aid program in Indonesia with the understanding that a large part of it would be designed to aid the regions and assist in the solution of regional problems.

I pointed out in conclusion that there were obviously other

elements that could and should be included in an overall settlement but that the above suggestions would indicate the lines along which a settlement might be reached. The five-year period prior to the transfer of sovereignty would give an opportunity to observe Indonesian action under point 5. I urged that serious and prompt consideration be given to some such action, and I reported that Subandrio would be in New York shortly for the UN debate and that I believed he would be receptive to any suggestions.

The telegrams containing the Embassy's suggested plan were sent to Washington on November 4, 1957. At a reception about ten days later at one of the foreign embassies, Deputy Prime Minister Hardi took me aside and anxiously inquired whether or not I had heard anything from Washington about officially proposing the plan we had suggested. Hardi was sure that if nothing was done, Sukarno was determined to expel the Dutch, and Hardi, as well as men like Hatta, the Anak Agung, Sjafruddin, the President of the Central Bank of Indonesia, and others, all knew that the expulsion of the Dutch would constitute a mortal blow to Indonesia's economy. I had to tell Hardi that I had heard nothing. In fact I never did receive a direct reply from the State Department commenting on our proposal. The only way in which I knew that Washington had paid any attention at all to it was that we did receive from our Embassies in Canberra and The Hague copies of messages they had sent Washington reporting Australian and Dutch official positions and damning the proposal, which had been sent to them by the Department for comment.

About that time John Steeves, a Foreign Service Officer acting as Political Advisor to the Commander in Chief, Pacific, in Honolulu, visited Djakarta in the course of an official tour throughout Asia. He was told the whole story and listened most sympathetically. After he had returned to Honolulu, and shortly before I left Indonesia, I had a letter from him dated January 13, 1958.

In view of my treatment by the Department this letter from John was most comforting. He said:

> Because I believe so strongly in the general thesis that you set forth some time ago and that we discussed again when I was with you in Djakarta, I have used whatever influence I have here to support your position. I did it through these channels rather than directly to the Department of State although I am formulating in my mind a communication by letter which I am going to send to Walter [Robertson] which will touch upon the subject again. Shortly after my return, however, and after talking with Gordon Mein [Department officer dealing with Indonesia] and learning that he held views similar to yours and mine, I did draft a very lengthy message from CINCPAC through his superiors urging that the highest levels in Washington give most urgent consideration to the proposals very much along the line you sent in to the Department and that we have since referred to among ourselves here as the "Allison Plan."

By the time this letter had been received it was already too late; the UN resolution had not received the required two-thirds majority, the Dutch had been expelled, and the regions were heading for open rebellion.

Before any of this had come about we had an interesting visitor from Washington, the late Congressman D. S. Saund of California and his wife. Mr. Saund was a native of what had been British India but had emigrated to the United States and had now been elected to Congress. I was happy to introduce him to my Indonesian friends as an example of American democracy and belief in racial equality. On the afternoon of November 15, I took him to Bogor to have an interview with Sukarno. Sukarno was as articulate as usual, and his whole theme was West Irian. He began by repeating his well-known statement that if only America would agree in principle with the Indonesian stand on West Irian, he could relegate the Communists to a position of no influence. He went on to say that the United States should not think that economic and other material aid was the only thing important in this age of nationalism in Asia.

Sukarno paused a moment and then, looking Mr. Saund straight in the eye, continued: "While raising the living standards of the people is important, remember, 'Man does not live by bread alone.'" For the first time in my presence, Sukarno then added that the important thing was to agree on the principle that West Irian was Indonesian; the details of how it should be turned over could be worked out over several years, if only the principle were agreed to.

Washington kept saying that Indonesia was extremely important, but it was hard to tell in Djakarta just how much they really meant it. About the same time as Congressman Saund arrived, Val Goodell, the CIA Station Chief, who had been in Washington on consultation, returned and told me of the great interest Washington had in Indonesia and the concern with which developments there were watched. On November 19 I wrote a personal letter to Walter Robertson reporting my talk with Goodell and saying that if this concern was real, "I would assume the Department would wish the best possible staffing in Indonesia and would give more than routine attention to the situation here."

I then pointed out that with respect to policy matters the Embassy had cabled on September 13 its comments on the conclusions of the Ad Hoc Committee concerning policy toward Indonesia and that even now, more than two months later, "the Embassy has had no indication of any sort from the Department as to whether the Committee's conclusions were finally approved . . . and the request in the Embassy's message for clarification of certain points has remained unanswered. In effect we do not know what present U.S. policy is toward Indonesia except by deduction from the Department's instruction on individual matters."

Turning to the staff, I reported that I was the only Foreign

Service Officer in all of Indonesia with prewar experience. At that time we were operating with an Acting Deputy Chief of Mission, the regular Deputy being on extended sick leave, an acting head of the Political section, an acting head of the Economic section, and an Administrative officer, all of whom had less than one year's experience at the post. In all of Indonesia we had only two language officers, one in the Embassy and one in Surabaya. They were both good men but were junior in grade and lacked extended experience in the country. There were numerous other deficiencies which I mentioned, and I said that if Indonesia is as important as I thought it was and as the State Department apparently did, as indicated by Goodell's report to me, I believed greater effort should be made to secure able and experienced personnel. I concluded by saying that I did not believe the Embassy was getting the detailed attention it needed if it was to do a proper job for our government. While I believed I should come home on consultation as soon as possible, I hesitated to press the point in view of the personnel situation in Djakarta. I was never destined to get that consultation in Washington. Instead, the Department sent Gordon Mein out to consult with me in Djakarta.

Gordon was then head of the Office of Southwest Pacific Affairs in the Department and had previously served in Indonesia and was well known to, and favorably looked upon by, many of the leading figures involved in the Indonesian political world. He was an able officer and all of us who knew him were shocked and grieved when in 1968 he was assassinated by left-wing toughs in Guatemala, where he was serving as American Ambassador. I looked forward to his arrival in Djakarta, but before he came the Dutch had been expelled, Sukarno had been attacked, and I had another set-to with the Department.

On November 29, the UN resolution calling upon the Dutch and Indonesians to undertake negotiation on the West Irian issue had failed to receive the required two-thirds majority. The

United States had abstained in the voting thus officially maintaining its neutrality, but I was informed that in private conversations in the UN corridors it was made clear that the United States would not be offended if the resolution should be defeated. It was not long before the Indonesian Government was informed of this, and it did nothing to reduce Sukarno's suspicions of Washington.

The very next day, while Indonesian passions were heating up as a result of the UN action, there was an attempt to assassinate Sukarno, who was leaving a ceremony at the Tjikini primary school where two of his children were enrolled. A total of five hand grenades were thrown, and although two landed close to Sukarno, he escaped uninjured. Nine people were killed, three policemen and six children, and over a hundred were wounded. Early rumors that this attempt had been Dutch inspired were fortunately found to be completely untrue when members of a fanatical, anti-Communist Moslem group were arrested and brought to trial, where they admitted their guilt.

Sukarno did not lose much time in carrying out his threat to expel the Dutch and take over their properties. As a result of their stubbornness in refusing even to discuss the problem of West Irian with the Indonesians, the Dutch lost close to $2 billion worth of properties, and almost 50,000 Dutch citizens were sent back to the Netherlands. A substantial portion of these were Eurasians who had no real roots in the Netherlands, and their plight was pitiful. I couldn't help but reflect on what might have been the case if only Washington had backed our Embassy's plan which would at least have gotten talks started and taken Sukarno off the hook of having to expel the Dutch. And our plan did have certain safeguards which were ignored five years later when, at American insistence, an agreement was finally reached to turn West Irian over to Indonesia.

The late Alfred Duff-Cooper, British writer, former Cabinet Minister, and Ambassador to France, has a sentence in his memoirs, *Old Men Forget,* which immediately called to mind the experience of the Dutch with regard to West Irian. He writes: "It would be interesting to collect historical instances of harm that has been done by the reluctance of men to accept readily what they know they will have to accept in the end."

Walter Robertson had sent me finally a full reply to some of my previous messages and had given an indication of what type of action Washington was prepared to take. This turned out to be mostly military and covert.

After Gordon arrived, and I had listened to his accounts of Washington thinking on Indonesian problems, I realized that it would be hopeless to get Washington to come out directly in support of the Indonesian stand on West Irian. While Gordon agreed in general with my approach, he was too junior to make his voice decisive. Most of the decisions on Indonesian policy were being made in the Secretary's office. We decided the best we could do would be to keep Washington from coming down on the side of the Dutch and to urge action in various spheres, both economic and military, which would encourage the Indonesians to believe in the friendship of the United States. We didn't have much success.

While Gordon was in Djakarta it became increasingly evident that leaders of the Masjumi party and the right wing of the PNI were developing plans for the establishment of a definitely non-Communist government. We told the State Department it would be necessary to give these people active encouragement if their efforts were to bear fruit. We did not believe, as Washington seemed to, that it would be sufficient to indicate that if a satisfactory new regime was formed, the United States would promptly open negotiations on assistance programs. Mein and I said we believed it was essential to determine in advance what we were prepared to do for such a government and that if this was known, it would give those working for a change added leverage to bring it about. While stating that detailed recommendations would be brought back personally by Mein, we did state that immediately upon the formation of a satisfactory new government we should be prepared to offer military and economic assistance and "most important to be able to give the new government some assurance that we would use our influence to get talks with Netherlands opened." We stated that we believed a new, more conservative government might be able to control local agitation if talks were opened, even if it was not specifically stated that they were dealing with New Guinea.

It was not clear to us whether or not any new government which might be formed would oust Sukarno or be strong enough to dominate him while keeping him in his titular position of President. When Gordon flew back to Washington just before Christmas, I gave him a personal message to deliver to Walter Robertson with the request to pass it on to the Secretary. I expressed the belief that there were two ways to handle the present Indonesian situation. The one which I preferred was to work through Sukarno, to whom I was accredited, but this would require the Department to give me some bait with which Sukarno could be tempted into the American camp. This Washington seemed reluctant to do. If Washington was convinced that Sukarno was beyond redemption, then the other course was to work for the establishment of a government in which Sukarno would not appear, or if he did, would have no decisive influence. I said I believed either course would work providing Washington followed it through one hundred percent, including, if the second alternative was adopted, putting pressure on the Dutch to open talks. If Washington did this, I was prepared to go along, otherwise I did not believe I should remain in Indonesia. In the end, Washington did neither. It gave half-hearted support to the rebels which was quickly discovered by the Sukarno government, and which proved ineffective. The rebels were defeated. The United States fell between two stools, and its influence with Sukarno fell to a new low.

At the New Year's Day reception at Merdeka Palace, President Sukarno seemed more than usually friendly and greeted both Mrs. Allison and me with broad smiles and a hearty handshake. Other members of the government were also attentive, and I attributed it to a desire to demonstrate publicly that they did not give any credence to the spate of anti-Allison cartoons and stories in the Communist-dominated press, all of which implied I was working against the government. Even General Nasution, the Army Chief of Staff, who generally kept aloof from all foreigners, shook hands briefly with me and said a friendly "Good Morning." After the palace reception we gave a smaller one at the Embassy residence for members of the Diplomatic Corps and a few Indonesians. It went off well, and when the New Year's celebrations were over we drove up to our weekend cottage in the Puntjak, hoping to have a relaxed few days away from the stifling heat of Djakarta.

While sitting on our verandah reading and sipping a gin and tonic before a late lunch on January 4, Greg Hackler unexpectedly came in with a message for me which he had just brought up from Djakarta. It was a personal cable from Loy Henderson, Deputy Under Secretary of State for Administration, a good friend and extremely able officer, who had done much to improve the Foreign Service in the postwar years. I was dumbfounded when I read it. Without any preamble except to state it was in response to my message sent to Walter Robertson through Gordon Mein, it said that the Department would like to recommend to the President my appointment as Ambassador to Czechoslovakia. I was asked to reply immediately whether or not the appointment was acceptable, as the present incumbent, Alex Johnson, was leaving shortly. Loy, a kind and understanding man, put in a paragraph saying that Prague was one of our key posts in Eastern Europe and that it would be helpful to have there an Ambassador with my experience and knowledge of Communist objectives and tactics.

The next paragraph of the message was really startling. It suggested that I begin to make arrangements for leaving Indonesia by the first of February but instructed me in the meantime, until I heard further from Washington, not to discuss this matter with anyone except my wife. How we were to make preparations to leave within little more than three weeks, which would entail beginning to pack, making reservations by air or ship, and getting rid of our weekend cottage, without talking to anyone but ourselves I could not envisage. I knew nothing about Czechoslovakia except for the brief time spent there with Doug Poteat in 1946, before it had fallen into the hands of the Communists.

My initial reaction was to tell the Department to go chase itself around the block and to submit my resignation accompanied by a request for retirement from the Foreign Service. Toots was also mad, but we decided to sleep on it. After considerable thought and discussion with my wife I sent off a reply on the morning of January 6. I stated that from the first sentence of Loy's message I assumed that the policy to be carried out in Indonesia lacked the elements I had told Mein I considered essential and that if this was so, it would be difficult for me to carry out such a policy and the government would be better served by another Ambassador in Djakarta. While neither Mrs. Allison nor I was happy about going to Prague, we agreed that, as a career officer, I should be willing to go where the Department wished. I then pointed out the difficulties involved in trying to leave by February 1, and I requested our departure be delayed until March 1. During two weeks of almost daily cable exchanges with the Department about plans for our departure and the proper public announcement to accompany it, Loy Henderson was most helpful. It was finally agreed that while we should leave Djakarta about February 1, we did not need to arrive in Prague until about the twentieth of March and that, except for two weeks' consultation in the Department, we could divide the time between February 1 and March 20 as we wished between travel and leave. But I still was not supposed to tell anyone of my impending departure, although, in almost every message to the Department, I repeated that it would not be possible to delay an announcement much longer. On January 13 I reported that in view of recent press stories about my alleged subversive activities as well as stories from Washington claiming differences between me and the Department, the announcement of my departure would create a real public relations problem in Djakarta, and I requested early guidance as to what line to take.

It was not until January 15 that I was able to tell Prime Minister Djuanda about my early departure. I explained I was being transferred as a result of a far-flung, interrelated series of diplomatic transfers. Even then I had to ask Djuanda not to give any publicity to my impending departure, and I was not able to tell him who would succeed me. Djuanda commented that eleven months seemed a short time to leave an Ambassador in a post and pointed out that my predecessor had been there over three years.

While not making any public announcement of my transfer, I did not think it right to conceal the matter from my senior staff. I therefore called in each member of the country team one by one and told them the story. Greg Hackler already knew, but the head of the aid program, Jim Baird, Lionel Landry of USIS, and the Army, Navy, and Air Attachés were all surprised. I was flattered by what seemed sincere expressions of regret, but I was profoundly shocked, although not greatly surprised, at the story told me by my Naval Attaché, a Lieutenant Colonel in the Marine Corps Air Force. He had come to Djakarta several months after I had, and he told me that prior to his departure from Washington he had had an interview with my predecessor. After a brief discussion he had been told that he should report everything just as he saw it and that he didn't have to worry about what the Ambassador was reporting, for he, the Ambassador, was only a second-rate officer. The Colonel went on to say that after he had worked almost six months in Indonesia he found that his estimate of the situation agreed substantially with what he knew to be my position. That was the first and only time in thirty years in the Foreign Service that I had experienced this type of backbiting and apparent personal jealousy. One of the chief attractions of the Foreign Service as I had known it from the time I entered as a clerk in 1930, was that it was possible for an individual officer to get ahead on his own, without having to step on the necks of his fellow officers. I hope this is still true, but from the agitation for union-type organizations and grievance committees by some of the younger men who have recently come into the Foreign Service, I have my doubts. I wonder what I would have done had there been a grievance committee on whose shoulders I could have wept, during my' frustrating year in Indonesia and upon my unwanted transfer to Czechoslovakia.

The Department finally informed me it wished to send Howard Jones to replace me and requested me to obtain the agreement of the Indonesian Government. Howard was at that time Deputy Assistant Secretary of State for Far Eastern Economic Affairs. He had previously served in Indonesia as head of the economic aid mission, and he had also served as Deputy Chief of Mission in Taipei. He was an able and hard-working officer, and I knew he had been well liked by the Indonesians with whom he had worked.

While all these exchanges had been going on I had requested my staff to prepare a roundup of the recommendations we had made to Washington for action in Indonesia, and on January 16 I cabled the State Department about five closely related problems affecting relations between the United States and Indonesia which apparently were either ignored or misunderstood or were being treated as if they were completely separate and unrelated problems. These were: (1) arms for internal security; (2) inter-island shipping; (3) an American airline to serve Indonesia; (4) technical assistance for Garuda, the Indonesian airline; and (5) additional aircraft for Garuda.

I stated that press reports had recently indicated that Washington was looking with renewed interest at Japanese Foreign Minister Kishi's Southeast Asia Development proposal and that Congress might increase foreign aid in the coming year. It was indicated that both these policy shifts were designed to help the United States regain prestige lost as a result of the Russian success with Sputnik.

The issue regarding arms will give an indication of what we were up against. The State Department's position about supplying arms to Indonesia, as we understood it, was that it feared such arms might be used to attack separatist movements in the outer islands, or that they might be used to attack West Irian, or, in the third place, that in the event of a Communist conquest of Java, our arms would fall into Communist hands. Our military attachés had assured us that any amphibious operation would be impractical and highly improbable with the weapons that the Embassy proposed giving to the Indonesians. With regard to the fear that United States arms might fall into the hands of the Communists, we pointed out that if the United States would not supply arms, the Indonesians would accept them from the Soviet bloc. We emphasized that the United States was putting itself in a completely untenable position by refusing to grant arms for fear that they might fall into the hands of the Communists and by that refusal actually encouraging the Indonesians to seek arms from the Communists. We heard nothing from Washington before my departure. It was with a rather sardonic grin that I later noted that on the following April 7, the State Department spokesman declared, "We regret that Indonesia turned to the Communist bloc to buy arms for possible use in killing Indonesians who openly oppose the growing influence of Communism in Indonesia."

At the end of December, Jim Baird, head of the semi-independent economic aid mission had sent a twelve-page memorandum to his superiors in Washington which in large measure supported everything those of us in the Embassy proper had been saying. Jim gave me a copy. I noted that at one point he said: "A further source of distress is that while there is almost complete unanimity in Djakarta among responsible American government officials . . . as to how our country should proceed, this advice is not being followed."

On January 25, shortly after the news of my transfer had become public, Charles Tambu in an editorial in the *Times of Indonesia* stated that I had "brought courage and a fresh mind to bear on some of the problems which have dogged our relations, both with the United States and the Netherlands." After commenting at some length on my transfer he concluded:

Mr. Allison's departure marks a significant victory for the extreme left wing in Indonesian politics — and anyone who doubts our statement should read the Communist and fellow-travelling papers to savour their uninhibited glee at Mr. Allison's abrupt recall. Indonesian-American relations have come to an all-time low: further deterioration is impossible because we have struck rock bottom. The United States could not have worked harder or more diligently to connive with those forces which seek the destruction of the Republic of Indonesia.

On January 27, Prime Minister Djuanda gave a farewell luncheon for Mrs. Allison and me which was attended also by Deputy Prime Ministers Hardi and Leimena, Foreign Minister Subandrio, and Roeslan Abdulgani, Vice Chairman of the National Council, all accompanied by their wives. The Prime Minister made a long and touching speech of farewell and in order to undercut stories being put out by the Communist press that my transfer was due to my interference in Indonesian Government affairs, at one point he said: "There is one thing I do want to make clear, though. The Indonesian Government appreciates the services you have rendered to your government in order to build up, stage by stage, closer relations between our two countries."

Mr. Djuanda concluded by saying: "When a friend leaves us, he takes a little part of ourselves with him. We hope that you will take with you a little part of Indonesia, and that wherever your fortunes take you in the future, you will remember with warmth your year among us. I can assure you that we shall remember you."

We have not forgotten. Since my retirement my wife and I have gone back four times to see our friends in Indonesia, and we have rejoiced to see the progress they are making in building an economically stable, modern Indonesia under their new government. We have been particularly happy to note that the American Government is now playing a most constructive part in what has become an international cooperative effort to restore this great country and its friendly people to a position of influence and responsibility in Southeast Asia.

# XII

# Through the Looking Glass

## 1958–1960

WHEN WE STOPPED overnight in Tokyo on our way home from Indonesia friends there supplied me with clippings from the American and Japanese press, all of which indicated that I had fallen out with Secretary Dulles and was strongly opposed to our policy in Indonesia. I was not surprised, therefore, when I went before the Senate Foreign Relations Committee in Washington, prior to my confirmation as Ambassador to Prague, to have this matter raised. Senator Fulbright took the lead. He aimed his bushy eyebrows at me and demanded: "Isn't it unusual for an Ambassador to be transferred after only eleven months in a country, and isn't it true that you disagreed with the Secretary of State?"

I pointed out that my predecessor in Tokyo, Robert Murphy, had only been there eleven months when he was recalled to Washington, but I did admit such short terms were not normal. With regard to my disagreeing with the Secretary of State, I stated that it was not unusual for an Ambassador in a particular country to differ with the State Department on a particular policy with respect to that country. The Ambassador looks at the matter from the viewpoint of the information available to him at his post and makes his recommendations. The Secretary of State has to view the matter from a world policy point of view, and he may decide that the world interests of the United States might not be served by adopting the policy recommended by the Ambassador, however sound it might seem from the viewpoint of the country involved. I admitted there had been differences between the Department and the Embassy in Djakarta, but I maintained this was not unusual. Some of the Senators tried to get me to be more specific and spell out the differences, but I said I did not wish to say more than I had. Senator Fulbright was most understanding and suggested that, as a serving career officer, I had probably said as much as I should, and he moved on to other topics.

While in Washington I had two other interesting meetings. One was a debriefing at the CIA. Everyone was extremely polite and, though there were a few sharp disagreements with some of the CIA men, I was listened to carefully as I explained the reasons for the policies the Embassy had recommended. When the meeting ended, and I was being conducted by one of the senior CIA men out to my car, I was astounded to hear him say, "You should know that several of us here agreed with your reports and recommendations from Djakarta. I think you will be proved right in the end."

The other meeting was with my old chief, former Secretary of State Dean Acheson. Dean had never looked with much favor on Sukarno and normally would look at Asian matters from a Western viewpoint, but he was an intelligent and realistic man. After my first drink at his house in Georgetown I was emboldened to tell him about our six point plan for a solution to the West New Guinea problem. He listened carefully, asked a few questions, and I nearly spilled my drink when he said, "You know, I think I could have sold that policy to the Dutch." Foster Dulles never tried, and yet he, too, was an intelligent and realistic man. But Sukarno disgusted him and communism appalled him. Even a slight possibility that the two might unite blinded Dulles to any possible courses of action other than passive support of the Dutch and opposition to Sukarno. So I went to Prague.

Once I got out of Indonesia the Department apparently decided it wasn't so urgent for me to get to Prague, for in looking at my records I see we didn't arrive there until the middle of April.

We were met in Vienna by Bill and Barbara Crawford from our Embassy in Prague with a car to drive us to our new home. Bill was to be my Deputy during most of our time in Prague. He knew Eastern Europe well, had served in Moscow and Paris, and was gifted in languages. He spoke perfect French, good Russian, and could get along in Czech. I think he also spoke German. The Crawfords were a great help in getting us adjusted to life in Europe and particularly behind the Iron Curtain, which was vastly different from our previous life in Asia.

It was our first visit to Vienna, and the two and a half days we spent there were delightful. The American Ambassador was an old friend, "Doc" Matthews, whom I had first met during the war in London. His wife had been associated with the American Consulate in Kobe and then the Embassy in Tokyo and had been on the *Asama* and the *Gripsholm* when we were evacuated from Japan after the attack on Pearl Harbor. We had a pleasant lunch with them, and Helen was able to give Toots some good pointers on what to do in Vienna. She insisted we should have dinner at Vienna's most famous restaurant, the Drei Huzzaren. Bill and Barbara took us there that same evening, and we agreed that everything Helen Matthews had said about it was true. As we were leaving I heard someone call, "Hey, John, what are you doing here?" It was General Lawton Collins — known to his troop as Lightning Joe — whom I had last seen in Manila at an Asian Ambassadors' Conference, when he was Ambassador to Saigon and I was Ambassador to Tokyo. He had retired from government service and was now in Europe on business. Apparently, if we had stayed in Vienna long enough and gone to the

Drei Huzzaren every night, we would have met all our old friends.

Our Czech chauffeur, Friedrich, was a tall, slender man with a worn, intelligent face who was most pleasant and efficient. He was obviously not a Communist and had had a more responsible position before the Communists took over. But, as was true of all our domestic staff, he had to report regularly to the secret police about our activities. I'm afraid he was not a happy man. He smoked constantly, and not too long after we left Prague he died of tuberculosis. After we had been in Prague a short time I realized that Friedrich was on duty from early morning, when he took me to the Chancery, until late at night, if we were going out in the evening, and that this was true seven days a week. One of my first recommendations to the State Department was for a second chauffeur so that neither one would have to be on duty such long hours. It took several messages to Washington, but eventually we did get permission to hire another.

Our drive to Prague was uneventful, although we were held up at the border by the Czech immigration police for almost an hour, while they apparently read our passports word by word, and their armed sentries at the barbed wire gates watched our every move. All this in spite of the fact that all of us had diplomatic passports, and our car bore the red and orange license plates indicating we were diplomats. We arrived in Prague in time for dinner in our new home and what a home it was!

The Embassy residence was a huge three-story building with, I believe, ninety-three rooms (I never counted them all), an elevator in an iron cage running from the kitchen in the basement to the third floor, thirty-two telephones (all bugged), a furnace room which looked like the boiler room of an ocean liner and had a small railway train which brought coal to the boilers, and a huge indoor swimming pool which we were never able to use. We learned it would cost at least $1500 to fill the pool with water and heat it, and the United States Government did not think this a necessary expense. Neither did we, but we did use one of the dressing rooms, in which we could seat forty people, for a theatre, where on Sunday evenings we would often invite members of the Diplomatic Corps to watch American movies that the army sent us every week from Nuremberg.

The residence had originally been built in 1929 by a Czech Jewish coal baron who is said to have spent $7 million on the building, its decoration, and the grounds. All the plumbing fixtures, for example, were gold plated, the toilet seats were ivory, and there was one room paneled with wood taken from a decaying old seventeenth century church. After Munich and the coming of Hitler the owner had been forced to sell his home with most of its furniture and fittings and a wonderful art library to the Czech Government to get enough money to enable him to leave the country. His brother had built a similar residence on another hill about a mile away. At the end of World War II, the Czech Government, which at that time was playing no favorites, sold one residence to the Americans and one to the Russians for Embassies. The American Government was able to pay with counterpart funds accumulated during the war and just after, so the expense was not great. I have always believed that it was a mistake for us to have such a huge and luxurious house in a Communist country. The Russians stripped their residence of much of its luxurious fixtures and art and shipped them back to Moscow; they used the building not only as residence for the Ambassador but also for many of his staff. The Communist Czech Government could point to the American Embassy and claim it was a typical example of the conspicuous consumption of the capitalists.

In spite of its elegance the residence was surprisingly livable, and from a purely physical point of view our two years in Prague were delightful. For this huge edifice, far larger than the residence in Tokyo where we had a domestic staff of fourteen, we had a staff of nine. The cook was a jewel of great price. He had been trained in France and was the best cook in the whole Diplomatic Corps, and probably in all of Prague. Our butler, Charles, was a large, rather rotund, elderly man, who, properly dressed, would have made a fine Santa Claus. We were told later that although he was a devout Catholic, he was also the most ardent reporter among our staff to the Communist secret police, about what we did and said and whom we had in the house. But Charles had feet which pained him, and he wore large black shoes which had a rather far-reaching squeak. We always knew when he was near. When we had no guests or were not going out we would often have a couple of drinks in the library before dinner. Sometimes, if dinner was a bit late, I would have an additional half. I taught Charles the Japanese word for "half" and he greatly enjoyed using it. I think he often had the cook delay dinner a bit so he could come squeaking into the library and, with a broad grin, inquire, "*Hanbun?*"

Our own Embassy Chancery was housed in an old baroque palace with over one hundred and fifty rooms. It had been built originally in the middle of the seventeenth century and then rebuilt about 1715. It had belonged to the Schonborn family, and one of their descendants, who had been born in the building, still lived in Prague. Before the Communists came into power he had often been a guest of the American Ambassador and told me he had played bridge there. He now ran a second-hand book, map, and print shop a short walk from the Embassy across the famous Charles Bridge. In a sad voice he once asked me not to visit his shop too often as merely selling a book to the "Imperialist American Ambassador" might get him into trouble with the police. I tried to keep away but it was hard to do, as a second-hand bookshop has always tempted me the way swinging doors of the old saloons used to tempt some of my elders. I was quickly learning that in a Communist country one watched one's step. At least this was true of Prague in 1958, when the Novotny regime in power was more Stalinist than Stalin.

Protocol Chief Jecny told me that before the Communists

had taken control he had been a lawyer. He was now a loyal member of the party and was later to be rewarded by being sent as Ambassador to Tokyo. He was one of the only two Czechs I ever saw wear a dinner jacket. The other was Deputy Foreign Minister Jiri Hajek, the only Communist official for whom I ever felt any real friendship. After about an hour with Jecny, during which arrangements were made for presenting my credentials the following week, Bill Crawford and I returned to the Chancery, and I had an opportunity to examine this old palace in which we worked and in which many of our small staff had apartments. In 1949, during the time Ellis Briggs was Ambassador in Prague, the Czech Government expelled, on two weeks' notice, over three-quarters of the American staff, leaving only the Ambassador and twelve others. All American diplomats were said to be spies, and trumped up charges were made against some of the Embassy's Czech staff who were tried and imprisoned after "confessing" that they had been forced to spy for the "Imperialist American diplomats." Of course, Washington reacted by expelling most of the Czech diplomats. The restrictions on the size of the staff had gradually been lifted, and by the time I arrived we had a staff of eighteen Americans, including an Army and an Air Attaché and their assistants, who were Master Sergeants. Although the USIS Library had been closed, we did have an officer of the USIS who acted officially as a Press Attaché. It was a good staff, and I'm sure we got as much work done as many Embassies with a much larger staff.

I had a large, high ceilinged, pleasant office with a huge fireplace. I was warned that it was not safe to dictate letters or dispatches to my secretary, as it was assumed microphones were located in all strategic spots. On the third floor of the Chancery we did have an area which we believed was comparatively safe. No one but American members of the staff was allowed in this area, and members of the staff took turns sleeping there on a cot so there was an American present around the clock.

The night of my first full day in Prague we went to bed early, wearied by all the tasks involved in getting settled in a new place. About ten-thirty my bedside phone rang and Bill Crawford asked if I could come down to the Chancery. He said he would send Dick Tims, our first secretary and political officer, up to get me and Dick would explain what it was all about. As we drove down to the Chancery Dick told me that Joe Jacyno, our second secretary and economic officer, had been arrested by the secret police, charged with espionage, and had been held for several hours, in spite of the diplomatic identity card he carried. He had just been released and was at the Chancery ready to tell us his story. It was almost worthy of Alfred Hitchcock.

Several months before my arrival a party of Western businessmen, including several Americans, had been taken on a conducted tour around the country. Jacyno, who spoke Czech, went with them, and on the trip he struck up a friendship with a young Czech interpreter as a result of their mutual interest in hi-fi, stereo, and all forms of modern music. Upon their return to Prague, Jacyno had kept up the friendship and had given his Czech friend some records which were not otherwise available in Czech stores. They would meet from time to time at a café for a beer or two and sometimes exchange records. On this particular afternoon the Czech had telephoned Jacyno and urgently requested a meeting at their usual place. Jacyno went and foolishly allowed himself to be talked into going to the Czech's apartment to listen to a new machine or new records, I forget which. When they got to the apartment, the Czech told Jacyno he had some interesting information about, I believe, the Czech munitions industry. He then took some papers from behind a picture on the wall and handed them to Jacyno, who said he was not interested. The young Czech told him to take them home and look them over and then shoved them into Jacyno's pocket. About two minutes later, while Jacyno was wondering what to do, the door flew open and in dashed the secret police, who took the papers from Jacyno's pocket, where they obviously expected to find them. Both Jacyno and the Czech were arrested, and although Jacyno protested he had diplomatic immunity and showed his credentials, he was kept for questioning. Finally, as I remember his story, he was permitted to call a friend in the Foreign Office, who eventually secured his release but warned him he would probably be expelled from the country.

We reported the facts to Washington at once, and early the next morning we received instructions to make a strong protest to the Foreign Office stressing the prolonged questioning of a diplomatic officer. As I had not yet presented my credentials, it was Bill Crawford as Chargé d'Affaires who made the protest. We had some reason to believe that the Foreign Office had not been consulted about Jacyno's arrest and that it was somewhat embarrassed about the incident, coming, as it did, just at the time of the arrival of a new American Ambassador. The secret police apparently were restive because there had been no anti-American news in the local press for some time, and they were afraid that the arrival of a new American Ambassador might be the occasion for some friendly sentiments being voiced. They won. The press was full of stories about American spying on the people of Czechoslovakia. Jacyno was declared persona non grata and was ordered to leave the country within twenty-four hours. His wife was in Nuremberg shopping and consulting doctors at the American Army hospital there. Jacyno was not permitted to await her return but was taken to the Austrian border at 5 P.M. April 19, just forty-eight hours after his arrest.

On April 24, 1958, for the third time I went through the ceremony of presenting credentials. I was told by the protocol chief to wear a morning coat, striped trousers, and a Homburg. Fortunately I received the instructions well in advance, for when I opened the hatbox containing my Homburg, which I had not worn since I left Djakarta, the box was empty. Somewhere along the line the hat had been extracted by someone whose need was apparently greater than mine. My wife figured that the tips we had paid for its transfer from airplane to hotel to ship, to another airplane, another hotel, another ship, and to the train all the way through Singapore, Hong Kong, Manila, Honolulu, Washington, New York, Genoa, and Vienna totaled almost as much as the hat had originally cost. And now it was gone. One of the Embassy secretaries was going for a couple of days to Vienna and she kindly offered to get a new one for me. It arrived in time, and my senior staff and I set off for the imposing Hradcany Castle, the official, but not actual, residence of President Novotny. Prague was still cold in April, and we wore overcoats which pleased me, for I felt a bit silly wearing a Homburg instead of a silk hat with a morning coat. If one is going to dress up at all, I believe it should be done properly. The Indonesians were sensibly less formal and only expected white suits.

We were met in the courtyard by a guard of honor, and, in company with Protocol Chief Jecny, I marched down their ranks trying to look severe and properly military. We then were taken up stairs into the castle and through several gorgeously furnished rooms, unchanged, I was told, since the days when the Hapsburgs had ruled there. Finally we reached our destination, and my staff was lined up behind me. Large doors opposite us were opened, and in came President Novotny, the Foreign Minister, and various other officials. Novotny stepped forward, we both bowed, I read my formal statement, he read his, and we then shook hands. I was then led into the room from which the President had come, where I was seated at a table with Novotny, Foreign Minister David, one or two other officials, and Jecny, who acted as interpreter. For well over half an hour I was questioned about American policy in Europe with particular reference to our policy toward West Germany. It soon became obvious that the chief fear of the Czechs was the possibility of another attack by the Germans. I tried to reassure them but was not able to convince them that the policy of arming West

Germany was not directly aimed at Communist Czechoslovakia. They seemed to believe we were furnishing the Germans with atomic weapons. My explanation that no American atomic weapons could be used without the express approval of the President of the United States and that America had no intention or desire to attach Czechoslovakia was obviously not particularly reassuring to them. The interrogation finally ended. We all stood up, bowed slightly, and shook hands with each other, and I was led back to where the poor staff had been standing first on one foot and then on another. Everyone had been correct and polite during the ceremony, but there had been no warmth.

The Swiss Legation was just across the street from the castle, and the Minister was greatly intrigued by the length of my stay with the President. He reported to other members of the Diplomatic Corps that the American Ambassador had spent forty-five minutes inside Hradcany Castle, while the usual time for presenting credentials was fifteen or twenty minutes. Obviously something important must have taken place. When I told my diplomatic colleagues what had really happened, they seemed to find it almost as hard to believe as the Czechs had found r y statement that America was not giving West Germany atomic weapons with which to attack Prague. But at any rate I was now official and the long, boring round of diplomatic calls began.

The main substantive business with which the Embassy was concerned while I was there was the effort to get the Czech Government to pay compensation to American concerns whose property had been confiscated by the Communist regime when it came to power. The chief claimant was International Business Machines. Negotiations over these claims had been going on before I arrived, and they were still going on when I left two years later. For me the chief result was the friendship developed with Jiri Hajek, a Deputy Foreign Minister who was in charge of the negotiations on the Czech side.

Before World War II, Hajek had been a professor of history at Charles University. After the Communists came into power he had spent two years in London as Czech Ambassador. His English was fluent, and after we had come to know each other he confessed that he was a lover of Shakespeare. Hajek was obviously an intellectual Communist and not from the ranks of labor. He told me that he had become a Communist while a student at the University and that his conversion began in a YMCA discussion group where he had studied and discussed the works of Lenin. At times Hajek was obviously embarrassed by some of the things he had to say in the course of his official duties. I later discovered that one could still appeal to his bourgeois instincts. At that time there were many official visitors to Prague from neighboring Communist countries and during their visits there would always be a reception given by the President at Hradcany Castle to which members of the Diplomatic Corps would be invited. Speeches would be given, and almost invariably the "British and American imperialists" would be gratuitously insulted as would other nations from time to time. The Yugoslav and Austrian Ministers, who spoke Czech, each walked out at least once while I was there when their countries were insulted. I decided to take the matter up with Hajek.

I called on Hajek and told him I was coming to see him, not as the American Ambassador and not under instructions, but only as his friend John Allison who had a problem he wished to discuss. I referred to a recent reception at Hradcany Castle for, I believe, the Bulgarian Foreign Minister. After the reception was over I learned from one of my colleagues who understood Czech that both my country and Great Britain had been grossly insulted. I could, of course, refuse to attend future receptions, but I had been taught that when the President of the country to which I was accredited issued an invitation it was considered a command, and if I did not go, I would be insulting the President. I had no desire to insult the Czech President. On the contrary, I was there to make friends and improve relations. I could bring with me to future receptions a member of my staff who understood Czech, and if my country was insulted, I could walk out. That, it seemed to me, would be even worse, as it would be a public demonstration which could not help but attract considerable attention. What should I do?

Hajek explained that when representatives of Communist Governments got together it was their custom to make speeches and exchange views about the world situation and to condemn unfriendly powers. I replied that if the Communists wished to do this among themselves that was their privilege, but why did they then invite the Diplomatic Corps to come and listen to their countries being assailed? Did Hajek have any suggestions? The poor man looked embarrassed and said he could not advise me; I would have to do what I thought right. I thanked him and explained I wanted him to understand how I felt so that he would not be surprised at any action I might take in the future. We shook hands and I left. From that day until I left Prague, the United States and Great Britain were never again mentioned by name in unfriendly speeches at Hradcany Castle. It was not a great victory, and the negotiations concerning IBM's property were not made any easier. Long after my departure from Prague, Hajek became Foreign Minister in the ill-fated regime of Prime Minister Dubcek. I was not surprised when I read that he had protested in the United Nations, in August of 1968, when the Russians invaded his country. I was also not surprised to read that he had had the courage to return to Prague to what he must have known would be imprisonment if nothing worse.

Shortly after we arrived in Prague the annual Spring Music Festival opened with guest artists and conductors invited from many nations. Dean Dixon, an American Negro conductor who lived at that time in Sweden, was among those invited, and we decided to give a reception for him after the concert to which we would invite Czech artists, musicians, critics, and a few members of the Diplomatic Corps. On the day of the concert Mr. Dixon's wife had to be taken suddenly to a hospital, and, while he went ahead with his conducting, he didn't feel like coming to a party afterward. However, this did not keep the Czechs away and over a hundred of them came and ate and drank until almost three o'clock in the morning. We went to bed exhausted but with the feeling that we had made a start in getting to know the Czechs and getting them to realize that although we were capitalists we could still be friends. We were wrong. It was the last party we had to which any large number of unofficial Czechs came. In the future only Foreign Office officials, a few military officers, and once in a long while an unofficial Czech who had some special reason to be seen at the American Embassy, came to the residence.

It was almost a year later before we found out what had happened. The late Julius Katchin, a young American concert pianist who had visited us in Tokyo and Djakarta, came through Prague on his way to give a concert in Bucharest. He stayed with us at the Embassy and told us he would return in a few days for a longer stay. We thought it would be a splendid idea to have a party for him and invite some of the Czechs who had been at the previous party. Julius knew several of these people and said he would sound them out. He came back that evening and sadly told us to forget about a party. He had found out that when the guests had left our party at the time of the Spring Music Festival they were stopped by the secret police as soon as they emerged from the Embassy Compound. Some of them were questioned for several hours, and many were searched to see if they were carrying away any capitalist propaganda. None of Julius's friends wanted to go through that experience a second time.

From time to time American tourists and a few businessmen came through Prague, and whenever possible we would have them over for tea or a drink. They almost universally had nice things to say about the hotels, the kindness of the hotel staff, and the friendliness of the Czechs whom they had anything to do with. As far as they could see there were no invidious restrictions put on their movements or on what they could see. Communism didn't seem so bad to these visiting Americans who didn't realize that their hotel rooms contained hidden microphones. But it was different for those of us who lived in Prague. Shortly after my arrival I applied through the Foreign Office for permission to visit some Czech factories and industrial establishments. When I left the country two years later I still had not been permitted to visit a single one. In company with the American Agricultural Attaché to the American Embassy in Warsaw, who was also accredited to Prague, I did get to visit one collective farm, not a very impressive one. But a factory? Never. Nor did we succeed in getting Czechs to visit our home even when we went through all the required steps recommended by the Foreign Office.

At one time a Foreign Office official told me I should see more Czechs and get to understand their point of view. I said I would be delighted and told him I had just been informed that a party of American doctors, who had recently been in Moscow and were now in Warsaw, would be visiting Prague the following week. I told the Minister that we would like to give a reception for the doctors and invite some Czech doctors and public health officials to meet them.

The American doctors arrived in Prague and were met by the Czechs who showed them their hospitals and gave them a large reception at the then new Yalta Hotel. Several of us from the Embassy were invited to the reception, and this was the first time we had met the Americans. The Embassy reception on their last night in Prague had been set up in accord with Foreign Office suggestions. The American doctors and their wives were loud in their praises of how the Czechs had treated them and the facilities they had been given to see what they wished to see. Surely, there wasn't any really heavy oppression in Czechoslovakia. We told them we had invited some twenty Czech doctors to the reception and so far not one had shown up. At six forty-five, a junior official from the Protocol Office of the Foreign Ministry arrived. At seven o'clock when none of the Czech doctors had put in an appearance my wife got a bit annoyed. She had learned since coming to Prague that if she acted in the normal polite manner she had been accustomed to use in Tokyo and Djakarta that the Communists paid no attention to her. However, if she said frankly what she thought and began to adopt the tone of a fishwife, the Communists seemed to understand and became most cordial.

Toots finally went up to the Czech Official and asked where the Czech doctors were.

He replied, "Many of them are on vacation."

"All of them?" asked Toots.

"Well, some are on duty at their hospitals."

"All of them?" insisted Toots.

The poor man wasn't given a chance to reply, as Toots went up close to him and in a voice which the American guests couldn't fail to hear, said, "I know why no Czech doctors are here. They knew that you or some other official would be here to make a list of any Czech doctors who showed up and they were afraid."

The Protocol officer finished his drink and quietly slunk away. But the next day he greeted her with open arms at a National Day reception at another Embassy.

There was always a large number of Czechs at the National Day receptions given by the various Embassies. Many of them were comparatively minor officials, and it was pathetic to see how their wives all carried large handbags in which they squeezed as much as they could of the fruit, cakes, and other food available at Embassies but not available generally on the local market. The diplomats all tried to look the other way when this was happening, because this was one of the few ways in which foreigners could do something for the local people. Another was to make purchases in the many antique and jewelry shops which were filled with articles confiscated by the Communist Government from the non-Communist Czechs. We were told the original owners got from ten to twenty percent of what the items sold for, and this was often their only source of income.

It was not a pleasant atmosphere in which to live, and Toots often commented on how glum the people whom we saw on the streets looked. We hardly ever saw a smile on any face; but we did once. It was on one of our periodic trips to Nuremberg on a cold February weekend. We were traveling in the large Embassy limousine, because Toots's sister was with us, and our smaller private car would have been too crowded. As we approached the ice-covered bridge leading into the smoky factory town of Beroun, we saw ahead of us a smaller car which seemed to be having trouble, and it finally came to a complete halt. Aust, our Czech driver, had slowed down and managed to stop just before hitting the smaller car. But the car behind us apparently didn't have such good brakes, and it banged into our rear bumpers at almost full speed. Its front end was completely crushed, the windshield was in splinters, and the driver's face was bleeding from broken glass.

Almost instantly a large crowd surrounded our cars, and we noticed that many of the people were pointing at the damaged car and then our car and laughing heartily. Toots was shocked. She called Aust and asked him what the people were laughing at, saying it seemed cruel to laugh at the misfortunes of the people in the rear car. "Oh," said Aust, "they're not laughing at the people in the rear car. They're laughing, they say, because that is what happens to a Russian car when it hits an American car." The Cadillac had a small hole in the luggage compartment, no other damage. We didn't tell President Novotny what Aust had said!

There were other ways in which the Czech people showed their true feelings about their Russian overlords. We had noticed during the Spring Music Festival that when conductors from non-Communist countries appeared, such as Dean Dixon and Sir Malcolm Sargent of Great Britain, the auditorium was packed, and the people would give standing ovations to the guest conductors. When the guest conductors were from other Communist countries the auditorium would never be full, and large numbers of those who did come left at the intermission. The applause was polite but never enthusiastic. When an American ice hockey team defeated a Russian team during an international tournament in Prague, the applause of the Czech audience was deafening. No individual Czech would dare show preference for the Americans or any Western country over the Russians, but when several hundreds or thousands joined together in a peaceful demonstration the government could do nothing to curb them.

The second Easter we were in Prague our good Catholic butler Charles took us to Easter Service at one of the beautiful old Prague Catholic churches. The church was packed, and the singing of the men's and women's choirs was wonderful. Even an old tone-deaf Scotch Presbyterian could appreciate it. When we left the church there was a crowd of Czechs from the church around our Embassy limousine which was flying the American flag and the Ambassador's flag. They politely gave way so we could enter the car, and I found my throat choking up as I noticed one white-haired grandmotherly lady cautiously point at the flags on the car and then turn to us and give a quick wave of one hand before any watching secret police could see her.

Just before Christmas of 1958 I received an invitation from Chancellor Clifford Hardin of the University of Nebraska, my old school, to give the commencement address in the following June. We had wanted to take a long overdue leave in the

United States, and I therefore wrote Loy Henderson, who had been so helpful when I left Djakarta, to report this invitation and inquire whether I could take leave at that time. Loy at once replied that I should certainly accept the invitation.

In April of 1959 I received another letter from Chancellor Hardin informing me that the board of regents of the university had approved a recommendation of the university senate that I be awarded the honorary degree of Doctor of Laws at the June commencement exercises. I was tremendously pleased and also a bit amused. I had been informed several years earlier that when I was Assistant Secretary of State under President Truman I had been recommended for an honorary degree, but the university board of regents, good Republicans all, had not approved. Now that I had served President Eisenhower for some six years as an Ambassador I was apparently purged of all sin and fit to receive the accolade from my alma mater.

There were three noteworthy things about my commencement address. The most important was that it was short, not more than fifteen minutes. The second was that I began by pointing out that when I had been graduated from the university thirty-two years before, we considered it quite an event if our commencement speaker came from the East coast. Here I had come all the way from Czechoslovakia and no one considered it strange. I then said, what just thirteen years later seems not at all impossible, that "when one of you comes back some thirty years from now to make the commencement address he may come from the moon." The third important thing connected with my address was that, after the 1959 commencement was over, it was decided not to have commencement addresses in the future. But I did get the honorary degree, and several years later when I had retired to Honolulu and began teaching at the University of Hawaii, it came in mighty handy. No one knew what to call a retired Ambassador, but *Who's Who* said I had an LL.D., so I became Dr. Allison and all the pedants were happy. A mere Ambassador had no standing in the scholarly community, but a Doctor was different. It took me over twenty years to become an Ambassador but only fifteen minutes' speaking to become a Doctor.

We had flown back to Washington but were able to return to Europe on the *United States* and then have two or three days in Paris before returning to Prague. While both the official and domestic staff seemed glad to see us return, the most enthusiastic welcome came from our little dachshund, Trinka. The very night after our return Trinka was to prove her worth. She slept on a chair in our bedroom, and about eleven-thirty she let out a sharp yelp. Toots was sure there was a burglar around, but I claimed Trinka was only cold, as her blanket had slipped off. Toots insisted, so I opened the bedroom door and looked out into the hall but saw no one. Then Toots said to look on the balcony outside the bedroom window. This seemed utter nonsense to me, for I was certain it was impossible to climb up the thirty feet of sheer concrete from the garden below. But I had learned it never pays to argue with your wife, so I took my small flashlight and beamed it out on the balcony. Sure enough, there was a man out there, calmly smoking a cigarette, who began talking to me in Czech and waving his arms. I called Toots to telephone Bill Crawford, whose house was in the same compound, to come over and translate.

When Bill arrived below our window he called up that there was another man down there. He finally persuaded the man on the balcony to climb down, and I then put on a robe and joined Bill down on the terrace. In the meantime, Toots had awakened Charles, who joined the party and was able to persuade the two men to show us their identity cards, which all Czechs had to carry at all times. The cards said they were students and were eighteen and nineteen years old. They looked to be at least thirty.

The men claimed they wished to defect, but we thought that they were agents provocateurs sent by the secret police in an attempt to frame a charge against the American Ambassador in much the same way as they had framed a charge against Jacyno a year earlier. We told the men we had called the police, but this didn't seem to worry them. We shortly heard cars driving at fairly high speed around the compound, and we sent Charles out to stop and tell the police the Ambassador had given permission for them to enter the compound, which was American property. Just before the police finally entered the compound the men dashed off into the darkness. We had kept their identity cards, which we gave to the police, and the next morning I reported the incident to Hajek. We never did hear from either the police or the Foreign Office whether or not the two men had been found, but no charges were made against the American Ambassador or the Embassy.

One of the sad things about our luxurious residence was the State Department's indifference to keeping the residence and its many art objects in good condition. There was a fine Gobelin tapestry hung on the wall over the main staircase leading to the second floor. It obviously needed cleaning, and we found it would cost $75 to have a good job done. The State Department said there were no funds available so Toots got up on a ladder and did some de-mothing and scrubbing herself. We also urged the Department to send someone out to make an inventory of the house and its possessions, for this had never been done, and we had reason to believe that some of the smaller pieces were being appropriated from time to time by members of the domestic staff. But it would cost $4,000 the Department estimated, to send a man out to do the inventory and how could such an expense be justified?

One day Toots found on a bottom shelf in the library a carved glass vase trimmed with early French enamel. It was filled with rubber bands and broken light bulbs and was filthy. She took it out and cleaned it, certain that it was a piece of considerable value. About the same time she found a silver chalice, the bowl of which was made from a coconut which had scenes of the Nativity carved on it. One of the art books in the library had a picture of a similar chalice and said there were only about five of these sixteenth-century pieces known to exist and that they were in various museums in Europe. Shortly before we had gone on home leave, Bill Hughes, head of the State Department Foreign Buildings Office, visited Prague, and Toots had persuaded him to take these two pieces back to Washington and get them properly valued. She was able to point out that, according to a London newspaper, a piece similar to the coconut chalice had sold at auction in London for more than $12,000. She told Bill she thought the glass vase would be worth at least $5000. When we got back to Prague after our leave we found waiting for us a letter from Loy Henderson reporting on the pieces. He said:

> We are arranging to have the glass vase studied carefully by the Smithsonian. It would appear to be of considerable value, having been appraised in Paris at about $20,000. The Customs Service in Baltimore informally declared it to be an antique and placed a value of "something in excess of $10,000" on it. The other piece — the coconut cup — was left in London, where a professional opinion is being obtained from the Curator of the Victoria and Albert Museum.

As a result of the effort Toots had made and the fact that just one piece which she had discovered in the residence was worth more than $10,000, the Department at long last agreed that it might be worthwhile to send someone out to make an inventory. I suppose we will get our reward in heaven, but I sometimes wish that Toots had just wrapped those two pieces up and put them in the bottom of one of our trunks.

One of the most useful activities of the Embassy was the primary school which we ran for the children of our staff and the staffs of the other diplomatic missions in Prague. The American Government contributed the necessary rooms from the 150 in our Chancery, and the wife of one of our Embassy officers acted as unpaid principal and general supervisor. The school, of course, charged fees and with this money paid two Czech lady teachers and bought books. When we were in Prague there were children of eighteen different nationalities in the school. The Communist Embassies all had schools which their children had to attend, but the Yugoslav Ambassador sent his oldest daughter to our school as well as to the school for Communist children in his Embassy. She was one of the star pupils and took a leading part in the Christmas pageant which our school put on.

The Yugoslav Ambassador and his wife became our good friends. They had lived for several years in New York, where he had represented his country at the United Nations. At the many National Day receptions given by the various Embassies considerable interest was aroused among the diplomats as well as among the Czech officials present by the fact that the Yugoslav Ambassador was often seen interpreting for the Russian Ambassador and me. The Russian was a burly, rough looking man who actually was most pleasant. During World War II he had been Mayor of Yakutsk in northeastern Siberia when it was visited by Henry Wallace on his trip to Asia. The Ambassador therefore felt he had a special interest in Americans and was always friendly. However, he only spoke Russian, hence the services of the Yugoslav Ambassador were gratefully accepted.

At one of these receptions the Russian Ambassador asked whether my wife and I would be willing to dine some night at the Russian Embassy. The answer was, of course, yes, and about ten days later we were informed that the British Ambassador and his wife had also been invited, and a date was agreed upon. When we arrived at the Russian Embassy we found that the only other guests besides the British and American Ambassadors and their wives were Deputy Foreign Minister and Mrs. Hajek. After gorging ourselves with at least twenty varieties of *zakuska* washed down with innumerable small glasses of vodka, we were served a five course dinner accompanied by very good Russian wines. After dinner the ladies were taken to one room where a young member of the Russian Embassy staff acted as interpreter, while the four men went to another room and Hajek acted as interpreter. For over an hour we had a comparatively frank discussion of some of the matters on which the British Ambassador and I disagreed with the Communists, but nothing of great significance occurred. However, the atmosphere could not have been more friendly, and when we left we agreed we would have to meet more often in the future. It was not to be. At the next National Day reception the Russian Ambassador was not present. A week or so later when I asked Dick Tims, our Czech expert, to see if he could arrange a date for the Russian Ambassador and his wife to come to dinner at our Embassy, I was told he had been recalled to Moscow. The rumors soon began to circulate among the Diplomatic Corps that the Czechs had requested the recall of the Russian Ambassador because he was getting too friendly with the British and American Ambassadors. When Moscow hesitated to agree, we were told that the Czechs, in orthodox Communist style, had produced some photographs of the poor Ambassador in a compromising position with a Czech lady. None of us believed the Ambassador guilty, but he did disappear from Prague without making the usual farewell calls on his colleagues.

When we were on home leave my wife had discovered that she had emphysema and that, while it could not be cured, its development could be arrested if she would take certain precautions, among them to stop smoking. This she did at once. The second year we were in Prague, however, both the physical and the psychological climate began to get her down. During the winter we seldom saw the sun, and there was a continual smog over the city. Within the residence the servants were continually at each other's throats. In order to keep in good with the secret police the servants would not only report on what we did but on each other. If one servant seemed to be on more friendly terms with Toots than another, she was reported on, and therefore Toots had to watch her actions at all times. It did not make for a happy life. We had one favorite upstairs maid who came to us during our second year, and since she is no longer in Czechoslovakia, her story can be told.

Anna was a lawyer whose uncle was a political prisoner in Bratislava. She, too, had been a political prisoner for three years, and when she was released the only work she could get was that of maid. She spoke good English, and when she came to the Embassy immediately told Toots that she must report once a week to the secret police. She was told not to worry, that all the other servants did too, and if she didn't have enough material just to make up something.

Anna was permitted to visit her uncle in prison twice a year, and her next visit was scheduled for just after New Year's in 1960. Shortly before the New Year holidays one of the other upstairs maids took sick, and the junior maid broke her wrist in a fall. They were both due back at work in about ten days and in time for Anna to get off for her trip. One morning she came in to see Toots in her bedroom, her eyes brimming with tears. The secret police had just telephoned to say that if she wanted to see her uncle, she would have to depart that very night, and Anna was not willing to leave Toots without a maid. Knowing that the bedroom was bugged and that the secret police would hear everything she said, Toots sounded off.

"Anna," she said in a voice which carried, "you get packed right away and be prepared to get on the train tonight. The secret police know the other maids are not here, and they're just trying to inconvenience me. Well, if they think I can't make my own bed and clean up the bedroom they're sadly mistaken. If the Communist government spent more time thinking how they could do something for their people instead of wasting time trying to inconvenience the wife of the American Ambassador they would be better off. You pack your bags; you are leaving tonight to see your uncle."

Anna thanked her and went off. In about an hour she came

back, her face beaming. "Oh, Mrs. Allison, the secret police have just telephoned to say I didn't have to go tonight after all. I can wait until the regular time."

The climate and the general strain, however, did not let up, and Toots had to spend more and more time in the Army Hospital in Nuremberg. In February, in an effort to get more sunlight than Prague offered, we took two week's leave and drove to Berchtesgaden where we were given a suite in the American Army hotel there at the "outrageous" rate of $4.50 a day for the two of us. It was a fine two weeks. The sun shone almost every day, and although there was a lot of snow, it only added to the beauty of the scenery. One day at lunch an Army Major General came to our table and introduced himself as the Commanding Officer of the area and asked if he could join us at lunch. During the course of our conversation I inquired whether the army made any money on the army hotels. I didn't see how they could on the rates they charged us. We were told that in the General's command there were three hotels, including the one we were then in, and that they lost $1 million a year. I couldn't help but compare this loss of a million dollars, which the army seemed able to take with equanimity, to the $950,000 that Congress grudgingly granted the State Department for entertainment allowances for all their officers in more than one hundred posts throughout the world. This allowance had been approximately the same for the past ten years in spite of rising prices in the meantime. It was now easier to understand why my Air Attaché in Prague had a larger entertainment allowance than I did, even though the peculiar conditions prevailing in an Iron Curtain country made it impossible for him to spend more than about half of it.

Congressman Rooney of Brooklyn, Chairman of the House Appropriations Subcommittee which considers the State Department appropriations, was not so lenient. He looked into everything, big or small. However, Mr. Rooney also understood many of the problems the Foreign Service faced. On our last Thanksgiving in Prague Mr. Rooney descended on the Embassy with Mrs. Rooney, his staff assistant, and several others. The Congressman was given a briefing at the Embassy in the afternoon, and in the evening we invited him and his party to join us at the residence, where Toots and I were giving a Thanksgiving dinner for all our American staff and their wives, a total of about thirty-three people. The whole staff was there, including the two Master Sergeants and their wives from the Army and Air Attaché offices. This impressed the Congressman as being a symbol of true democracy, although they had not been invited to impress a Congressman. They were nice people and, in addition, able and efficient members of the staff. One of the wives acted as secretary to the Air Attaché, and one of them taught in the Embassy primary school. Mr. Rooney seemed to enjoy the group and stayed until a late hour. The next morning before the departure of his group, his staff assistant gave me a check for $100. Mr. Rooney knew that the cost of the previous night's dinner, which he considered a good morale booster for the staff, would have to come entirely out of my pocket, because there were no Czechs or members of the Diplomatic Corps there to justify the expense being covered by the official entertainment allowance. Ever since, I have had a fondness for the Congressman.

In spite of the frequent visits to the Army Hospital in Nuremberg, Toots got no better. Then in the early spring of 1960 the army doctors decided (on the basis of what later proved to be a false diagnosis) that she had tuberculosis, and she was sent to the other side of Germany to an army hospital specializing in respiratory diseases, located near the Luxembourg border. By motor car it took almost thirteen hours to reach the hospital from Prague. Toots was frantic when they told her she would have to stay there for a least two to four months. I drove down with her to get her settled and then made another trip about a month later. About twelve o'clock on the night before my birthday, April 6, I received a telephone call from the doctor in charge at the hospital telling me I should get down there as fast as I could if I wanted to be sure of seeing my wife alive. My Czech driver who had to have an exit permit from the Czech police was home in bed, and anyway it would take thirteen hours to drive to the hospital and that might be too long. However, I called Charles and told him to get in touch with the driver and to tell him to get his exit permit as early as possible in the morning. I then called George Weinbrenner, the Air Attaché, and asked him if a small plane could meet me when I crossed the German border and take me the rest of the way. George was, and is, a fine officer, and he took charge at once. By eight-thirty the next morning the driver had his exit permit, the Czech authorities for once being accommodating, and we were off for the German border. We took our private car, which could make faster time on the narrow, winding roads than the big, official limousine. George told me a helicopter would meet me when I crossed the border and take me to a nearby army airfield, where a small plane would be ready to fly me the rest of the way. It normally took almost four hours to reach the German border, but Aust, our driver, knew it was an emergency, and we reached the border in less than three hours. There was no helicopter (its pilot presumably was counting on our arriving an hour later), so we drove on towards Nuremberg after telling the German border police our problem and asking them to tell the helicopter pilot, if he showed up, that we were headed down the Nuremberg road. About twenty minutes later we heard a loud buzzing, and there was the helicopter landing in a nearby field. I took my suitcase and climbed into the machine having told Aust to drive on to the hospital.

A fifteen or twenty minute ride took us to a small army airfield, where there was an L-19 plane ready to take off. To my surprise and pleasure the pilot was my friend Major Bill Maddox, whom I had met in Tokyo and who now was assigned to the Nuremberg area. Bill had married Jay Kurusu in Tokyo, the daughter of Ambassador Kurusu who had accompanied Ambassador Nomura on the final call on Secretary of State Hull the morning of Pearl Harbor. Bill told me that he had requested permission to be my pilot when he had heard about the message from George Weinbrenner.

As we landed on a small strip near the hospital, I saw the Colonel in command striding out to the plane to meet me with a broad smile on his face. I heaved a great sigh of relief and was doubly reassured when he told me Toots had come out of a long bout of unconsciousness and all the indications were that she was out of any immediate danger. She hardly knew me when I first went into her room, but by the next morning she seemed almost normal. I stayed there nearly a week, and during that time it was agreed she should be transferred back to the United States for better treatment. It was also agreed that she should be accompanied by an extremely efficient army nurse, Captain Liebowitz, who had been with Toots before and knew both her and her problem well. On the morning of Toots's birthday, April 13, the local nurses brought in a birthday cake, and after a brief celebration, Toots, Captain Liebowitz, and I piled into our car for the drive to the Army Hospital in Frankfurt from which she would be put on an air force hospital plane and flown to Walter Reed Hospital in Washington.

I had promised Toots to meet her in Washington as soon as possible. I had completed thirty years of service and was eligible to retire at a fairly good pension. At the comparatively young age of fifty-five I figured I could find something else to do in a location that would not in itself be a constant threat to my wife's health. It was almost the end of May before I finally got back to Washington, having sent a letter to President Eisenhower stating that I wished to resign "for personal reasons" and expressing my appreciation for the privilege it had been to serve under him. My old chief, good friend, and respected antagonist Foster Dulles had died the previous year. The present Secretary, Christian Herter, was a fine man, but I didn't feel as close to him as I had to Foster, and it was not therefore as hard as it might have been to sever connections with the State Department. Both President Eisenhower and Secretary Herter wrote me flattering letters expressing regret at my retirement, but no great pressure was exerted to get me to change my mind.

At the June Foreign Service luncheon Loy Henderson, still Deputy Under Secretary for Administration, asked me how I would like to spend a weekend in Baghdad. Never having been to Baghdad seemed to me a good reason for going there, so I said I would be delighted and asked what it was all about. The then Premier Kassim was celebrating the second anniversary of his coming to power and all the nations that recognized Iraq had been requested to send delegations to a two-day celebration. Jack Jernegan, the Ambassador to Iraq, would be the Chief Delegate, and I would be the other official representative of the American Government. My final consent to go was based on the condition that, either going or coming, I could spend two nights in London. This was agreed to and after a cursory briefing in the Department I was off. In a trip which lasted a total of just eight days I spent one night in Beirut, three nights in Baghdad, and two nights in London. My heavy baggage caught up with me the last night I was in Baghdad. But all had gone off all right and the dark, lightweight suit I was wearing was all I needed. It was my Last Hurrah and shortly after I returned to Washington, Toots was able to leave Walter Reed, and I was a member of the retired branch of the Foreign Service.

# XIII

# "It's My Own Invention"

TWELVE YEARS after retirement from the American Foreign Service I still find myself reading the *Foreign Service Journal*, a vastly better magazine now than when I was Chairman of its Editorial Board some twenty-five years ago. In the last issue to reach me, that of October 1972, I noted with some interest that the beginning salary of a newly commissioned Foreign Service Officer in the lowest grade, Class VIII, was more than the salary of an Officer of Class I in 1930. Of course, much of this increase is due to inflation, but a substantial portion is due to the increased realization by leaders in the executive and legislative branches of our government of the value of the Foreign Service Officer and his work. This development is good, but it has not silenced the legion of critics, in and out of government, who continue to expound what is wrong with the Foreign Service, the State Department, and all those who deal with foreign affairs. With the great prominence given the activities of Henry Kissinger, seemingly at the expense of the State Department and Foreign Service, during the last years of Mr. Nixon's first administration, the flood of criticism increased. The Foreign Service and the State Department as we have known them in the past are doomed; a whole new approach must be looked for. Or, so say the critics.

While some of the criticism is just and well deserved it seems to me that most is exaggerated and much of it misdirected. The Foreign Service is often blamed for the actions of its masters in Washington. For example, in the Summer 1972 issue of *Foreign Policy*, Stanley Hoffmann, a professor of government at Harvard, says, "What we need is diplomats aware of other nations' anxieties and neuroses." Later in the same article, in talking about the management of foreign affairs, he speaks of "another old fallacy: that of believing that what is evident to us . . . is also evident to others and poses no special internal problems to them." Dr. Hoffmann must not have known many Foreign Service Officers. It is not the Foreign Service Officers who are unaware of other countries' "anxieties and neuroses." It is Washington. Didn't George Kennan resign as Ambassador to Yugoslavia because he was unable to persuade his superiors in Washington and the gentlemen in the Congress that what seemed good and reasonable to them did not always seem so to the Yugoslavs. With respect to Dr. Hoffmann's second statement, one wonders if he has ever read of Ambassador Grew's warning to the State Department before Pearl Harbor that, in spite of superficial similarity of the Japanese official and businessman to his Western contemporaries, we "cannot judge these people with a Western yardstick." As I have pointed out, the same problem was encountered by me and my staffs in Tokyo and Indonesia after the war, trying to make Washington understand that these Asian peoples did not always view things in the same way we did.

Since the end of World War II the Foreign Service has made an increased effort, to the extent that Congress has provided the funds, to give its best officers special training in the languages and cultures of those countries in Asia, Africa, and the Middle East which in the past have so often been neglected in the normal American education. If, in the future, we do not have a sufficient number of diplomats "aware of other nations' anxieties and neuroses" it will not be because the Foreign Service and the State Department do not recognize the need. It will be because the Congress has not provided the means.

The budget for the Foreign Service would not need to be greatly increased to permit more of its officers to get the benefit of this special training. The Foreign Service is far too large at present, and if it were cut to a more reasonable size, the remaining officers could receive more and better training without increasing the present budget and even perhaps lowering it somewhat. Ambassador Ellis Briggs has told how the efficiency of his Embassy in Prague was increased when he was forced by the Communist Czech Government to cut drastically its size. I have told how we were able to eliminate fifty people from our staff in Tokyo without any loss of efficiency; and John W. Tuthill, former Ambassador to Brazil, has told in the Fall 1972 issue of *Foreign Policy* how he was able to cut the American personnel in Brazil by over thirty percent to the great advantage of American policy in that country.

As I look back over my thirty years in the Foreign Service and think of all the officers I have known or known about, I believe it true to say that the faults of the professionals, when there were faults, were more those of omission than commission. We have at times been too cautious, although this trait has often had the virtue of restraining the overeager activism of our less professional colleagues from the political sphere. Talleyrand's advice to the young diplomat, *"Surtout, pas trop de zèle,"* can be and sometimes is taken too literally; but it is well to keep the counsel in the back of one's mind, along with Edmund Burke's dictum that there are some problems which require a "salutary neglect." Having said this, I must also acknowledge that there are many times when imagination and daring are called for, and the best professional will not be held back by excess caution.

The most serious damage to our interests abroad has been caused by the impatient, well-intentioned amateur who, usually unconsciously, was convinced that anything that was good for America was good for the world. If something worked in Kansas City, it should work in Singapore or Tokyo or Bangkok. But often it didn't, and the poor professional had to pick up the pieces and often take the blame.

The Boston Sunday *Globe* of September 24, 1972, carried a long article from its Washington Bureau entitled "How State Department Plays Second Fiddle," and at one point it said:

> The trouble today is that the Foreign Service wants to make policy because it is persuaded that sometime in the past it did so. But the fact is that the Foreign Service is not equipped to give advice that fully takes into consideration national defense requirements, economic needs, or domestic political factors, one official explained.

That official could not have been a Foreign Service Officer. From the moment I became a member I was told that the Foreign Service does not make policy. We were supposed to contribute to the making of policy but in the final analysis foreign policy could only be made by the President. Certainly it is only the President and "the President's men," as one critic calls them, including, one hopes, the Secretary of State, who can be aware of all the factors which must go into any policy.

What the Foreign Service can and should do is give expert advice on how any policy can best be implemented in the foreign field. This will include advice on the timing as well as the manner of its implementation, so that the "anxieties and neuroses" of other nations may be taken into account. Much of our troubles with Japan over President Nixon's sudden decision to visit Peking and his later economic measures could have been avoided, I believe, if the Foreign Service had been permitted to advise on the manner and timing of their implementation. Both the visit to China and the economic policy were good and long overdue, but the way in which they were carried out needlessly impaired relations with our most important friend in the Pacific world.

When I place such stress on the professional Foreign Service it may be assumed that I see no place for the noncareer Ambassador. Not at all. I see no place for the purely political appointee, but this does not exclude all appointments from outside the Foreign Service. There are several categories of persons who can make a most useful contribution. One, of course, is the man or woman, who, because of special training or background, has a unique knowledge and understanding of the country and people of a particular country. Such a one was Professor Edwin Reischauer who was sent as Ambassador to Japan by President Kennedy. Another category is the man who has a strong personal friendship with the President and who, because of that friendship, will have immediate access to the White House whenever desired. Even a man who, for other reasons, might not be acceptable to a foreign country will often be accepted if it is known that he has the ear of the President. Still another type is the man who at a particular time, because of his background, may be of great value not only to his own country but to the country which receives him. I should guess that Ambassador Ingersoll, the Chicago industrialist, sent to Tokyo by President Nixon, is one of these. At a time when the economic and trade interests of Japan and the United States are of such great importance it is a good thing to have a man in Tokyo who can command the respect of both the Japanese and the American financial and industrial communities. But there is no place in my book for the man whose only qualification is the amount of money he has contributed to a successful Presidential candidate. I still believe that the majority of Ambassadorships should go to the best of our career officers. How can we develop a Foreign Service of real competence if the best men see that the majority of the top jobs go to outsiders whose only virtue is wealth?

If the Foreign Service is to furnish the majority of Ambassadors, it of course follows that during their careers, officers must not only be given the opportunity but the encouragement to enlarge their capacities and understanding of all the factors that enter into what President Nixon has called the New Dimension of Diplomacy in these final years of the twentieth century. This is being done but not on a large enough scale. Officers are being sent to leading universities not only to study the languages and cultures of remote countries but to study a vast variety of subjects that will help them deal with our constantly changing world. They attend our National War College and other military service institutions so that they will have a better understanding of the security needs of our country and its allies as well as the means of meeting these needs and coordinating them with our political, economic, and social needs. Unfortunately, there never seems to be enough money so that all those who could benefit from such training can receive it. In recent years there has also grown up the policy of assigning senior officers to universities as Diplomats in Residence where they can exchange knowledge and experiences with members of the academic community, both faculty and students. Too often, however, such assignments have come at the end of an officer's career, and instead of bringing back to the Foreign Service new ideas and inspiration from his year in academia he is retired and his experience lost.

Since the end of World War II the Foreign Service has been the subject of almost countless attempts at reform to make it not only more competent to meet the demands of the modern world but to make it more attractive to its members. Many of these reforms are sound, and it is certainly true that the Foreign Service today seems to be attracting a more dynamic, intellectually alert, and concerned group of young men and women than was sometimes true in the past. But I am afraid the Foreign Service will never live up to its true potential until the top leaders in the Congress and the executive branch of the government make it clear that they not only respect and admire the members of the Foreign Service but are willing to give them the means to do their job and reward them with top positions in the foreign field if they do their job well.

The young Foreign Service Officers today should not be discouraged if things frequently seem to go wrong and their favorite ideas are seemingly disregarded. When I look at what has happened in the lifetime of the one Foreign Service Officer I know best, I am far from discouraged about the future. For example, I have told how in the summer of 1952, the evil influence of Senator Joseph McCarthy almost prevented a distinguished Harvard Professor, John Fairbank, from receiving from the State Department a passport to go to Japan for study. Yet in 1966 and 1967 Professor Fairbank was a respected member of a State Department panel of advisors on Chinese affairs and a welcome guest at the home of the Assistant Secretary of State for East Asian and Pacific Affairs. I have told how in 1951, the economic outlook for Japan was so bleak that John Foster Dulles, then working on the Japanese Peace Treaty, was urged by the Japanese to give a written agreement to underwrite the Japanese economy for an indefinite period. Again in 1955, when Foreign Minister Shigemitsu was in Washington he was told by Secretary Dulles that Japan should not expect to see a change in its unfavorable balance of trade with the United States but should make up the deficit through trade with third powers. Yet in 1972, Japan is not only the third-ranking industrial country in the world but its balance of trade with the United States is favorable to the extent of more than $2 billion. In the late 1940s and the 1950s a monolithic communism seemed to threaten world peace. In 1972 this is no longer true and Under Secretary of State U. Alexis Johnson, in a statement before the House of Representatives Foreign Affairs Subcommittee on National Security Policy and Scientific Development, on August 8, 1972, was able to say: "The dreadful prospect of another world war, this time between the Communist and the non-Communist powers, seems now more remote than at any time since the mid-1940's."

If thirty years in the Foreign Service and twelve years outside the Service in which to observe its progress have made me generally optimistic about the future, the experience has also made me cautious. The younger officers who not only have achieved a material position far superior to any that officers of my generation had but who, more importantly, have also greater opportunities for service in a much wider field of foreign relations than we ever did, seem, from what I read, to be almost as much concerned about their rights and privileges as about their opportunities and responsibilities. I hope they will read what Under Secretary Johnson, in the statement I quoted from above, also said:

> The number of our critical national needs which can only be met through international action and cooperation is continuing to grow. Narcotics cannot be controlled any other way. Endangered species cannot be protected any other way. The flow of goods vital to our economy and health cannot be guaranteed any other way. The benefits of satellite communications cannot be enjoyed any other way. Let me stress that I am not saying these problems are made easier by cooperation between nations. I am saying that there is literally no other way to solve them.

In addition to all of these problems there is the perennial problem of war and peace. While war may be more remote than any time in the last thirty years it is still there. I hope the Foreign Service Officers of today will stop worrying so much about grievances, promotion problems, and their rights and spend more time in helping to solve some of these great unsolved problems. If they do, I know they will find the years of their service even more stimulating and satisfying than I found the years between 1930 and 1960. I wish them luck.

# Index

# Index

Abbink, John, 123

Abdulgani, Roeslan, 309, 343

Acheson, Secretary of State Dean, 78, 113; and Korea, 116, 130; and Japanese Peace Treaty, 145, 150, 169–70, 172; and treaty with Philippines, 159; and Allison's appointment as Assistant Secretary of State, 175; and Truman-Churchill conference, 180; Eurocentrism of, 183; and Indochina, 183, 191–92, 194; and Asia, 183, 346; and 1952 ANZUS Council meeting, 196–99; meeting with Romulo, 199–200; and Mrs. Allison's trip to Asia, 202–3; and Indonesia, 346

Adams, Ware, 78

Aizawa, Colonel, 25

Allied Maritime Conference, 89–90

Allison, Jeannette, 18–19, 27–30, 45, 47, 73

Allison, John: and A. Jorgensen, 1; in college, 1–2; first voyage to Japan, 2–3; teaching in Japan, 2, 3–7; with General Motors, 8–10; joins Foreign Service, 11; at Shanghai Consulate, 11, 14, 32–33; 1930 return to U.S., 11–12; and Foreign Service exams, 11, 12–13, 19; at Kobe Consulate, 13–15; and book collecting, 17, 21, 79–80; marriage to Jeannette Brooks, 18–19; in Dairen, 23–25; in Tsinan, 25–29, 30–32; in Nanking, 29–30, 24–45; and *Panay*, 33–34; third promotion of, 46; and Pearl Harbor, 48–55; internment during World War II, 54–72; at Division of Economic Warfare, 74, 77–82; at main London Embassy, 82–104; death of father, 84–86; at Allied Maritime Conference, 89–90; at Whaling Conference, 90–91; and European Inland Transport Organization, 91–94; and Red Cross tour, 104–5; at United Nations, 106–8, 145; as Assistant Chief of Division of Japanese Affairs, 109; as Chief of Division of Northeast Asian Affairs, 109; as Deputy Director of Office of Far Eastern Affairs, 110; as Assistant Secretary of State for Far